MW00324554

DEATH OF A "JEWISH AMERICAN PRINCESS"

DEATH OF A "JEWISH AMERICAN PRINCESS"

THE TRUE STORY OF A VICTIM ON TRIAL

BY

SHIRLEY FRONDORF

Villard Books
New York
1988

Copyright © 1988 by Shirley Frondorf
All rights reserved under International and Pan-American Copyright
Conventions. Published in the United States by Villard Books, a division of Random House, Inc., New York, and simultaneously in Canada
by Random House of Canada Limited, Toronto.

Library of Congress Cataloging-in-Publication Data

Frondorf, Shirley.
   Death of a "Jewish American princess."

   1. Murder—Arizona—Scottsdale—Case studies.
2. Steinberg, Elana, d. 1982.   3. Steinberg, Steven.
4. Trials (Murder)—Arizona—Phoenix—Case studies.
I. Title.   II. Title: Jewish American princess.
HV6534.S48F76   1988   345.73'02523   87-40576
ISBN 0-394-56854-0   347.3052523

Manufactured in the United States of America
9   8   7   6   5   4   3   2

He will swallow up death for
ever, and the Lord God will wipe
away tears from all faces.

—Isaiah 25:8

AUTHOR'S NOTE

The Steinberg murder trial took place in the month of February 1982, but people in Arizona have never forgotten it. The trial, and the verdict, shocked everyone. Most people thought that a miscarriage of justice had occurred in that stately courtroom on Jefferson Street—it was as if the law had taken a holiday in normally conservative Phoenix. A jury in a criminal trial is supposed to be a mirror of the moral values of the community, but no one seemed pleased with this verdict afterward. Years later, newsmen still write stories about the Steinberg trial, and people talk about it with a sense of wonder and frustration.

It haunted me. I used to be a prosecutor, and I know that there can be strange, unpredictable verdicts, influenced by deep-seated emotions and beliefs that no one ever guessed were there, emotions which are more compelling to a jury than the letter of the law. It must have been so in *State* v. *Steinberg.* The newspaper accounts of the trial were intriguing, but they only hinted at what may have really happened. I decided to peel back the layers and see what lay beneath—to see if the majestic structure of the criminal justice system had worked wonderfully in the trial of Steven Steinberg, or whether it had failed. My goal was to be a reporter after the fact, a sociologist, of this verdict. It took almost three years to do that.

Most of the story comes directly from court records of the trial, police reports, and newspaper accounts. I've simplified the legal points, trying to keep the essence of them, so that the courtroom tactics and psychiatry will be more understandable to nonlawyers. I've tried to identify the points where the course of the trial turned in a certain inexorable direction, what I would call the vital signs, the trial's pulse and temperature. Some of these turning points were unexpected and purely emotional; some were calculated and skillfully directed. In hindsight, the signs of what was happening seem clear, but I know that they were not so clear to lawyers in the heat of battle.

Over the last three years I talked to scores of men and women who had a part, if only tangential, in this tragedy. They were thoughtful, introspective, and generous with their time. Some of them appear in the narrative by their true names; others requested anonymity, and I've complied with their requests and used names that are not their own. For my hindsight view of trial strategy I have called on the expertise of friends who are more knowledgeable in their fields than I. To all of these individuals who gave their time so freely, I am extremely grateful. It was hard to stop interviewing, I found. I kept wanting to go back to each one and say, "But what about this?"—for I believe there are questions still unanswered.

The most compelling reason that I could never put the Steinberg verdict out of my mind was what had happened to Elana Steinberg in this trial. First, I must identify her and her position. She was the victim, and normally you would think that nothing else could ever hurt her after she was killed by her husband on that May night in 1981. But there was more to come. According to the news stories and the talk among people who had seen the trial, a new defense had been born. The dead woman had been characterized throughout the trial as a terrible person—someone who was materialistic, who shopped and spent, nagged and called her husband at work. She was the one on trial, not the man who had killed her. Unlike him, Elana Steinberg was defenseless in the courtroom. When it was over, her memory was tarnished, and her loved ones were desolate.

I don't particularly think of myself as a crusader, but I sensed that the justice system had done a terrible wrong to this young woman. It was the same system that I believed in and had sworn to defend when I passed the bar; it was the same system that was supposed to protect people like Elana Steinberg. I knew one thing—if someone I loved was murdered and this was what was going to happen in the courtroom, I would prefer the justice system to forget about it and let the person who had done it go. At least that would leave the memory intact.

Once I heard the noted criminal lawyer Alan Dershowitz explain that it was necessary, in some cases, for the defense to "desanctify" the victim. The Steinberg trial is an extreme example of what Dershowitz was talking about. If justice does require what happened to Elana Steinberg in the courtroom, that is a tremendous cost whose benefits should be weighed against its heartaches. People should be aware of what is happening in the trial and why it is happening. Only then can jurors weigh it for themselves.

In the end, I became a crusader in spite of myself, an advocate for a young woman who desperately needed an advocate in this trial. I learned that she was a woman who was fun, a woman who laughed a lot, who had spunk and a zest for life. She was cruelly treated by the law, but she is not forgotten. Now it's time to balance the books.

CONTENTS

INTRODUCTION

I went to Elana Steinberg's grave the other day.

I had finished the last chapter of the book, or at least I thought it was finished. It should have been a milestone event, the kind of event you celebrate, but I wasn't entirely happy. Melancholy would have been a better description of the way I felt, although it is hard to be melancholy on a brilliant blue day in Arizona. I wandered around the house moving stacks of notes and newspaper clippings, and the unease didn't go away. Suddenly, I felt that it was absolutely imperative for me to go to the cemetery, to Elana's grave. I'd been there once before, so there was nothing new to see, but maybe the trip would drive away the melancholia.

Elana's mother, Edith Singer, went with me. I had brought flowers wrapped in that wet dark green tissue. I knew that you don't take cut flowers to a Jewish grave, but it was instinctive for me. We drove in my car out to Greenhaven without talking. This was unusual for both of us.

Arizona is not a good place for cemeteries. A tree has to struggle for survival in the desert sun. The few species that thrive here, like the acacia and paloverde, give little shade. Their leaves are narrow and spiky and not like real leaves, the kind that trees have in Ohio, because in the desert even the trees have to save precious water. The grass can be green in Arizona, and it is green in Greenhaven—a harsh artificial color and a coarse strange texture. There are no graceful hedges of forsythia or bridal wreath that make cemeteries in other climates so beautiful. Greenhaven is acually a desert wash. It is stark outside of the cemetery gate, sand and power poles. For a Midwesterner like Elana Steinberg it is a strange place to lie.

After I parked the car we walked to the Jewish section of the cemetery, marked off with a chain. The segregation is not some bit of anti-Semitism. Jews must be buried in consecrated ground, and their graves are always separated. In the middle of the section there is a large stone monument with an inscription:

BENEATH THIS MEMORIAL

THE SACRED PARCHMENTS

RETURNING TO DUST THEIR

ETERNAL TRUTH HOVERS

ABOVE THE SOCIETY OF MAN

When I began to write this book about Elana, I didn't know what this meant; I didn't understand the reference to parchments in a graveyard. I'm not Jewish, and I did not know that damaged Torah and prayer books were buried there. I had learned a lot these two years. Trying to be careful not to cover the carving on the stone, I laid my flowers on Elana's grave marker, flat on the ground like all the markers. It was done with Elana's maiden name—Elana Joy Singer 1947–1981.

Edith's grief was instantaneous and primitive. The tears

rolled down her pink-and-blond face; her sobs were uncontroll-
able. An older man and a woman in a blue dress who stood in
the next roadway turned and stared at us. Edith's misery always
surprised me, because it had been more than four years since
her daughter's marker had been dedicated. Though I knew
Edith well by now, because we had talked together for two
years, I was still amazed that she had so much pain. No one
could ever doubt that the grief was genuine, but it was so fresh.
I come from a family of cool and unemotional Dutch from
Cincinnati. None of my relatives would dream of such outward
mourning. For them the dead were buried with an expensive
funeral in Spring Grove Cemetery and that was it for the most
part, except for a hardheaded assessment of the estate that had
been left behind. Edith's grief was so pure and primal. The
intensity of her mourning resembled those funeral processions
one sees on TV newscasts which show women dressed in black,
following a coffin. It was not a sound you expect from a well-
groomed Scottsdale grandmother dressed by Lillie Rubin.

I looked down at the flowers and the headstone and wondered what Elana would think about what I was doing. Would
she approve? It is important to remember that Elana Steinberg,
née Singer, was first and foremost a traditional Jewish wife and
mother. Jews have always believed that it is the role of the wife
and mother to nurture, to raise the children and to keep alive
the Jewish culture. Elana did that. She kept close ties with all
of the relatives, she celebrated the holidays with food and gift-
giving, she cared for her husband and children and her home
with single-minded attention. By the standards of family life
which have been so essential for Jewish survival, Elana's life
was traditionally correct. What happened to her was not.

If Elana were able, I wondered if she would say, "Leave it
alone—let him live in peace. You're only making it worse, and
what's more, you're embarrassing me!" Or perhaps she would
be like her mother and father, seething with frustration and
bitterness at the failure of the justice system to punish her
killer or even acknowledge that her murder was a crime. I tried
to think like Elana, but of course I could not. She left no

writings behind. She did not know that her life and feelings would ever be of special interest to a whole community who could never forget her death.

Even now after two years of talking to people who knew Elana, of interviewing those who were her friends and those who were her enemies, and of tracing the history of Elana's vibrant immigrant forebears, I do not have an idea of how she would react. I do know that Jewish women have complex concepts of themselves. Added to the choices and decisions that all women have there is the responsibility of carrying on the cultural heritage as Jewish women have always done. In Judaism, marriage is tight and loyal, and it has always been so. Elana Steinberg was no exception; she had proved that over the years. She was a loyal wife to the very end.

Of course, there was something that Elana could never have imagined. Not only was she stabbed to death in her bedroom on McCormick Ranch, crying out to her children for help, but she was to be killed a second time in a Phoenix courtroom with the blessing of the American judicial system. Elana Steinberg could never have dreamed that being her own version of a wife and mother was fault enough for her to be judged and found guilty of causing her own murder. And certainly no one could have imagined that this particular brilliant strategy would be conceived and carried out by a team of men who were Jewish themselves.

People in Phoenix still shift uneasily at the mention of the Steinberg murder trial. With the exception of Steven Steinberg's attorneys and psychiatrists, the verdict made everyone uncomfortable. Perhaps it was because no one spoke for Elana Steinberg in that courtroom. No one objected when she was transformed from being the victim of a particularly brutal homicide to being the real defendant. But after it was over, most people felt a little ashamed.

It was cooler now in the cemetery. The man and the woman in the blue dress had gone, and it was time for Edith and me to leave as well. I came to the conclusion that Elana Steinberg would not object if another voice was heard now. Her friends said she was spirited and not afraid to speak out—

"gutsy," according to one neighbor. She just might want to redress some of those mortal wounds that had been inflicted in the courtroom. I hope so, but I will never know.

Judaism has a body of law known as the Halakhah. The word means literally "the way to walk." The Talmud and generations of Jewish scholars have set forth a way of rules and guidelines for living the correct, the ethical, life. The Halakhah covers things great and small—how to cook, how to eat, how to dress, how to marry, how to act and react to virtually every situation. The directions, and they are good ones, have served the Jewish people well for centuries. But in the Halakhah there is no guide, no commentary, nothing, that deals with what happened to Elana Steinberg in that Phoenix courtroom. On this occasion the friends and the lawyers had to find their own way to walk, and the way they chose did not leave much room for Elana Steinberg.

When Edith and I left Greenhaven that day I think we both felt better. Edith had regained her composure. We talked about other things all the way out to the Singers' house in Scottsdale. Outside the duplex, Elana's youngest daughter, ten-year-old Shawn, was riding her bike in circles. Everyone says that she is amazingly like her mother, petite, lively, with long red hair and freckles. Edith has a photograph of Elana at the same age taken back in Skokie in happier days, and the resemblance is striking. Shawn is bright and cheerful, full of personality. She hugged her grandmother in a burst of affection. She is obviously loved and cared for.

Will someone, someday, call her or her dark-haired sister, Traci, a Jewish American Princess? It is possible, if someone doesn't know how bitter the phrase would be for these young women. The phrase dies hard. It has been a useful concept for Jewish writers and comedians for some years now and presumably still raises laughter on the Catskill circuit. It is not a phrase invented by the *goyim,* it is a Jewish joke. I do not believe it is likely that the phrase will ever again be an epitaph for a young woman as it was for Elana Steinberg; surely all the wrong stars and wrong planets couldn't come together for a second time as they did in that Phoenix courtroom in 1982.

So this is the story of Elana Joy Steinberg in life and in death. It is also a story of the criminal justice system in action, functioning in a way that is gratifying to some and troubling to others. This is a story of something known as forensic psychiatry, and of those men who practice it in courtrooms across America. This is the story of jurors who see Satan every day in visible form and who can speak directly to Jesus. And for all of us who do none of those things, but who sometimes wake in the night and look at our sleeping bedpartner, this is the story of the perfect husband.

PART ONE

DEATH BY VIOLENCE

CHAPTER ONE

SCOTTSDALE AT NIGHT

It was ten o'clock on the evening of May 27, 1981, in Phoenix, and a storm was in the making. May was early for the monsoon season, which is what newscasters call those rare summer nights in the Sonoran desert of Arizona when rain sweeps up from the Baja peninsula. This night there were lightning flashes in the south sky and an ominous still feeling in the hot desert air.

At B. B. Singer's restaurant on Central Avenue in the uptown business district a sparse group of people were drinking at the bar and at the restaurant's maroon mohair booths. The dinner hour was over and the serious drinkers were in charge. In the bare parking lot in back of the restaurant, all was quiet. Papers blew in an occasional gust of wind around the garbage bins. There was a steel door marked "Deliveries Only" in the brick wall, with a buzzer to ring. Inside, there was an alcove at the back of the restaurant's kitchen. It was noisy from the clashing of the dishwasher, but there was no one about. From the alcove, stairs led up to two dark and gloomy rooms on the second floor. One room was obviously a storeroom, stacked with folding chairs, paper chains, and forlorn banners printed "Happy New Year." To the left, the second room was grubby and dark, with no windows. There was a battered desk, a telephone, and an old-fashioned safe. This was the office of the two B. B. Singer's restaurants on North Central. Now it was deserted and still.

Bill Adamowitz, the night manager of the Brass Derby, having emptied the two cash registers, lumbered through the kitchen, all the way to the back stairs. It was the manager's job to put the register receipts in the safe—both of the Singer restaurants on North Central kept their cash there and made bank deposits in the morning. On this night the door to the safe was swinging open. The money that had been there at six o'clock from the lunch and dinner trade was gone, as well as the customer's wallet, flush with cash, that a waitress had found. Adamowitz swore.

"Jeez, I have to call Mitch." The manager thought glumly about Mitch Singer and his temper. Mitch's disposition had never been good, but he was now even more volatile with the increasing rumors that the three Singer's restaurants were going under even with the New York investors Mitch had found. Adamowitz also thought about the scene with the dishwasher Miguel earlier that night. Miguel had wanted his paycheck early and had been belligerent when Adamowitz refused. "Shit, I couldn't give it to him even if I'd wanted to," mumbled the manager to himself, as he dialed Mitch Singer's home. "This place is falling apart." Miguel was unlikely as a serious suspect, Adamowitz thought. The dishwasher wasn't sophisticated enough to work out the combination to the safe—he was sure of that.

In Scottsdale, Mitch Singer and his wife, Bonnie, were asleep in their new house. Mitch could always sleep, even when things looked bad, as they did with the B. B. Singer's restaurants just then. Mitch was a pragmatist. If the restaurants couldn't make it with the money from the New York group that David Goldfarb had found, something else would turn up. Mitch traveled light and didn't worry about things like that. The phone rang—it was eleven-thirty.

"Goddammit, what are you guys doing down there— sleeping? Okay, I'll take care of it in the morning. Close it up, call the police," he told Adamowitz.

After all, burglaries at B. B. Singer's were not exactly news. In the last two years, Phoenix burglary detectives had been called to the restaurants six times—all by Mitch's brother-in-law, Steve Steinberg, who then managed the Singer's restaurant called the Brass Derby. Mitch didn't know it, but to the people who worked at Singer's the burglaries were a joke. Some thought it was Mitch's form of self-help, but many thought it was Steve Steinberg. Steve had all the employees take polygraph tests, and most of them resented it; none of the tests had ever turned up anything. Neither the police nor the insurance company found the burglaries unusual—no one had ever complained. The call from the restaurant that night was annoying to Mitchell Singer, but not something to worry about. He turned over and went back to sleep. It was almost midnight. Scottsdale and Paradise Valley were quiet, waiting for the storm to break.

On McCormick Ranch, Officers 23 and 82 of the Scottsdale Police Department were patrolling in separate cars. Violent crime was almost nonexistent in Scottsdale, and there was no need to have two-man teams on patrol. In 1981, the city was sparsely populated to the north. The ranches on Scottsdale Road and at the foot of Pinnacle Peak were home only to a few Arabian-horse breeders and numerous rattlesnakes; Paradise Valley was enjoying a last reprieve from the bulldozer and the Nicklaus-designed golf courses that were on the way. Developers had just begun to discover what could be done with the lush high desert north of Scottsdale. McCormick Ranch was the first to emerge from their drawing boards.

On these choice acres the heirs of International Harvester's Cyrus McCormick had found a refuge from Chicago winters. There they had bred Arabian horses. When the family sold the property in 1976, they gave a park to the City of Scottsdale and kept an Arabian show ring for the All-Arabian every

spring. The rest of the land became a planned community—
the first in Scottsdale. The planners did their work well. The
Ranch has two lakes which glisten in the desert, a resort hotel,
two beautiful golf courses, a mix of condominiums, luxurious
homes, and apartments. The streets were plotted as a maze of
circles and cul-de-sacs. All of the streets back on fairways of the
golf courses or on lakes and greenbelts. Every street has a
Spanish name. McCormick Ranch bustles with croissant shops,
stores for pool supplies, travel agencies, and investment counselors, because these are among the critical needs of Ranch
residents. Ranch restaurants are trendy; they are the first to
feature Cajun food or *nouvelle cuisine.* One restaurant is a
replica of Rick's Bar in Casablanca with waiters in bush jackets
from the Banana Republic and a pianist playing "As Time Goes
By."

The Ranch is a potpourri of middle-class society. There
are senior fugitives from the Midwest here, but the Ranch is
not a senior-citizen enclave like so much of Phoenix; most
residents are upwardly mobile professionals who have children.
There is even a new elementary school, unusual in Scottsdale,
where schools are closing, not being built. There is a mix of
professions and religions, working women and stay-at homes.
If there is a common theme among the residents it is a devotion
to the good life. To preserve the pristine character of the Ranch
the planner thoughtfully built a five-foot stuccoed wall for
miles, to surround the enclave.

The Ranch is beautifully kept, full of oleander in bloom,
Jacuzzis and hot tubs. Bougainvillea falls in showers of fuchsia
over stucco walls, and the greenbelts are clipped and green. In
Scottsdale the sun shines 340 days of the year, and with all
of this everyone on the Ranch should be happy. But there is
a subtle undercurrent of dissatisfaction, a hidden malaise of
a community that is not in harmony with itself. There is a
strange frequency of juvenile vandalism on the Ranch that cannot be explained. The ducks on the lakes are mysteriously
killed; cars drive over the newly planted ryegrass in the night,
ruining the turf with ruts; black paint is thrown on one garage
and then another in a regular pattern. The local newspaper

reports fierce battles in the Ranch homeowners' associations, in which slates of antagonistic candidates for thankless nonpaying posts are usually engaged in life-or-death struggles for control. As in much of Phoenix, the newcomers on the Ranch are somewhat rootless and isolated. But even with these problems the typical resident, if asked to set a contentment grade, would say that he (or she) is happy with the choice. Anyone who bought property on McCormick Ranch in the early days when the first houses were being built could hardly be displeased. By 1981, property had doubled in value. The planners had done well; nothing was cheap or ill-favored. As Ranch residents slept that May evening in 1981 they were slowly but perceptibly growing richer.

It was midnight. In her buff adobe brick house on Via de Luz, Pawan Nandam was still up hemming curtains in her family room. Her husband and two children were asleep. Pawan is from the Punjab. Her East Indian good looks and slow accented speech mislead people who do not immediately recognize the sophistication of Pawan and her husband, who is considered a genius by his colleagues at a Phoenix electronics plant. The Nandams are cosmopolitan travelers, at home in London as well as in America. Pawan herself is a shrewd observer of American social customs.

At midnight Pawan heard a woman screaming, then a man's voice raised in anger. She went to the sliding glass door. "I looked out, but you know, there is a park behind the back wall, and you hear noise there a lot." Four years later, Pawan still frowns and worries at the memory. "I thought maybe Elana was having a party. . . . " Her voice trails off. "After I didn't hear anything else, I went to bed." Pawan doesn't like to think about it now, and that is understandable, since the sounds that Pawan heard were her friend and neighbor Elana Steinberg's last few moments of life.

A mile away, David and Rhona Goldfarb had just gotten to sleep, after the storm had cleared the air. Their elegant adobe desert home in north Scottsdale was a cut above the houses on

McCormick Ranch. There was a tennis court and a winding glassed-in stairway and a circular drive. The address fit David Goldfarb, who was on the verge of making it big in the business world. Goldfarb had a business brokerage and was beginning to franchise his operations. Ever since the big snowfall of the winter of 1979, when the city of Buffalo almost disappeared in a mountain of snow, it seemed as if everyone wanted to move to Arizona. A good number of the new pioneers to the desert wanted to realize another lifelong dream—to buy their own business. Many of the dry cleaners and restaurants, cheese shops and boutiques bought in such optimism would not prosper. In due time these failed businesses would be sold to another eager buyer. Goldfarb was a good businessman in the right place at the right time. He and his wife were social and entertained often. Their friends were a circle of businessmen and professionals in Scottsdale, and their closest friends were Steve and Elana Steinberg.

Five minutes after midnight the ringing of the phone woke them. Rhona Goldfarb answered, since the telephone was on her side. A man's voice screamed, "Rhona, come over right away—right now!" The phone clicked off.

Rhona Goldfarb didn't recognize the voice, because she had awakened from a deep sleep, but she knew immediately that something terrible happened somewhere. Her first thought, and that of her husband, was for the next-door neighbors—"I thought, who else could be calling me?" The Goldfarbs threw on robes and ran to see if everything was all right next door. The neighbors were still up, and reassured them that there was nothing wrong. Neither Rhona nor David could settle down after this. "The call was so genuine—it wasn't just the kind of call you get at night from a drunk. It was real, and it was meant for me, I know. And it was not something that was going to go away." Her husband felt the same way. It was his idea to make a second contact with the neighbors next door— this time a phone call.

"We thought that maybe they couldn't talk to us when we were there earlier, that maybe somebody was in the house. I know it sounds crazy, but the call was so compelling," says

Rhona. "You knew it was *real.*" The neighbors were again re-
assuring when David called. Finally the Goldfarbs went back to
an uneasy sleep.

Pat Eldridge was on duty in the dispatcher's room of the
Scottsdale Police Department. It was midnight and a slow night
for her. The Scottsdale police station is nothing like the average. The building is one of three city buildings which were the
prize-winning work of Arizona architect Bennie Gonzales.
A reflecting pool bisects the complex of these beautiful white
structures. The pool is the home of two swans, whose health is
carefully guarded. Art galleries and French restaurants ring the
grassy plaza; fountains play everywhere. The elegance of this
setting is incompatible with crime.

The call came in at 12:07; the recording machine was on.
A man screamed, "My wife was just murdered, and they walked
in the house, my God please—I'm bleeding, I'm trying to stop
the bleeding!" Then a child's voice took over, screaming hysterically—"This is his daughter, please hurry. I'm here, I'm Traci.
I'm scared." The control room quickly mobilized. There was no
doubt that the department had a Code 3 emergency to deal
with, and that was unusual in north Scottsdale. Eldridge tried
to keep the terrified child on the phone—in 1981 if a Scottsdale
officer lost the caller before he could get an address there was
no way to trace location. At the same time another dispatcher
was sending out a Code 3 to cars on patrol, her voice tight with
urgency. There was a possible, if not probable, dead body on Via
de Luz, and children could be at risk as well.

It is impossible to drive straight across Via de Luz. The
street started and stopped in cul-de-sacs a dozen times. It was
a pleasant pattern, a triumph of the subdivision planner, but a
definite hazard in an emergency. Officer Mark Barnett was patrolling north of the Ranch when he heard the call, Kevin
Chadwick and Paulette Kasieta south. All three arrived at the
house on Via de Luz together in a miracle of response time.
Barnett, sandy-haired, with a thin expressive face, is one of
those men who seem to be able to handle life's emergencies. He
is the kind of person a man would want for his buddy on Gua-

dalcanal or in Nam, or that a mother would want to lead a search in the woods for a missing three-year-old. He is soft-spoken, calm, and collected. Barnett is still a little bit surprised at the short time it took him to thread through the maze of streets on the Ranch that night.

Although he left the department a year after the Steinberg murder, Kevin Chadwick remembers that night well. Now Chadwick studies psychology at Arizona State University and runs a truck pumper station. The call to Via de Luz was something he will not easily forget.

"The first thing I heard on the radio was what we call a hot tone, and you listen real hard to that. You have to listen to the dispatch tape to get the full effect of the call. The dispatcher's voice was really different—very dramatic and tense. You knew it was really a crisis, it was real. She was feeding us bits and pieces all the way. 'Looks like a knife, possible dead body, there are children.' I went right into Code 3—that is, full emergency lights and siren. Most Code 3s didn't turn out to be anything much in Scottsdale, but I knew this was different. I don't know how I got there, it's such a mess of streets up there. Mark and Kasieta were there."

Chadwick didn't hit the right cul-de-sac and had to sprint over the grass that separated two circles. A barefoot man in a short bathrobe ran out of one of the dark houses, shouting and waving his arms.

"They killed her, they killed my wife!" he shouted. "There are two of them, they're gone, they went out the back door and over the fence!" He pointed to the back of the house with one hand; the other hand was wrapped in a towel.

Barnett stayed with the man out in the street while Chadwick and Paulette Kasieta ran up the walk of the buff adobe block house; their guns were drawn. Chadwick pushed open the front door. It was dark in the entryway and what looked like a sunken living room—a faint light came from a hallway to the right. "All I could hear was this horrible screaming, it sounded like kids. We walked down a hall. In one of the bedrooms there were two children. One dark-haired girl, the oldest, was on the bed screaming hysterically into a telephone. A little red-haired girl was sitting on the floor all huddled up. I said, 'Calm down, we're here!' "

The hall was a long corridor with rooms off one side. At the end of the hall was a door that was closed. A faint light shone underneath.

"You could tell that room was the master bedroom. I thought to myself, I do not want to go down there and open that door, because it is obvious what is going to be there. I am going to find a dead body and maybe two murderers besides." Chadwick still remembers his trepidation. Dead bodies and violence were not standard fare in Scottsdale, where crime is minimal and generally of a quiet white-collar variety. It is true that skeletons are sometimes found in the high desert outside of town, bleached and sexless and remote. But bodies were not found in north Scottsdale, or most of all, in a bedroom on McCormick Ranch with children screaming.

Chadwick pushed the door. A light illuminated a bedroom with plush white carpet and silver marbleized wallpaper. There was a platform bed across the room from the door. A huge stain of blood in the middle of the bed dripped off onto the floor in a pool. Reddish splatters were at the head of the bed, in a fan pattern against the beautiful wallpaper. Slumped sitting on the floor, one leg crossed under her, leaning against the side of the bed, was a young woman in a short light blue nightgown. She was covered with blood, and there were numerous wounds in her arm and side—each wound looked like a hole with a glob of blood on it. The woman was small-boned and petite, almost frail. Her long auburn hair was swept aside by the pile of stained bedding and a comforter that had fallen on her. On the other side of the room, one drawer to a dresser was pulled out. Three pairs of underpants were on the floor near a sliding glass arcadia door to a patio. The door was open, and the warm muggy air was flowing in.

"I felt her carotid artery, but it was just routine. There was no question in my mind that she was dead; no one could be alive that had been mutilated that way. We checked the closets and the dressing room and there was no one there. The children's screaming had stopped, and I was glad about that. Kasieta had calmed the little dark-haired girl."

Outside, an ambulance drew up. Out in the street the barefoot man in the brown robe broke away from Mark Barnett and ran toward the front door. "Sir, don't go in there!" Barnett yelled—his job was to keep the house clear.

"You asshole, it's my wife!" the man screamed at Barnett.

The man in the brown robe was Steven Frank Steinberg, age thirty-seven, late the manager of one of the B. B. Singer's restaurants, now unemployed. The battered body inside in the blood-spattered bedroom was Steinberg's thirty-four-year-old wife, Elana. Death had not come easily on McCormick Ranch.

CHAPTER TWO

THE HOUSE ON VIA DE LUZ

In 1981 the Scottsdale Police Department was not renowned for its skill in criminal investigations, and the force and the city manager were sensitive about this. It wasn't a secret; there were embarrassing hints of the department's ineptitude in the Phoenix papers. To be fair to Scottsdale, the art of criminal investigation is like any other skill; it improves with practice. A city with a high rate of violent crime is bound to have a more professional homicide team. Scottsdale had few murders and fewer muggings. In 1981 it was still a small town in spirit, catapulted into being a city.

For years, the town was just a crossroads of dusty gravel streets. There was a feed store for ranchers, a Western outfitter, and a few stores where the occasional tourist could buy Navajo and Hopi jewelry. A few very, very wealthy people spent the winter there, but most of Scottsdale's residents were small farmers or tradesmen, or descendants of "lungers" who had come to the desert for their health. It was not unusual to see horses in the town streets. Scottsdale called itself "the West's Most Western Town"; the basis for this seemed to be that some of the stores had false Western fronts and hitching posts by the front doors. Most people in Scottsdale knew each other. They had coffee and pie at Lute Wasbotten's drugstore, and they followed a slow pace.

Suddenly with the perfection of central air conditioning everything changed for Scottsdale. The change did not come gradually but was an explosion; people poured into Scottsdale and Paradise Valley to live. They loved the shops, the Western atmosphere, and the unfailing sun. By 1981, when Elana Steinberg was killed, Scottsdale Road was not only paved all the way out to Pinnacle Park but was ringed with expensive resorts and condominiums. Executive business seminars and celebrity tennis tournaments were held in Scottsdale. For a small city it became nationally fashionable, a good place to live—if you were transferred to Scottsdale by your company, you were happy about it.

All of this quick growth strained the skeleton city services. The fire department was privately owned and the library was staffed by volunteers, which provided a quaintness that was prized by Scottsdale residents. This was fine, but it was a little frightening that the police force seemed to be more adept at riding in the city's annual Parada del Sol than at solving murders.

The first public criticism came when Bob Crane, the well-known star of the long-running TV series *Hogan's Heroes,* was found beaten to death in a resort apartment. Along with a lead pipe that was the instrument of the star's demise, the police found a library of pornographic pictures. Months passed and there was no hint of anyone's arrest in this intriguing case. News stories were increasingly vague about progress in the investigation. No one said so openly, but finally it was rumored that the murder investigation had been fatally bungled. Those in a position to know said that so much damage had been done at the crime scene that there could never be a successful prosecution, even though the police felt sure that they knew who had killed the TV star.

The preservation of crime-scene evidence is critical to a prosecution. Nothing should be moved or destroyed; unauthorized persons milling around and leaving prints compromise the integrity of evidence. "Contamination" is the word a prosecutor would use, and it can spell doom. There was another rumor about what went wrong—somebody said that there had been some incriminating statements made by the chief suspect, but the police had not given *Miranda* warnings. In a situation like that, not only does the prosecutor lose the statements themselves, but the problem spreads out and can poison the whole investigation that comes afterward. What was wrong with the Crane investigation was all speculation, though. No one knew exactly what the problem was, and the police weren't talking. One thing was known, and reported. When the Scottsdale police turned over their departmental reports—the "DRs" —to the Maricopa County Attorney's Office, the prosecution was politely but firmly declined. The police did some more work and submitted the case again with the same result.

The defects in the crime scene, whatever they were, were apparently such that they could never be repaired. The County Attorney's Office was discreetly silent about the problem. After an initial period of huffing, spokesmen for the Scottsdale Police Department were silent too. Someone had gotten away with a high-profile murder in Scottsdale, and it was embarrassing in the extreme.

After this debacle, the police department was reorganized and began to upgrade its personnel. When Elana Steinberg was killed, the revamping had just begun. There was no trouble with recruitment; policemen liked the Scottsdale force and there were plenty of applicants. The department could be selective, and it was.

One of the first acquisitions was an identification and crime-scene expert from Washington, D.C., named Cecil Kirk. Kirk, a photographer, was a twenty-year veteran of crime-scene work with the Metropolitan Police Force in the capital; his biggest assignment had been with the Congressional investigative team in the Kennedy and Martin Luther King assassinations. He had been connected with two hundred murders in one way or another over the years, and he was expected to gather and preserve crime-scene evidence, Scottsdale's Achilles' heel in the TV star's murder. Kirk was eligible to retire when he saw Scottsdale's advertisement in a professional magazine, and his wife was immediately enthusiastic. He now has a tiny and crowded office in the Scottsdale department's pueblo-style building in the plaza.

Kirk was only one of the dozen Scottsdale police officers called out the night Elana Steinberg was killed. Detectives were called at home and told to report to the house on Via de Luz. The cul-de-sac was soon packed with police cars. Cecil Kirk stayed longer than anyone else. He spent more than five hours in the Steinberg bedroom with the marbled paper, measuring and photographing. He was down on hands and knees searching for scraps of fiber and hair, or for objects that didn't belong in that room. He had officers search the house, turning over cushions on chairs and couches and examining drawers and papers. He spent two hours matching slashes in the bedding against Elana Steinberg's wounds, trying to see if her killer had stabbed through the comforter as she slept. He took dozens of photographs. With the Crane fiasco still on his mind and everyone else's mind as well, Kirk was a perfectionist on this scene. It was almost five-thirty when he left that morning, releasing Elana Steinberg's body to the mortuary drivers who had been patiently squatting in the living room through that long night.

The house swarmed with police. Alison Livermore, the Scottsdale crisis intervention officer, arrived and spent her time calming the two hysterical little girls and Elana's parents. Barnett and Chadwick were told to secure the bedroom until the investigation was complete; Barnett stood at the hall door and Chadwick at the patio. But the master bedroom was the only room that was intact, because there was chaos in the rest of the house as people that Steinberg had called arrived.

While the dispatcher had been trying to calm Traci and keep her on the telephone, Steve Steinberg had been busy on another line in the den, calling family and friends. He called Elana's brother, Mitch Singer. He called the Goldfarbs—it was his call that had frightened Rhona. He called an acquaintance on the Ranch, Mike Berkovitch, who is still puzzled by that call.

"We really didn't know him that well. I don't know why he would have called me. But he yelled, 'Come over right away. They've killed Elana and the house has been robbed!' I asked him if he had called the police, and he said yes. I got dressed and I drove over there as fast as I could. I didn't know what I was going to find."

Mitch Singer got there before Berkovitch. He brought his wife and their baby along, and a pistol. Barney and Edith Singer were there; Mitch had called them. Steven Steinberg's mother, Esther Goodman, and her husband came—no one knew how they heard about it. All of them were milling around in the house. There were ambulance attendants in the living room squatting on the floor, waiting for the detectives and Cecil Kirk to finish. Elana's father, Barney Singer, felt faint and collapsed—someone called a Scottsdale physician to look at him.

Mistakes of the Crane murder were still haunting the force. Two of the officers were reprimanded later for the confusion on the scene at Via de Luz. Fortunately, no major damage was done—the master bedroom had been kept secure. No one could enter that room with Chadwick and Barnett on the doors, although Steven Steinberg tried.

Steinberg was still barefoot and in his brown robe; he had a towel wrapped around a cut on the palm of his hand. He wandered in and out of the rooms; sometimes he went outside into the street. He cried a lot and complained about the pain in his hand. Some of the people who saw him that night thought he acted dazed, some thought he was controlled. Once he hit his head against the wall. He tried to force his way into the bedroom, shouting, "I've got to see her! Is she dead?" Barnett told another officer to hold him back. Then he tried to come in the sliding glass doors from the patio, but Chadwick was there and kept him out.

Mark Barnett's impression of Steinberg that night was that there was something off-key in his reactions, almost an underlying hostility in his manner. "The first time I saw him was when he came screaming out of the house saying, 'They killed my wife, there are two of them, they went over the back fence!' I stayed with him trying to get information while the other two officers went in the house. The thing I remember about Steinberg then is that his attitude was just not what you would expect when a loved one is hurt. The vibes were different. There was something about the way he responded that I would call 'passively hostile' to me, to the police. It just wasn't what you would expect under the circumstances. It's a subtle thing. Like when he said 'you asshole' to me—that's a funny thing to say at a time like that, and it kind of points up what he was like. He was pretty calm, though. When his lawyer interviewed me before the trial I could tell that he wanted me to say that Steinberg was like a wild man, you know. But that wasn't the way it was."

Steinberg did not have much to say to his wife's family— he avoided Barney Singer's eyes. Edith cried, "What were you doing when they were killing my daughter, you're a big strong man, what were you doing?" Steve turned away from her. He could talk to Mitchell, but not to Elana's mother and father. When Steve talked to Mitch that night, it was to justify his failure to protect Elana. Mitchell remembers their conversation. "When I got to the house that night after he called me, I went up to him. He was sitting in the kids' room and I was very upset that my sister had just been stabbed to death and Steve was sitting there with just this little cut on his hand and two guys supposedly held him down while all this was going on. I was mad and I said so. He held up his hand and said, 'How in the fuck do you think I got this?' Then, later, we were both out in the kitchen. He took a drink of water and he emptied the water in the sink and he told me, 'There goes fifteen years down the drain.' I'll always remember that."

To everyone else in the house that night, Steinberg talked nonstop. He told Paulette Kasieta that two men with long hair and bushy beards had come in through the glass sliding door. He said they were white men, and that both the beards and the hair looked like they were fakes. He told Barnett that the two men asked "where the jewelry was."

He expanded the story about the bushy-haired men to
Mike Berkovitch. When Berkovitch got to the house, Steinberg
was sitting in the hall on the carpet looking dazed. "He cried a
lot and he told me these two guys came in, and they wanted to
know where the jewelry was, and that he told them, or else he
got it for them. And then he said that the two men said it wasn't
enough, and that they wanted more."

Berkovitch accepted the burglar story without question.
When he got home the next morning, he ordered an alarm
system installed in his own house.

Elana's mother and Mike Berkovitch believed the story
that Steinberg was telling everyone, but the Scottsdale police
were immediately suspicious. There were no signs of forced
entry into the Steinberg bedroom. The grass outside was damp
from the rain. There were no footprints on the grass as there
should have been if someone had been there that night. If there
had ever been two bushy-haired men in the Steinberg backyard,
they had not touched the ground when they left. The gate in
the back wall to the park was padlocked, and the picnic table
that blocked the gate had never been moved.

In the silver-and-white bedroom, Chadwick and Barnett
agreed about Steinberg's account as they stood watch. "We
talked about it while we were there and it was obvious his story
was a phony. First of all, this was a tiny, delicate-looking
woman. She was no threat to anybody, anywhere. Why would
she be just mangled, and the husband just have that little
scratch on his hand? He wasn't hurt enough for what he said
happened."

Barnett thought it was obvious that Elana had been
stabbed in the back and the side while she was lying in bed,
probably by someone in bed with her. There was a slash right
through the mattress, leading to the chilling thought that she
might have been impaled. The underpants on the bedroom floor
were wrong; they were laid out on the floor meticulously, almost daintily. In Barnett's experience that was not the way
burglars operated; they just heaved things around. Barnett and
Chadwick agreed that it was highly unlikely that there were any
burglars, with or without bushy beards.

Steven Steinberg was not just a bereaved husband. He was rapidly becoming a murder suspect. Although some officers were cruising the neighborhood, there was no serious manhunt for the two bearded strangers that Steinberg had described. Everyone's attention was focused on him.

At this point the department made a case assignment. The lead detective was to be Frank Hylton, a seven-year officer with a soft West Virginia drawl. It was Hylton's first murder assignment. The city was using a system known as team policing that year: officers shifted in and out of assignments every two years. In some ways the team policing was a good idea, but it had a disadvantage. Hylton lacked experience in preparing homicide cases for trial, and that experience would be missed down the road.

Hylton was a serious man and not given to theatrics. If anything was worrying him on this night it was the thought that the Crane fiasco should not be repeated. He moved swiftly to clear the scene—detectives were assigned to interview witnesses and neighbors. Hylton's partner, Chris Bingham, was assigned to take Steinberg to the hospital for treatment and then to the police station. Before he left, Hylton asked Steinberg to sign a "consent to search" form so that Kirk could begin the work on the bedroom. He remembers the incident vividly:

"He was sitting on a bed in this den or the child's room. Barney Singer was there and some other people. I said, 'Mr. Steinberg, would you sign this search consent?' He got real white and said he didn't feel like reading it just then and would I read it to him. So I did, and then he did a real strange thing —he just slid right off the bed to the floor, like it made him feel faint or something. His father-in-law was there, just glaring at him."

In the master bedroom, Chadwick and Barnett had noticed drops of blood on the foot of the bed which were not connected to the pool of blood on the floor where the young woman's body was slumped. When the evidence team began their work, they lifted the mattress and box spring where the blood drops were. Tucked in the hollow of the wooden bed platform under the box spring they found a long, bloodstained knife. "It was long and thin and razor-sharp—the blade was at least ten inches long," Kirk recalls. "There was no guard between the handle and the blade—it was kind of molded all the way down. It was a meat-carving knife, good-quality, the kind you would use for a roast, or for Thanksgiving." Cecil Kirk was confident. "There's a fork for this, I know it."

Kirk and Barnett walked out of the bedroom to the kitchen —the Steinberg house was built in a U shape, and it was a long walk around the U, sixty-six feet, to be exact. In one of the drawers in the perfectly ordered kitchen was the carving knife's mate, a matching fork—Kirk was right. Elana Steinberg had been killed with a carving knife from her own immaculate kitchen, and her murderer had taken a long walk to find exactly what he wanted.

At two o'clock that morning, Frank Hylton put in a call to the County Attorney's Office. The county attorney, Tom Collins, believed in sending a prosecutor from the major felony trial group out to a murder scene with the theory that having the prosecutor on the spot would head off technical problems that could destroy a trial. With the Scottsdale Police Department still smarting from mistakes made at the Crane murder scene, it seemed like an especially good idea. On the night of May 27, deputy county attorney Jeff Hotham was on call. He arrived on the Ranch by three o'clock.

Hotham was thirty-two, a five-year veteran of the County Attorney's Office with an outstanding string of convictions to his credit. Unlike Frank Hylton, Jeff Hotham had some experience with murder. He was feeling very confident at that point in his life.

Since he had been in major felonies, Hotham had never lost a jury trial. Even more impressive was his string of death-penalty cases. The death sentence was not imposed easily in Arizona, and when it was, it was a sign that the prosecution had done a good job on the trial—evidence had to be overwhelming and well presented before a judge would consider the death sentence. But there were five men on death row at the prison in Florence who were there because of Jeff Hotham. His colleagues in the office were impressed—to them, Hotham was on a roll.

The trial record suggested flamboyance, but that was not Hotham's style. Soft-spoken and polite, the darkly handsome prosecutor took a very low-key approach, concentrating on physical evidence like fingerprints and ballistics, rather than dramatics.

Hotham had been with the County Attorney's Office since graduating from law school at Arizona State in 1975; it was his first job and the only one he ever really wanted. The office considered itself fortunate to have someone of Hotham's quality —he had a picture-perfect background. He had been an Eagle Scout, a National Merit Scholar at Illinois, an army captain in intelligence in Vietnam; he had been outstanding in everything he had ever done.

Hotham worked his way steadily up the ladder in the County Attorney's Office, ending up in the plum unit known as the major felony trial group. It was where he always wanted to be. He liked the constant trial work and the easy camaraderie of the prosecutor's office. Hotham's supervisors respected him as a hard worker, and he was considered a solid trial attorney, not flashy but dependable.

Prosecutors in Maricopa County were very independent. The deputies ran their own cases without any interference or even any suggestions as far as strategy was concerned. Unlike lawyers in private practice, a prosecutor has no difficult clients to please, except in an abstract way. There was no one looking over a prosecutor's shoulder—some plea bargains had to be approved from above, but that was all.

Independence was typical of the office since Tom Collins had been elected county attorney in 1980. Collins had rescued the office from a swamp of politics and personal vendettas that had plagued his predecessors. At the time of Elana Steinberg's murder, Collins was enjoying a period of bipartisan popularity. The Democrats had not even bothered to field a candidate against him in the last election. Collins ran the office in low key—a considerable relief after the belligerent personalities of former county attorneys. The office was considered to be un-corrupted, reasonably competent, and without political preten-sions.

If there was a weakness in the prosecutor's office it was that there were no stars—no deputies who could be counted on to bring in a conviction in a high-profile case. Big cases, like the bombing assassination of investigative reporter Don Bolles, were usually farmed out to the State Attorney General's Office. Generally, prosecutors went to trial opposing public defenders who also worked for Maricopa County. There was a state of comfortable coexistence between the two offices. If there were some acquittals, prosecutors tended to be philosophical about them rather than bitter. In most cases there was no great harm done, and it was considered good for the public defenders' mo-rale to win one once in a while. The chances were very high that an acquitted defendant would be back in court again very soon, because that was the way of the criminal. Unless a dep-uty's trial record was abysmal, there were no reprisals or assign-ments to preliminary hearings in remote desert outposts in Apache Junction or Tolleson. It was pleasant to work in the County Attorney's Office. It was also a system which did not lend itself to self-criticism.

When Hotham arrived at the Steinberg house, Steve Steinberg had been taken to the hospital. There were civilians milling around in the living room and bedrooms. Hotham was irritated. "Don't they ever learn?" he mumbled to himself, and he was referring to the Scottsdale police. Except for the bed-room, the scene was contaminated. Hotham liked physical evi-dence, and he looked at murders from a strictly technical standpoint. If a prosecutor couldn't show that the murderer, and *only* the murderer, could have left the incriminating evi-dence at the scene, a good defense attoney was halfway home. This was just the kind of carelessness that had doomed any prosecution in the Crane murder. Hotham was annoyed—al-ready in his mind was a shadow of uneasiness that was to persist and grow.

Hotham and Frank Hylton met in Elana's bedroom, where Cecil Kirk was beginning his work. Both men had been at murder scenes before, but the mutilation of this body shocked them. "It was very vicious," remembers Hylton. "Stabbing always is, more so then using a gun or a club. It's what you see with rage, this kind of multiple stab wounds; it's overkill, but pretty typical of people who know each other very well. It shows hatred for a person."

At the autopsy the coroner was to find at least twenty-six separate stab wounds in Elana's body, ranging from three quarters of an inch to four inches in depth. At least four stabs pierced vital organs, spleen, liver, stomach, and heart; one was in the temporal lobe of the brain, but because the victim was near death at the time, that wound was deemed to be "postmortem." At least four of the wounds were fatal. The lesser stabbing on the arms and through the webs of the fingers suggested that the victim had tried to defend herself. All of the blood in the bed showed the place of Elana Steinberg's struggle —she had tried to sit up and get away, but time ran out as she bled to death and toppled over onto the floor.

Hotham and Hylton watched Kirk search the house. Behind a mirror in the bath and vanity was a pile of jewelry, gold chains, earrings, and a diamond watch. The vanity had a man's toilet articles and belongings on it, and it seemed to be the man's half of the dressing room. The jewelry was not near the drawer where the ladies' underwear was thrown out on the floor; that was on the other side of the room by the open arcadia door. "We wondered why the jewelry was piled over here, tucked behind a mirror. It didn't fit with Steinberg's story at all, but it did fit with our theory of what happened. It was our belief that he was going to take the jewelry, say it was a burglar, and that would be that. Either she was supposed to sleep through it all, or else she was supposed to be killed by the burglar too. Probably the second, because he had to go out to the kitchen to get the carving knife, and that is one hell of a long walk," Kirk says.

The crime-scene team searched the rest of the house and found nothing of any significance. They moved the cushions and opened drawers and cupboards, but there was nothing unusual. Meanwhile Steven Steinberg's story was being relayed to

Hylton in phone calls from Chris Bingham at the police station. It didn't hold up.

"What does he say about the knife?" Hylton asked his partner.

"He says the two men had plastic gloves on and the knife must have been long, because he put his hand on it underneath theirs, he says. He's sticking to the story that the men came in the back and wanted jewelry."

At five o'clock Hotham and Hylton agreed. There was cause to believe that Steven Steinberg had murdered his wife.

Hylton called Bingham and told him that he would come down to the station for a final interview and then they would book Steinberg. Before going to the station, Chris Bingham and another officer, Harry Cipriano, had first taken Steinberg to the hospital. Bingham is still with the Scottsdale force. By now a fifteen-year veteran, he supervises the major felony unit. Bingham is an attractive sandy-haired man with the look of a Scotsman; like all Scottsdale officers, he looks as if he had just stepped from the shower, and he is exceedingly polite. Steinberg's palm was stitched in the emergency room. The cut was not serious—a flesh wound with no nerve or tendon damage; there were some small nicks on Steinberg's body that could have been defense-inflicted wounds. Taking his fingerprints had to wait until the palm healed, but the emergency-room doctor took fingernail scrapings and blood samples.

From the hospital it was just a few yards to the beautiful police building. Bingham and Cipriano took their suspect to an interview room. Its atmosphere was not intimidating. On the wall in the carpeted room were posters for the Parada del Sol. In the office across the way was a handsome cowboy bronze and a signed sketch of the President, a sometime visitor to Scottsdale. Cipriano and Bingham sat down with Steinberg, still barefoot and in his short brown bathrobe. Bingham remembers the interview well: "Talking to him that night, I was struck with how cool he was, composed. I thought, here is a cool customer. He said he wanted to talk to us; there was no reluctance.

"We just listened and took it all down—you do that even

if the story sounds improbable, because you never know if it's improbable until it's checked out. And persons on the scene are always suspects, so we wouldn't rule Steinberg out even from the very beginning. And as he went on talking, I think you could say his story was improbable, all right, it was unbelievable. I think that's a better word."

Steinberg told the police that it had been a peaceful night on Via de Luz. He had played in a softball game in Paradise Valley, taking Shawn, the six-year-old, with him. Elana and Edith Singer had taken Traci to a school concert at Kiva School —Traci played the flute. Everyone was home by ten o'clock. Elana went to bed early. The last he heard from his wife was when she asked him to open the sliding glass doors to let the breeze in.

According to Steinberg, he followed his usual routine of staying up in the den, watching *Hollywood Squares* and *Cell Block H*. When he went to bed, Elana was almost asleep and the glass door was open. Steinberg told the police that he woke up to hear Elana screaming, "Steve, Traci, Shawn!" There were two men in the room bending over Elana; he felt a weight on his chest. One man held him down while the other stabbed Elana over and over again. He said he tried to stop the hand from "going up and down," and the burglar's hand had a plastic glove on. He said he told the two men where his wife's jewelry was by shouting, "It's in the drawer!" The men just disappeared, presumably out the door. Steinberg told Bingham that the two had bushy Afro hairstyles and bushy beards, and both the hair and beards looked false. Steinberg said he ran down the hall to Traci's room when he heard her screaming, "What's wrong?"

"Her door was shut and she was on her knees in bed screaming. I asked her to call the police and she said she didn't know how. And I said just dial 0. And she said, 'What's happened?' and I said, 'It's Mommy.' When I went back into the bedroom Elana had slid off the bed and she was on the floor. Then I got my robe and put it on."

By this time the detectives had talked to Mitchell Singer and had learned more about Steven Steinberg's world and how that world was falling apart. They were told that Steinberg was a heavy gambler, that he was in a financial jam because of gambling losses, and that Mitch Singer was selling the restaurants to New York investors who had not wanted Steinberg to stay on. They heard that Steinberg had taken out loans to pay gambling debts that his wife didn't know about, and that the safe at the Brass Derby had been looted. The picture was more complicated than it had first appeared to be—Steven Steinberg was not a run-of-the-mill suburban husband, but a gambler in deep trouble.

Bingham told Steinberg that he was going to be arrested and booked. For the first time Steinberg was visibly upset; he trembled and shivered with cold. "I can't believe this is happening to me." Finally, he asked to see a lawyer. It was five-thirty in the morning.

On Via de Luz the crime-scene team was just about finished. Evidence had been tagged and put in plastic bags. The knife, the bloody bedclothes, and Elana's nightgown were carefully treated and packaged. There had been photographs made of the carnage in the silver-and-white bedroom, of Elana's slumped body on the floor, and of the underwear lying on the floor. Everything was done.

Traci and Shawn had gone home with Edith and Barney Singer. Edith was in a daze; she stumbled and fell getting into the car. Before she left the house, Edith cleaned up the glasses of water—"My daughter likes a neat house," she said. Through the rest of the night, Edith and Barney and Mitch Singer waited at the Singers' for Steve to come back from the police station. No one dreamed that he would be arrested. Edith and Mitch still believed in the burglars, but Barney Singer knew different. In recalling that terrible night, Barney says that Steinberg's avoidance of him made him certain that his son-in-law had killed Elana.

"I knew it the minute I walked in the house. He couldn't look at me. He looked away. And why would he call everybody else but not me that night? He called me twenty times a day, for everything he did. He was like my own son, maybe closer. But he didn't call me and he couldn't look at me that night because he killed her. He didn't have the guts to look at me. And I said when we got home, 'Edith, he killed her.' "

Edith protested; the idea was too preposterous for her. She was dazed and crying; nothing made sense.

Dawn came in a rosy flush on the McDowell Mountains, rugged and mysterious, to the east of the Ranch. Birds were beginning to sing on the desert. It was going to be a fine blue-skied day. Cecil Kirk was the last person to leave the house on Via de Luz. There is a softness in his voice when he speaks of Elana Steinberg even years later.

"When I picked her up to put her on a clean sheet we use for fibers, I was amazed how light she was. She was so tiny, and this was such a vicious murder.

"The house was kept so nice, everything was shining and perfect. The kids' room had all these toys, and this special wallpaper and a blackboard they could write on. It was just what a kids' room should look like. What I really remember, and I don't know why this stays in my memory, was how neat the kitchen was. When we went to get the mate to the knife everything was lying perfectly in the drawer. Everything had a place. What was really sad to me—again I don't know why because it is an insignificant thing—was that right next to the door to the garage there were pegs on the wall to hangs things on. There was a peg for her purse, and it was hanging there with all these little homely things in it like Kleenex and pictures of the girls and Mitch's little boy and a little gold pencil. My thought was, this is not a house where something like this happens."

CHAPTER THREE

MEMORIES OF CHICAGO

It was a brutal killing, but that is not unusual when someone uses a knife. Unless the killer has some knowledge of anatomy, it's not easy to stab someone to death—even someone as small as Elana Steinberg was. There was a particular ferocity in the attack on this ninety-pound woman. She must have been caught unawares and unsuspecting in her bed that night.

If the killer was her husband, as the police believed, the characters seemed all wrong for such violence. Elana was slim and pretty and young; her handsome husband was the model of an up-and-coming Scottsdale businessman. And as Cecil Kirk observed, the setting wasn't right for this carnage. The house on Via de Luz was immaculately kept and beautifully furnished —clearly a house meant for comfort and for entertaining friends. It was a house where children played the flute and were taught to erase marks from their school books before they turned them back on the last day of school, just as Traci was doing on the night her mother was killed. On the surface there was no hint of a dark current underneath that could explain what had happened here.

But there was a crack, a fault, in this shiny surface. A careful observer could discover and trace the vulnerable flaw in this marriage. The Steinbergs were living a very fragile existence and had been doing so for years. There was something troubling and inexplicable in Steven Steinberg's character—a seam of anger and impulse that had been building since his youth. Elana had seen glimpses of the dark side of Steve's nature at the end, but marriage and family was everything to her and she underestimated her danger.

The story begins more than a thousand miles away from the desert, in the northwest suburbs of Chicago. Steve and Elana and their families before them were Chicago people; they hadn't been in Arizona long enough to shed those ties. Whatever happened to flower into this tragedy must have had its roots back in Niles and Skokie and Rogers Park.

I went back to Chicago four years later. I wanted to talk to someone who knew the Steinbergs when they were young and fresh and full of optimism. I wanted to see where Elana Steinberg's grandparents had begun their life in America after they arrived in the great immigration from Eastern Europe, where they had lived among cousins and *landsleit* who cared about one another. I didn't think I could understand this family until I saw where Barney and Edith Singer met and married and raised their children when life still seemed good.

Edith's father, Samuel Lubin, came to America from the Ukraine when he was fourteen. There are no survivors of any of his family that stayed behind. As with so many Jewish families with roots in Europe, there is nothing left and that part of their history is forever lost. Sam Lubin met Edith's mother on the boat coming to America. It was an immigrant's shipboard romance—not unusual in its time.

Lubin became a manufacturing jeweler in Chicago, making pieces for other jewelers. He had his shop in the Loop on Michigan Avenue, an unusual location for his day. Most of the Jewish merchants and craftsmen stayed in the areas of first settlement, on Maxwell or Halsted Street. Edith's father was a

leader, aggressive and successful. The business he started is still
in operation and prospering under Edith's brother Morris.

Four children were born to the Lubins, three girls and a
boy. Edith is third in line, right after Morris. The Lubins are
fair; Edith has blond hair and is blue-eyed. Her youngest sister,
Sarah, had reddish hair much like Shawn's or Elana's. The
family lived a traditional and quiet life in Garfield Park, a shady,
pleasant spot that was one of the first stops for the more prosperous Eastern European Jews when they moved out from the
west side of Chicago.

Edith's father's rise came easier and faster than for most
of the fifty thousand immigrants from Russia and Poland who
settled in Chicago at the turn of the century. Making jewelry
and being a goldsmith had been respected crafts for generations. In czarist Russia, Jews were forbidden to own land, join
the guilds, or even attend schools, but goldsmiths were sometimes among the favored few who were allowed some special
privileges. Some could even live precariously outside the Pale
of Jewish Settlement in cities like Moscow and St. Petersburg;
their children were able to go to school and take music lessons
and live in a culture very different from the shtetls and crowded
ghettos of the cities where Jews were made to live. To any
refugee, jewelry has always had a practical and essential meaning. It is small and portable; it could be hidden and carried
when refugees were forced to move and to hide. Money had no
meaning in czarist Russia at the end. For the Jews, jewelry
could be the way to survive, to eat or to buy passage to America
for a son who was going to vanish in the czarist army. It was
the currency of survival. To Edith Singer's family, jewelry was
their livelihood and much respected.

As soon as she graduated from high school, Edith went to
work. College for a girl was not a priority for her family, especially in the waning days of the depression. The Lubins were
merchants and jewelers and did not particularly think in terms
of higher education—that was to come with the next generation. Even Morris did not go, but he was the natural inheritor
of the business and there was really no necessity for it. Edith's
first job was in the office of a commercial laundry, the largest

in Chicago, where she was the switchboard operator and ran office machines. Her instructor in the mysteries of these machines was the boss's nephew, a young Canadian named Barney Singer.

Barney's parents were part of the great immigration from Eastern Europe, too, but they had settled in Canada. The older Singers were old-fashioned, very religious. They lived in traditional Orthodox ways and were mystified by some things in America. Becoming "American" for first-generation women like Barney Singer's mother was not always easy. It is hard to comprehend that women like these were the sophisticated Elana Singer's grandmothers, but such was the speed at which the families of immigrants embraced American life.

The Singers sent the young Barney to Chicago to get a start in life with his uncle. The pattern of relatives helping each other to get a foothold in the New World was very much intact. Barney loved his uncle. All through the war he had Morris Heckman's name on his dogtags as his next of kin even though his own parents were still alive in Canada. Barney was easy to like himself. He was one of those individuals whose face seems to radiate good humor. Now he is overweight and balding and could be a double for the actor Ed Asner. The cheerfulness and simplicity are still there—everybody likes Barney Singer. He is known as a "softy," a "sweetheart," and until his daughter's death, nothing had ever made Barney angry. Even when Edith fell out with her South Side relatives in a long-lasting feud, her relatives were still partial to Barney, and he is the only person who can still communicate with all sides of the family. He is bluff and sentimental and a good friend.

When the war broke out in 1941, Edith and Barney were courting at the laundry, an office romance. Barney had the approval of Edith's family. By coincidence, years before, Lubin had sponsored Barney's uncle in the Masons, so there was a tie of acceptability to both families.

After Pearl Harbor, Barney had enlisted in the army and was sent to Fort Sheridan for basic training. Almost immediately he was moved to Tacoma, where everyone said Barney's outfit would be one of the first to be shipped overseas to the

Pacific. Barney and Edith were engaged by then, and Edith went west on the train by herself to get married, a daring trip for a nineteen-year-old girl who had never been away from Chicago before. Girls didn't take trips to see their boyfriends, particularly girls from families like Edith's, but it was wartime and everybody was doing it. Sam Lubin told her before she left, "If you go out there, you go to get married," but Edith had no thought of anything else. They were married by a rabbi at the base in Tacoma without the big wedding they would have had back in Chicago. Their wedding picture is a World War II classic. Edith wears a tailored suit with a gardenia corsage and looks unbearably happy. Barney is in his uniform, fresh and young, with a full head of hair, and he stares confidently into the camera. Ten weeks later he had shipped out to the South Pacific, and Edith was on the train going home again. Her husband did not return for four years.

Barney's outfit was the 1874th Engineer Aviation Battalion. The EABs of World War II were combat engineers attached to the Army Air Force and the counterpart of the Navy's Seabees. Most of the EABs were overseas by the first year of the war, and they stayed to the bitter end—the 1874th even landed on Honshu right after the surrender. In the South Pacific their job was to build airstrips as soon as the ground was captured from the Japanese. It was hard duty—the battalion lived in tents and mud for weeks. There was no fresh food, and the soldiers were subject to strange tropical ailments, like jungle rot that never seemed to heal, malaria, and dengue fever. The battalion would work twenty-four-hour shifts to keep bridges and roads open, often in complete darkness and driving monsoon rains. There were occasional Japanese snipers, and sometimes a plane dropping antipersonnel bombs as they worked. They did the job well—on one occasion the 1874th landed on Noemfoor Island in New Guinea and built a runway in record time; the first C-47s were landing in fourteen days. Barney was also in Leyte and Mindanao during his long overseas tour.

Elana's father keeps his wartime mementos in a cigar box in the Singers' kitchen. There are some faded V-Mails, crinkled gray tissue folded on itself that brings a rush of memories for those of Barney and Edith's generation. There is a collection of small faded photographs that now seem incredibly exotic for a Jewish boy from his uncle's laundry in Chicago. In one picture Barney is posed with two serious bare-breasted Micronesian women with draped skirts, almost as in a painting by Gauguin. There is a frame house on stilts in the background. In another snapshot a pig is being roasted in a pit for a feast—Barney's Eastern European parents and grandparents could hardly know what to think about this. His buddies posed in front of the construction equipment are thin, and the GI-issue pants ride low on their waists. There is a fistful of campaign ribbons in the box. It is the memorabilia of Barney Singer's four hard years of war for the country that his parents once called Columbus's Land.

In Chicago, Edith waited for the war to end. She had gone to work for her father in the jewelry business, learning to polish bracelets and rings that he had cast. Barney came home in 1946. Like many other returning veterans, he found that things had changed. His uncle Morris had died and two of his sons were grown and managing the laundry now. Barney felt superfluous. It was time to move on. He went to work for a garden and outdoor furniture store in Skokie; after the war there was a new market for the trappings of outdoor living. Sales of umbrellas, swimming pools, and barbecues boomed, and this became Barney Singer's trade.

It was the first year of the baby boom, and Edith was pregnant. All of their friends were having babies too, and moving north and west in the city to suburbs like Park Ridge and Skokie, areas where once the Germans and Irish had settled. One of Edith's sisters moved south, but the rest of the family went north in the perpetual game of displacement for various ethnic groups in Chicago. The Singers were renting a duplex in Albany Park when Elana was born on November 14, 1946. She was a tiny, pretty baby with a piquant face, and she was quickly Edith's pride. She loved to dress Elana and walk her in the big, old-fashioned black buggy of the forties.

From the first, Edith and Elana were inseparable—there seemed to be a psychic bond between them. When they were together they could shut out the rest of the world. One of Elana's friends in Phoenix told me that she had never seen a mother and daughter so close. "Elana used to tell me that she worried about what she'd do when her mother died. She didn't know if she could handle it or not, it would be so devastating for her," the friend recalls.

Elana was never a troublesome child. She was quick and intelligent in school, but there was never any plan for her to go to college. It was Elana's younger brother, Mitchell, not Elana, who went away to college, but that was in the tradition of Jewish middle-class families at the time. Edith says that Elana and Mitchell always got along and didn't fight; others don't remember it quite that way. There seemed to be a certain crosscurrent of rivalry or aggressiveness between the brother and sister. On the night of Elana's murder, Mitchell told Frank Hylton, "My sister is the type of person who is the boss, and who has not always been happy." Later on, when there was conflict between Elana's husband and her brother in the restaurants, Elana would always take Steve's part. There was a deep loyalty between brother and sister, but growing up must not have been quite the harmony that Edith Singer now remembers. These were two strong-minded children.

When Elana was ready for high school the Singers had moved again but were still in the northwest suburbs. In 1960, Elana enrolled in Maine Township East. Maine East is a proud and distinguished high school built in the thirties in what was once a German Lutheran neighborhood on Dempster Avenue —it is one of several fine Chicago high schools with national reputations for excellence. Maine East is still an imposing structure; if there were a model of what a high school should look like it could very well be Maine East.

By the time Elana Singer arrived as a freshman at Maine the student body had changed; the northern Europeans of German and Scandinavian ancestry who were the school's first students were beginning to give way to Italians and Eastern European Jews who were moving north and west in the city; it was the second wave of immigration on the move in Chicago. Scholastic achievement was still high—Maine East has always had that reputation. Elana's class was one of the last before the big student revolution; the class of 1964 was before Vietnam, protests, and drugs.

In the yearbook all of the girls have either beehive hairdos or "flips"—hairdos achieved at the painful cost of sleeping on rollers with brushes inside them every night. There was no need for dress codes at Maine East then. The girls wore knee-length dresses, cropped jackets, and little pumps in the style of Jackie Kennedy; the boys had short hair and wore thin ties. Everybody danced to the Twist and the Pony. It was the era of musical "girl groups" like the Shirrelles and the Supremes, Buddy Holly and Eddie Cochran; Dick Clark's Bandstand was in full swing, and the Beatles had yet to revolutionize music. It was an innocent era which was to change very soon.

Elana was always a social being. She loved to go out, to talk for hours with her friends, and she was very interested in boys. Her closest friend was B. J. Kaufman, a cheerful, pretty blonde whose personality meshed perfectly with Elana's. It was one of those friendships that start in school and go on through weddings and the birth of children. Today B.J. is a suburban Chicago matron, quiet and thoughtful when she remembers her friend.

"I met Elana at BBG; we were about fifteen then. That's B'nai B'rith Girls—it's an organization for Jewish girls that go to different schools. First of all, Elana was fun. If I had to describe her, I would say that first. She was lively, funny, told jokes, and was sort of outrageous sometimes. Wherever she was, there was something going on. She was never boring. And second, Elana was smart. I think of her as being very, very intelligent. Some people thought she was aggressive, but it wasn't like that, really. She was ambitious, she wanted to be somebody, and she was proud. Elana should have been proud, she had a lot to be proud about. She had beautiful taste, a very classy girl."

When she was a junior at East, Elana met Steve Steinberg in a time-honored way. They were introduced by Elana's cousin Louis, the son of Edith's sister Sarah. Elana was captivated immediately. She thought that Steve was "cool" and worldly. It was not only his undeniable good looks but an air of restlessness about him, a kind of tough-guy manner that was appealing. He was the kind of boy who wore a leather jacket, the kind who would have a pack of cigarettes rolled in the sleeve of his T-shirt, who did different, daring things; he was not like the milquetoast boys Elana saw at Maine East. Steve was almost nineteen, and he was out of high school. When Elana brought him home, Edith and Barney Singer were hospitable.

Steve had a family of his own, but to Edith he seemed like a waif. She liked to mother people, and Steve fitted right in. He flattered her, followed Barney around, and was soon more than just a casual boyfriend of Elana's. Steve wasn't the first choice for a husband for Elana in Edith's mind. She would have preferred a "professional man," a budding accountant or dentist, but that was an occupational jump that was not a practical expectation for the Singers then. So Elana's parents welcomed the good-looking Steve Steinberg with affection and generosity. Edith told me that she felt sorry for him.

"He only had one pair of pants and one pair of shoes when we first met him. We got the feeling he was starved for affection. Steve lived at our house. He was there all the time. If they went out late, he would stay here and change his clothes, take a shower. There was nothing wrong, because Elana was very strictly raised. We thought this was like a home for him always, and he loved it. Mitchell was just growing up, and he and Elana would take Mitch with them, like he was Mitch's brother, too. We made him part of the family."

Steve Steinberg was an early baby boomer. He was born in 1944 when his parents were living on the South Side of Chicago. Steve's father, a good-natured, handsome man, was a butcher and owned a small butcher shop. The Steinberg paternal grandparents were Maxwell Street merchants, poor and devoutly Orthodox in their beliefs. Steve's mother, Esther, was serious, strict, and religiously observant; there was a daughter, Gloria, three years older than Steve. The Steinbergs lived modestly. Steven was a beautiful baby, quick and active, with a sunny disposition. He was brought up with a traditional Jewish religious education.

In grade school, Steve made friends easily, a trait that was to follow him throughout his life and was to prove immensely valuable when he needed it. When Steve was twelve, he had an experience that was to change his life forever. Steve's father had stayed home from work for several days with a vague flulike illness. No one was terribly concerned; apparently he was well enough for father and son to wrestle and play on the bed as they often did. In the midst of the play, Steve's father gasped and fell back on the bed—he died before Steve's eyes. The vague illness must have been the precursor of a massive coronary.

The load of guilt on the twelve-year-old boy after this wrestling match can only be imagined. If the thought was not openly expressed, it must have been in everyone's mind—if he hadn't done that wrestling, would he still be alive? Twenty-five years later, Steinberg was still intensely emotional about the incident. All of the psychiatrists who talked to him in the jail noted that he wept not about Elana, but when he described his father's funeral.

Life changed immediately for the Steinbergs. Steve, Gloria, and their mother no longer had their own apartment; they moved in with Steve's grandparents on the North Side of Chicago, and Esther went to work. The children were enrolled in different schools on the other side of town.

Steinberg told psychiatrists that the years in his grandparents' home after his father died were idyllic. Everyone was "warm" and "close," his mother was strict but loving, the grandparents supportive. "Not once in six years did my grandparents interfere with my mother's decisions about the children," he said. There was something missing from Steinberg's nostalgic description about these adolescent years in Chicago —something he didn't tell the psychiatrists. These were also the years in which Steven Steinberg became a pathological gambler.

Compiling the case histories of compulsive gamblers is the province of Baltimore mental health expert Robert Custer, the acknowledged leader in the field. The psychiatrist is now engaged with the idea that there may be some chemical component in the metabolic system of the compulsive gambler—a certain brain chemistry which causes him to soar with almost a cocainelike "high" when he is gambling. Added to the possibility of a genetic base, the man who becomes a compulsive gambler, Dr. Custer believes, is a vulnerable personality displaying certain traits. This kind of gambler has most often experienced an unhappy or deprived childhood with either physical abuse or parental rejection and withdrawal of affection. Many compulsive gamblers have experienced something truly unusual—they have had a brush with death in their early adolescence, which Dr. Custer calls the "death experience." In Dr. Custer's case histories the disease progresses along an almost inevitable path. First the gambling is minor and innocuous, the gambler is successful and in control. Somewhere along the line, luck runs out; the gambler begins to lose, and from this point on the progress of the disease is rapid and grim. At the end, the compulsive gambler is likely to be destitute, sick, or in jail, with those around him destroyed. Dr. Custer calls this the "desperation phase." The pattern fits the life of Steven Steinberg as if it were made for him.

These early years of adolescence were the years in which Steve first began to gamble seriously in card games and on sports cards—by the time he was in high school he was gambling almost professionally. He was able to win, and the money in his pocket gave him an exhilarating feeling. When Steve was in high school he made his first big win—the final experience that Dr. Custer believes sets the compulsive gambler on his path.

This first big win is crucial to the compulsive gambler. If someone with the potential for this pathology loses and keeps on losing, he will eventually go on to some other activity. But with the first big win, the win that is out of the ordinary in its size and its scope, the picture changes. Gambling has now become a part of life; the gambler is hooked. One of the characteristics of the compulsive gambler is a fantasy that he is blessed with skills that no one else has, that things will always turn out right for him. Psychiatrists have coined a fine descriptive phrase for this—they call it "magical thinking." Magical thinking is the gambler's belief that he has a secret power to be on top, that he can win the lottery, he is "lucky." It is a fantasy that will sustain the gambler when things get grim later on and he has passed into the inevitable losing stage. When he begins to lose, the pathological gambler is confident that his magic touch has just left him temporarily—it will be back in the next hand or in next Sunday's parlay. For Steven Steinberg it is ironically true that there was a kind of magic at the end for him; he beat the system.

Steve made his first big win, the one that made a difference, playing cards on a Lake Michigan beach where he played regularly. He won a car. No one knows exactly whether Steve won enough money to buy the car, or whether the car itself passed hands in a game; it could have been either way. Whatever the circumstances, from that point on, Steve became and remained an expert to his friends. "He was good at it," they said, and they believed it.

In the early sixties, new schools were springing up everywhere in Chicago to accommodate the baby boomers. Steven Steinberg enrolled in one of them. The paint was not yet dry on Mather High School in West Rogers Park when his class enrolled; Steve's was the first graduating class to go all the way through Mather. Traditions had not been established in this school, and there was little school spirit; the clubs were just beginning to feel their way. Mather was 90 percent Jewish and strongly middle-class, "one of those schools where the football team is one and nine and there is a big chess club," says a contemporary.

There are Mather graduates who now live in Phoenix, and they have done very well. They are professionals and businessmen who have met with considerable financial success in Arizona. Only a few remember Steven Steinberg's face from the yearbook. "I kind of picture him wearing a leather jacket, and that had a connotation, you know, that was sort of tough. He wasn't your usual Mather guy that was going to go to college and who played the clarinet." In the yearbook, the 1962 *Dais,* most of the boys have nicknames like Artie and Shelly, but Steve's nickname is Modern. Steinberg was on the track team and had a letter sweater, but his life was slightly out of the mainstream. His best friends were still from the South Side; Mather was just a way station. The young Steve was handsome, but not as handsome as he would be later on at thirty. His face had not filled out; it needed another five years before his good looks matured. At eighteen, all of Steven Steinberg's personality traits were set. He was gregarious with his friends, he was impulsive, he liked to take risks. He was a worker—Steve always had jobs, and he had been working ever since he was twelve years old to get spending money.

Steve graduated from Mather in June, and in August his mother married a widower named Dave Goodman. Goodman was born in Germany and had arrived in the United States as a young man when the Nazis first came to power. When Esther met him, he was a prosperous widower who had two children almost the same age as Steve and Gloria Steinberg. David Goodman's son from his first marriage, Joel, was an academic achiever, educated at Michigan and Stanford, in contrast to Steve, who had dropped out after one semester of junior college because, as he said later, "I knew all I needed to know."

In 1964, Steve's sister, Gloria, was getting married; Steve was nineteen and without much of a home base when he met the sixteen-year-old Elana Singer. The cousin's house where they met was on the South Side of Chicago, where Steve still felt more at home and where his social life tended to center. As soon as Steve met Barney and Edith Singer, an emotional gap seemed to be filled. From the first he was ready to adopt the Singers almost as his parents, and they did the same for him. Apparently Barney was the father figure that was missing from Steve's life, minus the guilt of the wrestling match. He and Barney were inseparable. He charmed Edith totally. Edith thought that her daughter's boyfriend was not only good-looking, but sweet and attentive—even more than her own son, Mitchell, who tended to be difficult. She cooked for Steve and prepared fancy tidbits. Edith is a good cook with gourmet tendencies, and Steve Steinberg was thin and hungry-looking in those days. Barney and Edith fussed over Steve like a son. The age difference between the thirteen-year-old Mitchell and Elana's boyfriend was large enough to blunt any jealousy that

might have occurred. Steve made a fuss over Mitch as well—
he taught him to drive; they went to races. No one could understand when the South Side cousin said that he wished he
had never introduced Elana and Steve. "I can't stand the guy,"
he told Mitchell, who was mystified.

It was graduation time at Maine East. Elana had taken
business and secretarial classes for four years. Middle-class families like the Singers had not yet put the education of a daughter
on the same level as their boys'—the first educational break-
through in the Singer family was for Mitchell, not Elana. Marriage, children, and the home were paramount for girls; they
were geared and groomed to be attractive. Self-care, hairdress-
ing, and clothes became almost a matter of family pride for a
girl, and in this respect, Elana Steinberg at seventeen was no
different from any of her contemporaries. In 1964 she was
poised and exactingly groomed—Elana was extremely neat. It
was difficult to find clothes to fit Elana's petite figure, and her
clothes were carefully chosen. Edith and Elana spent whole
afternoons shopping together in the wonderful departments of
Marshall Field's and Carson's looking for just the right things,
a highly pleasurable activity for both of them. Steve and Elana
went to the prom at East that year, and Edith found the perfect
dress. It was yellow, with a full gauzy skirt to the knee and
spaghetti straps in the fashion of the early sixties. In the gym,
they danced to "What a Sweet Thing That Was," and "Crying at
the Chapel." It was an innocent happy moment, and there were
not going to be many more.

CHAPTER FOUR

THE GAMBLER

Elana got a job as a legal secretary in downtown Chicago. The office staff called her their "little doll"—throughout her life people were always referring to Elana in diminutives. The relationship with Steve Steinberg was getting serious. For a girl raised as Elana was, that meant marriage and nothing else.

In the sixties, couples tended not to date alone. Double and triple dates were traditional. Elana liked to fix up her Maine East friends with friends of Steve's—she was the catalyst for at least two marriages. One of Elana's best friends eventually married Steve's best friend and, in what later proved to be an excess of togetherness, even bought a house on the same street in Arlington Heights when Steve and Elana did. Generally, Steve's friends didn't care for Elana. She was too outspoken and quick-tongued for them. She didn't care what she said; she wasn't deferential, and they resented that. When the couple had a falling-out a year later, his friends were secretly pleased. For a while, Elana dated a Chicago attorney she met at work. Nothing came of this relationship, and eventually Elana went back to Steve. One of Steve's friends told me later that Steve was having a "freedom attack"—"he just didn't want to get tied into it and he could see it coming." Steve's friends thought he was being marched into marriage to a drumbeat; "Don't do it, guy," one of them had the temerity to say.

When I asked old Chicago friends about the Steinberg marriage as they perceived it, they divided into two camps of loyalty. Elana's friends told me that they didn't buy the idea that Steve was a reluctant bridegroom. B.J. said it was a romance on both sides, with maybe a little more coming from Elana. "She was crazy about him," she said. "He was so handsome; he looked like a movie star. Elana liked that—she was very young, you know." Steve was older, and there was something daring, reckless, about him which drew Elana. Another friend didn't see that as an attribute.

"There was always something a little lower-class about him," she recalled. "You got the impression that he had grown up on the streets. It was just different."

By 1966 they had been going together almost exclusively for nearly three years. Steve was virtually living at the Singers'. They both agreed it was time to get married. In those days, when none of their contemporaries had their own apartments, marriage was a way to gain some independence from your family. Steve had finished his National Guard service and had been promised a promotion at the pharmaceutical company where he was a buyer. With their combined incomes, they could make it. The date was set for May 29.

The wedding was going to be a traditional Jewish blowout at the Blackstone, but the cost was a tight squeeze for the Singers. As with so many weddings, trouble began to surface between the two families almost immediately. Steve and Elana's wedding was gorgeous, everyone said. The Singers had gone all out and had taken the grand ballroom at the elegant Blackstone. Everything was done in cyclamen pink and white. The *chuppah,* the wedding canopy where the bridal couple exchange their vows, was filled with flowers. There was an open bar and lavish food before the ceremony, as is the custom in Jewish weddings; then a sit-down dinner for two hundred and an orchestra for dancing.

No one will say what caused the rift between the in-laws. It involved money, and it was sensitive. Edith Singer told me that she thought Steve's family had reneged on some of their obligations. For one, they had left early from the dinner for out-of-town guests the night before the wedding, and the Singers had picked up the tab when they weren't expecting to. Years later Steve said, and it was usually the first thing he said about his wedding, "My folks paid for part of it." Edith claims that Steve was embarrassed about the problem—he and Elana made up for it after the wedding, she said.

Whatever happened at the Blackstone, relationships between the Goodmans and the Singers were strained for all time, although this cannot be seen from the wedding pictures. Everyone was very photogenic; Barney Singer and Steve both look particularly pleased. Elana's hair is the beehive then fashionable, and it almost carried her petite figure away. In one photograph Steve is gazing at his own image in a mirror—he looks like a young Tony Curtis. They are a handsome pair.

Elana was the first of her group to get married; she was nineteen and Steve twenty-two. Everyone thought that Steve was doing well. There always seemed to be plenty of money for whatever the young couple wanted to do. The Steinbergs dined out frequently, and Elana was beginning to buy furniture. Elana knew that Steve went to the track and was gambling a lot, but she was not too perturbed at first; Barney Singer had always done the same thing. She had grown up around gambling, and there never seemed to be any serious trouble. From the first, Steve and Elana had agreed that she would manage the finances and pay the bills. Elana was tight-fisted, and money seemed to slip through Steve's fingers. When he was doing well, he was generous, a big spender. He would leave lavish tips at restaurants and buy presents for Elana. He always carried a wad of cash. Sometimes Steve would win more than usual at the track, and would come home and give Elana several hundred-dollar bills—"Here, this is for you, buy something you want."

They took a vacation and went to Las Vegas, which was always Steve's favorite destination. In Vegas, Steve lost big for the first time. It was something he couldn't handle. The balance to his gambling had tipped—before that trip he would borrow twenty or twenty-five dollars from a friend to play poker or make a bet and he could always pay it back. But he had to take care of the big loss in Vegas differently. It had to be concealed from Elana. At this point, the losing phase in the metamorphosis of the gambler probably began for Steve. From here on, Steinberg was "chasing"—betting to recoup past losses, not betting to win new money. Dr. Custer writes that although it may take years, the terminal losing phase is inevitable. Either the compulsive gambler grows cocky and brash and loses the careful restraint that had kept him afloat before, or the gods declare that it is now time for losing.

Steve was beginning to duck Elana on the extent of his gambling. His friends knew it and generally supported him— they thought Elana was a nag. A staunch supporter of Steve's told me that he would help to hide some of it from Elana. "We would go to the track together and he would bet his five dollars or whatever and then he would go to another window and bet a lot more. He would say, 'Don't tell Elana.' We all thought he was a big winner, though."

It must have been a lonely life for Elana, worrying about Steve's gambling and not being able to confide in anyone. Sometimes her protective facade would slip. Her best friend was astute enough to know about it. When I talked to B.J. she told me that she had known for years. "I first got the drift of how serious it was when my husband told me that he didn't want to go bowling with Steve anymore. We were poor then, everybody was, but not that poor. I told him not to be silly, we could afford it. Bill said that the real reason he wanted to quit was because Steve bet so much that it made him uncomfortable. It was getting out of hand, he said, it wasn't just a game."

Elana did confide in her friend once, when she discovered that Steve had extended a bank loan without telling her.

"Once they went to Vegas and I think he lost a lot of money there. A few months later Elana found out that her car —her little Mustang—wasn't paid off when she thought it should be. She called the bank and said, 'Isn't it time my car has been paid off? I've made all the payments.' And the loan officer said, 'Didn't you know that your husband was in and extended the loan?'

"I don't know why Elana told me about this. I think she was embarrassed about it, and worried, too, in a way. She held a lot of things in."

Strange things began to happen now. The first in a rash of burglaries, kidnappings, and robberies that were to follow Steven Steinberg wherever he went occurred when Traci was a baby and the family was living in an apartment in Des Plaines. Two burglars broke in when Steve was alone. He told the police the two men had bushy hair and bushy beards, and that the men had tied him up and put him in a closet. Steinberg said that when he escaped he found that the bushy-haired men had taken all of Elana's jewelry—the fine jewelry that the Lubin clan had given Elana for wedding presents and gifts over the years. After the robbery, there was no problem with the insurance claim. No one doubted Steve's story about the two bushy-haired men—and the agent was a relative of one of Steve's friends. The story lingered in people's memories, though, and they talked about it years later. It was dramatic and just not the normal burglary in Chicago. There was a flair, an air of danger, whenever Steve was in peril.

Later there was another mysterious burglary. Edith Singer had kept a little cache of money in a cookie jar in a kitchen cabinet in her Skokie apartment. One day it vanished. "It wasn't much, one hundred and fifty or two hundred dollars. Just my little private place, but it upset me that somebody had been in my kitchen." Steve commiserated with Edith. He accused the janitor at the apartment building—"That dog, he took your money, Edie."

Edith was outspoken, with a sharp tongue like Elana's.

She let everyone in the apartment building know what she suspected. The janitor's wife called her in anger to deny it.

By this time, Steve had taken a job working for Barney Singer and his partners, who had opened several pool and patio stores. Steve managed one of them. One night, there was another mysterious theft—four thousand dollars disappeared from the cash register at Steve's store. He had been the last one there. Steve blamed the bookkeeper. The partners were upset, suspicion fell on Steve, and they blamed Barney Singer as well for standing up for his son-in-law.

Barney was outraged. Words led to more words, and the business relationship was never the same. Eventually the partnership broke up and Barney left. Years later, both Edith and Barney insist that they never connected their handsome son-in-law with the mysterious robberies and thefts that clustered all around him. In the Singers' protestations there is a certain naiveté. Did they know about it and tolerate it? It is hard to imagine that anyone could have been oblivious to all the crimes that seemed to happen around Steven Steinberg. He was like a lightning rod.

It was a measure of Steve Steinberg's charm that no one chose to think the unthinkable. The idea that their son-in-law could be a thief, and a thief within the confines of their own family resources, was inconceivable. He was Elana's husband and the father of Elana's children. They loved him and were blind to his faults.

If Elana was worried about the gambling, she kept most of it to herself. Experts say this is a common reaction for a wife who realizes for the first time that she is married to a compulsive gambler—psychiatrists call it "denial." At first, the wife tends to fool herself into acceptance of her husband's gambling as normal. She scales down her expectations of the marriage so that she can live with it rather than destroy everything she knows with a divorce. Typically, the wife throws herself into housekeeping and the children, tennis or golf—in Elana's case, redecorating. The gnawing worry that everything is out of control is pushed to the back of the wife's mind. She closes her eyes to his raids on bank accounts and the children's piggy banks, the missing jewelry and savings bonds, the wild inventive excuses that she knows are not true. Everything fades into the grand delusion of the gambler's wife: things will remain much the way they are and nothing will happen to upset the balance of their life.

Elana plunged into homemaking and an almost frantic social life. She liked to organize groups of couples who would meet for dinner or go to parties. She worked for three years after they were married, and then stopped when Traci was born in 1969. The Steinbergs were still in Des Plaines then, but they wanted to buy a house. The one they found was in a struggling new tract in Arlington Heights. The area still has a feeling of country: there are farms on the road out from Northbrook, and a prairielike quality in the flat landscape. This is farmland still. The developer of the subdivision in Arlington Heights was stretched thin, and Elana drove a hard bargain. The Steinbergs were able to buy the modest brick split-level for a bargain-basement price, and had some money left over for Elana's decorating.

Today the street where Steve and Elana lived is much the same. The yards are neat and well mowed, the houses well kept. Many of the same people still live there in modest middle-class comfort. At the end of the block there is a park where Elana used to walk Shawn as a baby and where Traci played on the swings. The Steinberg house has two ugly black stone lions on a ledge, someone's folly, but otherwise it is indistinguishable from its neighbors. In the essence of suburbia, Elana was a typical wife and mother. Steve was attentive to his family, but he was beginning to stray. Unlike his gambling, the next problem was something that Elana could not tolerate. She discovered that Steve was seeing another woman. He was traveling then, and she thought the woman was someone he met on the road. Elana reacted swiftly, angrily, and decisively.

When I interviewed a friend of Steve's about it years later, he was clearly annoyed at the way Elana had handled the crisis. I couldn't understand why Steve's friend felt that way—perhaps he thought it was humiliating when she brought Barney and Edith into it.

"She called them all together, Barney and Edith," he told me. "Steve had to make a formal apology to all of them. She told him that if he did not give up the woman, she would get a divorce and it would not be friendly—she would see to it that he never saw Traci again. Barney and Edith chimed in; Steve had no say in it. So he did it. He had to eat dirt." I could tell that Steve's friend counted this episode as a mark against Elana —she was so direct and fierce about it. Steve had been put on probation.

The Chicago friends would always come in on different sides, I soon discovered. In Elana's friend B.J.'s view, permanent damage had been done. Elana could tolerate the gambling, but Steve's infidelity hurt her. I could tell that B.J. agreed with her friend.

"She put up with a lot from him with the gambling and running around, and she always tried to make him look good. You know that takes a toll after a while. He was making her unhappy underneath, but a nice Jewish girl just swallows that. Marriage is everything in a Jewish family, and there just isn't anything else for a woman, at least not then. Elana was proud and she wouldn't let it slip very often, but sometimes she did to me," B.J. told me sadly.

"You know, I used to love Steve, I really did. When they were first married I used to go over to their apartment all the time. It was so fun to be there. It was like playing house. He was always very, very nice to me—he was a charmer. At first I thought Elana had done well for herself. It wasn't until years later that I got the picture on his gambling and I guessed that he was making her nervous, very nervous. She never complained about him, though, never. She always wanted to make him look good, to puff him up, and she wouldn't tolerate any criticism of him."

After Shawn was born in 1975, the family seemed to be at a dead end financially, although no one ever said so. Everybody acknowledged that Steve "could sell anything" but somehow it had never amounted to a solid selling career. It wasn't that Steve didn't work—he was always a worker. There was something glib about his salesmanship, too many shortcuts that didn't play out. The cloud from the incident at the pool and patio store lingered. In the end, Steve usually relied on his father-in-law to find him another job when he needed one, and Barney always obliged.

Now everything seemed to be turning to a new stage— Arizona. Mitchell Singer had been sent to Arizona State University, and there he had met and married the daughter of a well-known Phoenix businessman with a string of restaurants. Having visited Mitchell several times, Barney and Edith Singer decided to move west. Chicago people were doing it; Arizona was not as popular as Miami Beach, but it was a comer. There were friends and relatives to call upon in Scottsdale and Paradise Valley, and it was no longer an unfamiliar wasteland. The Singers had not left Chicago behind; it had come with them.

With Barney and Edith Singer gone, the Steinbergs were like half a person. When Barney suggested that his son-in-law come out to Arizona and that the two of them open a store in Phoenix, Steve was entranced. For the first time he would have his own business, which meant he could control his own time and, best of all, manage his own money. There would be no disputes with partners or problems with the register. If he needed money he could take it, because it would be his. Of course, starting a new business would take work, but Steve had always thrived on work.

The experts are amazed at the workaholic nature of the compulsive gambler. Every person I ever talked to about Steven Steinberg remarked how hard he worked. Dr. Custer says that all gamblers are like this—it's as if an enormous flow of energy has been running through these people since they were children. It is routine for a compulsive gambler to put in fourteen-hour days or work two jobs at a time. While it's part of his psychic makeup, the gambler has to do it because this kind of gambling saps enormous energy. The facade has to be kept up, the bets have to be made. The whirl can never stop or even slow down because the whole thing will collapse.

The course was set for the Steinbergs to follow Barney and Edith to Phoenix, but Steve needed money. There had been a steady erosion in his finances in Chicago. When it was time to leave, he had to borrow five thousand dollars from his step-brother. Steve promised Joel that he would pay him back. Six years later, on the very night that Elana was killed, Steve was still making the same promise—the loan had never been re-paid. Steve always paid his bookies and generally repaid his friends when he borrowed from them, but this debt stayed open —family obligations differed from gambling debts in scale of importance.

The house in Arlington Heights was snapped up at once, largely because of Elana's skill in decorating. It was just a tract house, but it looked wonderful inside—it was a real estate agent's dream of a good listing because of the things Elana had done. Elana flew out to Scottsdale with the baby and six-year-old Traci. They were going to stay with Edith and Barney until the house the Steinbergs were buying on McCormick Ranch was finished. Steve told Elana that he would stay behind in Chicago, then drive one car out and hire someone to drive Elana's Toronado to Arizona. Now another of the strange crimes, like tales of Ali Baba, that always surrounded Steve took place.

Elana and the girls were in Phoenix at Edith's waiting for Steve to arrive when there was a call one morning. A man with a harsh voice said, "I'm somewhere between Vegas and New Mexico and your car just blew up, lady. I'm leaving it here." Edith called Steve in Chicago, very upset. He told them to be calm, not to worry—when he got out to Arizona, Steve said, he would go back to New Mexico and pick up the Toronado; it was just a glitch. When he finally did go back to New Mexico, he didn't return with the car. Steve told Elana that it was gone, demolished. "I'm going to sue those bastards for every penny," he said, but nothing happened.

For his friends in Chicago, Steve had a different, more exotic story. People had tried to murder him, he said. "He told us that these people caught him and they tried to kill him, I don't exactly know why, but I remember he said they pushed him up onto the hood of the car and drove real fast and he had to escape. They were going to kill him, he said, and then they took his car and wrecked it, and it was just junk. In hindsight, I guess I always thought this was a very strange story, but then those things happened to Steve—remember how he was tied up once in the closet in Des Plaines?"

But it didn't matter. They were here in the sun at last, to make a new start as have so many desert immigrants. It was 1975, and they were going to have a fresh, new life in the house on Via de Luz.

CHAPTER FIVE

BY THE TIME I GET TO PHOENIX I'LL BE HAPPY

When people decide to tear up their roots and move to Arizona, they do so, for the most part, with expectations for a better life and for more success than they have had in the community of their birth. This desire for constantly increasing success is particularly pointed and traditional for the descendants of those who came in the great migration from Eastern Europe. The children of these immigrants are expected to fare better than their parents did, and sacrifices are made in the family accordingly. The success story of the Eastern European Jews in America is without parallel in American history—sociologists say that this ethnic group accomplished in one generation what other groups may do in three, if they do it at all. The great leap forward had been forestalled for the time being in both Steve's and Elana's families. No one seemed to be doing particularly well in 1975, and the rags-to-riches formula was certainly at a standstill for them.

The move to the sunbelt was to change all that, at least

cosmetically. There was a radical difference between the life-style Steve and Elana left behind in Chicago and the society they were to find in North Scottsdale. Gone was the down-to-earth mixed neighborhood of Arlington Heights where people went bowling, drove Datsuns, and walked their babies in the neighborhood park. In the Steinbergs' new Arizona setting the life-style was affluent and trendy. Everyone they met had a swimming pool in the backyard; decorating was California-style and made Chicago look dowdy; cars were luxury or foreign models. To an outside observer it would appear that the new residents had found wealth in Arizona. In reality the life-style was built on fragile foundations. The new residents started businesses, but they tended to be undercapitalized. The houses were impressive, but had huge balloon payments to be faced down the road. The cars were invariably leased. The newcomers were to discover that in Arizona there were few conservative blue-chip companies like the ones lining the tollway back in North-brook to pump money into the economy. Desert economics were marginal, based on hype and hopes. Everyone was in the same boat. Nobody worried. Any desert dweller can tell you that the sun and the blue skies are infectious to the newcomer; optimism is everywhere.

Mitchell Singer, fresh out of college, spurred the ambitions and changed the status of the Singer-Steinberg extended family. Mitch had become an overnight sensation in the restaurant world. True, he had married the daughter of Herb Apple-gate, who owned a chain of successful restaurants in Arizona and California, and that was good for a start. But Mitchell had earned his own way and had discovered that he had a gift for the restaurant business. Under his father-in-law's eye, Mitch had worked at every job in a restaurant—busboy, bartender, cook, manager. He found that he had talent in the incredibly tough business of running a restaurant in Arizona, where restaurants rose and fell daily.

When Herb Applegate died, Mitch started his own restaurant. He chose a location in downtown Scottsdale near the street of boutiques known as Fifth Avenue. From the night the place opened, it was apparent that Mitch had something big.

Everything that could have been right to start a restaurant was. First, there was a shortage of good dinner restaurants in Scottsdale for the well-heeled winter visitor. The location was perfect. The food was good; Mitch chose a California menu of lavish salads, crab, steaks, all beautifully prepared. The restaurant was the first of Scottsdale's fern bars, restaurants where young professionals and well-dressed swingers could meet, and eat Brie, and see each other in an atmosphere of Tiffany glass and soaring ceilings with well-placed spot lighting. Finally, one of the things that may help a restaurant get off the ground successfully is the right name. The name that Mitchell chose had, for some reason, just the right chemistry. "B. B. Singer's" sounded right, it sounded like a place to go. It was an instant success. There were lines every night waiting for tables from the smiling hostesses. B. B. Singer's began to be mentioned in newspaper columns in the *Republic.* People met there for lunch or had late dinners; it was nothing to wait for an hour for a table. Mitchell had a winner.

Unfortunately, no one in the Singer and Steinberg families really appreciated that Mitchell's prosperity in the restaurant business was ephemeral and built on an unstable base. Mitchell had put little or no capital into the project. The whole deal was a package arranged by the landlord. It was a turnkey operation; Mitch paid the rent and the equipment lease out of the proceeds, and he himself owned nothing. If the cash flow at B. B. Singer's ever ran dry, the operation would be in real trouble, because there was nothing to fall back on.

Mitch did have one piece of capital: himself. Mitch Singer worked incredible hours. Like Steve and Elana, Mitch was a workaholic. He was ruthless in making the restaurant go. In the eyes of the family, Mitchell had passed into a new dimension. He knew important people all over town; he moved into a fine Scottsdale house and leased a foreign sports car with a cellular phone, the real sign of Phoenix success. He was beginning to draw backers, like Phoenix attorney Al Spector and land magnate Skip Malouf. It was a heady atmosphere for a young man not yet thirty.

Soon he branched out and opened another B. B. Singer's, this one in the north-central business corridor in Phoenix. It was another instant success. For Steve and Elana, even being associated with the restaurants made a difference in their social status. Everyone said, "Elana is from the restaurant Singers." The friends that they now made in Scottsdale were different from the old high school and bowling pals in Chicago. Their new friends were also on an Arizona roll, intoxicated in the desert air and sunshine. They, too, had cast off their Eastern and Midwestern conservative life and drab clothes. They had bought gold chains, and unbuttoned their shirts, and were almost overnight caught up in a new social life. They dressed the little ones in Esprit clothing, they took up tennis. Some of them even bought horses, and those animals ate at great expense to their new owners. The children went to the same Hebrew school at the Reform temple and played in organized play groups. With her ebullient personality, good looks, and two exquisitely raised little girls, Elana was a leader. It was a high-powered group, and it was hard to keep up with the sometimes frantic social pace. No one could fall back. This was a culture that did not tolerate or even understand the New England concept of genteel poverty, where social standing could still be maintained for those who didn't match the income norm of the group. No one could stop in this circle.

At first, the pool and patio store started by Barney and Steve did well. The location was in a suburban strip center in a neighborhood that was booming with new construction. Almost every house in Phoenix has a swimming pool. When you fly over the city in the daylight, you can see thousands of aqua-blue dots. The supplies for these pools—the chlorine, inflatable rafts, and patio furniture—were all to be found at the store. Barney knew the business inside and out, and Steve was a prodigious worker. They kept the store open seven days a week until nine at night, and it was no problem for either one of them. It took self-discipline not to deplete the cash flow of the business, and the money in the register was always a temptation. It moved out almost as quickly as it moved in.

Steve was not always a favorite with the suppliers. I spoke with one of them who found him difficult to do business with when it involved paying his bills.

"Was I glad when he left that store! I called on them. He would really push the suppliers around, really abrasive. He knew how to run the law around, how to avoid his bills. He would give you the impression he had four or five lawyers. He would say, 'Why don't you see my lawyer,' in a real smart-ass way. I finally quit going in, because I don't do business that way. I knew one salesman who wouldn't go in the store any-more even though they bought a lot of his stuff. When we heard about the trial and how everybody had said what a great guy he was, I thought, 'Wait a minute, are we talking about the same guy?' "

A year after they opened the store in 1976, Steve was robbed again. This time Steinberg told Phoenix police that a young man on a chopper had driven up to the shopping center on a quiet Fourth of July weekend and forced Steve into a little office in the rear of the store. The robber fired a shot through the water cooler and into the wall, telling Steinberg, "This is what your head will look like if you don't give me the money." Steve told police he handed over a plastic bag with three days' deposits in it—$7,360 in cash. Then the robber roared away. There were no witnesses. The hole in the drywall in the little office from which the police dug out a .38 caliber slug is still there: the present owner of the store keeps it as a curiosity.

The police dutifully took a report. It was only the first of many robbery and burglary reports that Steven Steinberg was going to make in Arizona; he was a magnet that drew crime. Steve was routinely tied up, shot at, run down in the desert, or burglarized. What did Elana think? If she doubted any of his stories there is no record of it. Barney and Edith Singer said they didn't think the gunshot incident was unusual until after Elana's murder.

Steve now had a new bookie, or if not a bookie, someone who could fill that role. According to experts like Dr. Custer, pathological gamblers characteristically have a warm and friendly regard for their bookies. They are never adversaries.

The gambler invariably regards his bookie as a friend, loyal and true—or a fellow businessman. The description is particularly fitting for Steve's relationship with Ira Gaines. Gaines is a former over-the-counter broker from New York who became a salesman in Phoenix. Steve always said that Gaines was not a bookie in the traditional sense, but just a friend who placed bets through another friend in New York who was able to move them on. Ira and Steve talked at least two or three times a day, every day. At the end Steve was depositing money directly into Ira's checking account at the bank.

Ira and his wife were friends of the Steinbergs. If Elana objected to Ira's influence over Steve, she made no sign of it. The Gaineses went to the same parties, and their children were friends —they were an accepted part of the circle. Ira's wife and Elana talked on the phone often. "She was a very dear, close friend," the woman said. Elana was friendly to Ira—she would tease him at parties, "You are my favorite, Ira."

The size of Steve's bets was increasing. He was now working in multiples of hundreds and thousands. He would bet thousands on big sporting events like Monday-night football, Sunday pro games, the baseball playoffs, and the World Series. The ante had gone up. No one, least of all Steve, knew how much he had won or lost over the years, for the pathological gambler never keeps a record.

Elana, like her husband, had a boundless store of energy. She never seemed to stop moving. Her talent and energy were concentrated on interior decorating, and everyone commented about what Elana had done with her house.

I could never understand what made the house on Via de Luz so special, but it was clear that it was. Everyone—neighbors, friends, enemies—told me so. I've driven down the block, and there was nothing exceptional. The houses are modest and innocuous. They all look alike, with doors and windows reversed in some models. There's just a patch of desert yard, stuccoed walls with bougainvillea, no trees—typical middle-class suburbia in Phoenix. The people with whom I talked told me that Elana's decorating ideas were wonderful. She had an unerring eye for color and texture: she had furniture made out of white Formica for one room, and it looked terrific. She took a guest closet and opened it up, had mirrors and little lights put in. It looked like a jewel box, with crystal and a little bar inside, one friend told me. She spent money, on that there was no doubt, but a lot of it was her own labor. She had plants, beautiful plants, and that was a feat by itself in Scottsdale, where there is no moisture in the air and houseplants are a challenge.

It made some people cross that the house was done so well, and I could sense a little angry reservoir of disapproval in a few. I could see how this was a factor in what they were to do to Elana later on. Others were just admiring.

"That house was just gorgeous inside. I really can't describe it, beautiful furniture, beautiful plants. It was something very special. You would walk in and say, 'Wow!' " a neighbor said. "I would go home and look at my own house and think what a slob I was."

People were impressed by how immaculately the house was kept. Everything gleamed and sparkled, and this was all Elana. She loved to clean, one person told me.

"She had a little apron with pockets in it to keep Windex and things like that in. Sometimes she would get up at three in the morning and clean the oven or something. She'd laugh about it—we all did." Another said, "If there was an ash in an ashtray, whoosh, it was gone. If there was just a nick in the paint, the next day five painters would come."

Nothing was too much trouble if Elana was cooking. If someone was sick or if there was a funeral, Elana's food offerings were works of art—bowls of fresh fruit, cut and beautifully arranged; elaborate salads and casseroles that she must have spent hours preparing.

But Elana's energy was still not fully tapped. Elana was vigorous and capable. In retrospect it's hard to escape the conclusion that her vitality and intelligence may have been wasted in her Scottsdale life-style, but being in business was not a viable option for women of Elana Steinberg's age and background. In a way, she was one of the last of the breed—her own daughters will be educated for careers. It was traditional for women of Elana's background to stay at home and, as a former member of the group told me somewhat cynically, "overtend the children." The two little girls had beautiful manners— Elana stressed that—and she was a conscientious mother. She read to them, took them to music lessons, was always there or picked them up when they came home from school. The children were a delight and a credit to Elana, "beautiful, lovely children," everyone said. Elana was nervous and hyperactive and brutally outspoken, but whatever she did she did very well —being a mother was her pride.

Socially the Steinbergs were now moving at high velocity, and part of the new aura of social success was the prestige of B. B. Singer's. Elana and her mother would eat breakfast there or drop in for lunch with friends. It was exciting to be part of such a popular Phoenix restaurant, and the upward mobility that would have been hard to come by in Chicago was natural, like a new skin, in Scottsdale.

In the winter of 1978, Barney and Steve's relaxed financial management of the pool store was about to have adverse consequences. The Christmas season was disappointing, and creditors were beginning to be vocal. There were no reserves for this kind of dry period. One of Steve's new friends, David Goldfarb, asked Steve if he could list the business for sale in his business brokerage. Barney and Steve were relieved, because Christmas had been such a bust and they were not prepared to wait it out until business improved. The store sold quickly, because, despite the financial drain of the salaries, it was a healthy business. In the short term, the sale looked good. Steve and Barney made a profit, and Steve had been promised a job working for Mitchell in the restaurant business. Elana bought two certificates of deposit: "These are not to be touched," she said sensibly. Elana had learned to be protective, and she was not going to let Steve have the money.

Steinberg testified in the trial that he went to work in the restaurant because he thought that Mitchell would make him a partner and pay him a large salary, an unrealistic idea. If Mitchell needed anything, it was a cash backer and not an impecunious relative. Working for Mitchell did provide Steve with a salary, a Lincoln Mark II, and fringe benefits, as well as the prestige of being the manager of one of the B. B. Singer's restaurants. To Steve and to their friends, the Steinbergs were moving up in the world. He loved it.

Eventually, I located a number of people who used to work at the restaurants. It wasn't easy, because people move around a lot in that business. As I found everywhere when I asked people about Steve Steinberg, there were two camps, poles apart. One group thought Steve was the greatest boss that ever lived—it wasn't unusual for them to say things like "I loved the guy." The second group found him arrogant and a bit of a con man. When I talked to one former employee, she told me about Steinberg's first day at work.

"I was working at Singer's on Central and Barney brought him around and introduced him. They were going to bring him in. He was really arrogant and throwing his weight around. I had the busboy watching the desk while I was doing something else, and he said, 'I'm going to go in your office and report you to Mitch for that!' And I said, 'I don't know who you are, buster, and you're not going into anybody's office.'

"I put up with him because I liked Mitch so much and he asked me to. I even used to run bets for Steve, take them to this place somewhere up on Northern, and I thought, 'Why am I doing this for this guy?' But he could talk, and be very cool, so smooth, he was really very convincing; in my opinion, a total bullshitter."

I asked if it was true that Steve was the force behind the restaurants rather than Mitchell Singer—Steve's supporters always said that. She was incensed.

"That's ridiculous. Mitch was really a whiz at the restaurant business, but he went down the tube eventually. It was very sad. He just let himself go. I always had the impression they were just making a place for Steve, because he was a relative and he was somebody they had to take care of."

Nineteen seventy-nine marked the start of Steve Steinberg's restaurant career and also the start of a new phase in his gambling. It was the year he began to resort to bank loans for bailouts, concealed from Elana. Steve had done at least one bank transaction before in Illinois on Elana's car, but so far in Arizona he had been able to keep on an even keel. In 1979 he started to borrow to gamble with a complicated fabric of bank loans. Case histories of pathological gamblers recount the astonishing ability of these individuals to get loans from different sources, juggling and overlapping them and then getting new loans to make payments on the old. Eventually the whole structure falls apart like a house of cards. The pathological gambler is so persuasive that he seems to be able to get money almost at will, or at least until the vein runs out.

In the two years following the sale of the pool store, Steve Steinberg got loans from four different Phoenix banks, banks that were usually a hard sell. They were all welcoming to him, and the backup paperwork they did on the transactions was slim. Steven and Elana Steinberg were very solvent, if anyone had inquired. Steve always turned his paycheck over to Elana. She paid the bills, and they were all current; charge cards were within their limits, and she was holding tight to the two certificates of deposit, although one was missing when she died. The loan officers knew that Steve was working at B. B. Singer's, and they needed only to look up North Central to see the lines at noon waiting for tables. Another B. B. Singer's, the third, was getting ready to open right on the corner of Central Avenue and Osborn, the heart of the business district in Phoenix. The loans Steve applied for were relatively small; none was over ten thousand dollars. Generally he would tell the loan officer at the bank that he was a partner and was making an investment in the B. B. Singer's restaurants, but for the most part it wasn't necessary to say anything at all. Steve signed Elana's name to all the applications, and she knew nothing about them. The loan money was intoxicating to him—he felt "up." He had a new source of gambling capital.

Besides the loan proceeds, something else helped Steve to recover his confidence. He went to Vegas in 1979 and won big —the last big win he was to have. On that trip he returned with cash in hand. In a burst of exuberance, the first thing he did was to buy Elana a new white Cadillac with her initials on the side. The Steinbergs' status was quickly growing. With Steve at the restaurant playing host and getting tables for people when they dropped in, the friends they were making were stockbrokers, attorneys, and investment counselors. The men would come to Singer's to eat, some every day, and nothing was too much trouble for Steve's friends. "I want a table for these people *now,*" he would say. There were parties every week, many of them involving the group's children, who were approximately the same age. Cars would line the cul-de-sac on Via de Luz. Elana entertained beautifully. She had a gift for parties—nothing was too much trouble for her to do.

By Phoenix standards, the Steinbergs made a lot of friends for a couple who had lived in Arizona only six years. Phoenix is a city where friendships are hard to find and harder to sustain. Everyone is from somewhere else, everyone is trying to start a new life. There are no old school friendships; no one knows your old neighborhood or your cousins, no one shares your memories of where you were on the day John Kennedy was killed. You meet a lot of people in Phoenix, but the friendships are drifting.

This was not true of the Steinbergs. Their social life revolved around a circle of some fifteen couples, divided into several interlocking circles that shifted and overlapped with different degrees of intimacy. Most of the Steinbergs' friends knew each other, although some did not. Some were friends that Steve or Elana knew in Chicago. Some they met through the Reform temple on McDonald Drive, the choice of the upwardly mobile Jewish family in Phoenix. Some were acquaintances from the Singers' businesses. The closest circle, the one that really mattered, began with a children's play group that had expanded into a social group for the parents. The most striking characteristic of Steve and Elana's friends was that they were all so alike they could have been cloned—"You could just stack people next to each other and you couldn't tell the difference," a former group member said years after the trial.

All of the Steinberg group were in their thirties. Most had children the ages of Traci and Shawn Steinberg, but there were some babies. There were no bachelors, no divorced men or women, and no working wives. The men, with few exceptions, had their own businesses or were professionals with their own practices—they didn't work for anyone else. They owned stores or brokerages; some were accountants. There was a podiatrist, an ophthalmologist, even a psychologist. All of the families had the trappings of success. They spent money freely and drove late-model luxury cars. They ate out a lot. No one stayed home on Saturday night—that was the big social evening. Like Steve Steinberg, all of the men were hard workers. Wives and children were "coasters" and always spent the dog days of Phoenix summers on the beach in California or Hawaii, but the men stayed behind, because they could not leave their businesses.

Sex roles were clearly defined. In the group, the women stayed home—there were no midlife careers. The group was not particularly interested in politics or intellectual pursuits; life revolved around the husband's work and the carefully raised children. Everyone knew everyone else's children; birthday parties were always well attended. The groups entertained at barbecues and swimming parties and took holidays and quick trips together to Tahoe and Las Vegas. Finally, there was the long summer exodus of the wives and children to the California beaches, where they stayed in little clusters.

Even the group's houses were almost identical. They all lived in the desert north of Phoenix within a few miles of one another. They chose houses that were of the same design, although in different price ranges—some houses were very expensive, others relatively modest. The house was usually a sand-colored or white adobe of vaguely Spanish style. All of them had red terra-cotta half-roofs and wooden french doors. The yards were left in carefully tended desert. Everyone had a pool and a few had tennis courts. The homes were new, as houses generally are in Scottsdale, but even so there was seldom a time when there was not a remodeling project in progress—there would be a clutch of trucks parked in front of the house with painters and carpenters at work on a new family room or installing wooden shutters on the deep adobe windows. The group liked to keep their houses well and there was no tolerance for an unkempt yard or shabby furniture.

Inside the cool dark houses the wives busied themselves

at cooking and child care, isolated during the day except for brief forays to chauffeur the children or do errands. The wives were pretty, with pert thin faces and lively manners. They wore fashionable sports clothes, jeans, bikinis. They were meticulous in their grooming and in their housekeeping. Their children, seldom more than two to a family, were exquisitely cared for. All but one couple in the Steinbergs' circle were Jewish; the group did not believe in assimilation. Except for the men who saw the *goyim* in business, the group had few acquaintances who were not Jewish. Even in Phoenix, where little ethnic and religious pockets have never had time to develop as they have in other cities, the group held together voluntarily in a form of clannishness. The ghetto of their great-grandparents in Lvov or Warsaw, the ghetto of the first-generation Jewish immigrants on Delancey and Maxwell Street, had been reproduced in the desert. It was a ghetto that was self-imposed and luxurious, but it was a walled society nonetheless.

This was the society that Steve and Elana were part of now. One couple who knew them back in Chicago were irritated by the new group and didn't hesitate to tell me about it. "Steve and Elana only wanted to be around people who had money," the husband told me. "If they thought you didn't have it anymore, they didn't want to have anything to do with you—it was like you had a contagious disease or something. When Brenda told Elana my shop was going under, Elana said, 'Don't say that. Just say you sold it. Don't tell anybody that.' She was really shocked, and you could see she thought it was a terrible embarrassment. And then we didn't see much of either of them for about two years, until Brenda's father died, when Steve called, and then Elana. You could tell they wanted to know how much money Brenda's father left her, and then we saw them again. I definitely connected the two things together."

Among the Scottsdale group Elana was a dynamic force, as she had been everywhere since high school—laughing, exuberant, flirtatious in an innocent manner. She was fun, she was always joking and telling crazy stories, never dull. A friend said that "she made everything go, because she had so much vitality —she sparkled. My kids loved her. I think that was because she was so little, and she would get down on the floor and talk to them, as if they were adults." Children understood Elana immediately because there was no facade. If she thought something, she said it. If there was a question, she asked it, often without thought for the consequences, but always without malice or guile. Beyond the frankness that some people found upsetting, there was a generosity of spirit. Elana Steinberg was a complex personality. Those who loved her had to accept her as she was—there was little room for neutral ground.

Not all the Chicago transplants to Arizona felt the same way as Brenda and her husband did. To another man, Elana was still Elana, even if this was Phoenix. He described her to me vividly.

"Elana was effervescent, jokey, loud; she was fun. She would say right out what she thought, like a child. I'll give you an example. When we first came out here from Chicago, she said, 'Dennis, you look terrible, your hair is getting gray. You've got to color it and lose some weight.' I told her, 'Are you crazy, Elana? I'm not going to do that.' But I went back to the motel and I finally ended up getting some hair color and I did it. I got black all over my forehead, and it didn't come off for weeks. But Elana said, 'Dennis, you look wonderful,' and she kissed me on the forehead. That whole exchange—that describes Elana."

CHAPTER SIX

DESPERATION

In December of 1980, the third Singer restaurant, the Brass Derby, opened and Steve moved over to be the Derby's manager. While Steve was working so hard, the crime wave that followed him was still flourishing. From the time he began to work for Mitchell until he left, there were six thefts of cash from the register. Usually the sums taken were between three and five thousand dollars. Steve would make a police report, but the burglaries were never solved. At Steve's suggestion the employees were told to take polygraphs, with negative results —everyone who worked at Singer's thought it was a joke, but an attitude of paranoia spread, as it does whenever there is money missing from the till. The bookkeeper, a serious woman in her forties, told me how she felt about it. She had walked into the office one morning and there were bags of cash from the safe all over the floor. "I ran downstairs and said that I wouldn't touch anything until someone came upstairs to watch," she said. "I didn't want them accusing me."

At work the relationship between Steve and his brother-in-law was volatile, but Mitch always had the upper hand. One of the cooks told me that they screamed at each other all the time. Mitch would yell, "I'm going to toss your ass out of here!" and Steve would scream back, "You can't do it!" But really, said my informant, Steve would jump. The semiviolent scenes made everyone uncomfortable, but running a busy restaurant is a tough and unforgiving business. Mitch had a terrible temper. Once he tore a phone off the wall; on another occasion he went into a fury over some dirt in the kitchen and had it completely torn apart and steam-cleaned all in one night.

Steve was explosive too, according to a bartender I talked to. "You know, the newspaper said that Steve Steinberg was so gentle and wouldn't hurt a fly. Steve had a temper. I've seen it. You saw it at work. He could be a son of a bitch to do business with. I never told this to anybody because they never asked me —I was waiting to see if anybody would ever ask me if I ever saw him with a knife. I saw him go after a delivery man once. He was making this meat delivery and they were arguing about something and Steve went for a knife. I broke it up." I asked him why he didn't say anything about it at the trial. "Jeez, that's not my problem, is it? Aren't they supposed to ask about it? Nobody asked."

Steve was the buffer between Mitch and the employees and Mitch and the creditors. It was a good thing, too, because everyone agreed that Mitch "didn't give a damn" about what he said. A supplier regretted the eventual demise of the restaurants: "Mitch was the brains of those restaurants. He really ran a class operation, but he expanded too much—Albuquerque killed him," he told me. "Even though we lost a lot of money in Mitch's bankruptcy at the end, I'd go back if he ever started up again."

When Mitchell leaned on him too much, Steve would come home and tell Elana. They were united in any controversy at the restaurant. Elana invariably sided with Steve, and didn't hesitate to let her brother know about it—Elana was never one to suffer silently, and her loyalty to her husband was intense.

When Steve wasn't working at night, he was playing poker

frantically. Poker players all over Paradise Valley remember him. He could never drop out of a pot no matter what he held, one man told me. When he ran out of money, he would try to borrow from someone in the game. "I just had been introduced to him," another poker player said, "when he grabbed my arm and tried to borrow four hundred bucks. I said, 'Hey, fella, I don't even know you, why would I lend you money?' "

Steve's favorite gambling was sports betting, but he was chasing and making wild bets. "He was a lousy gambler—a dumb gambler. He would bet a three-game parlay on three Sunday NFL games. Now, this is a dumb bet. You have to get all three games, with the point spread, and that's next to impossible. Steve was always thinking he would win, and win big," a bookie said.

In December, Elana's watch with a diamond band was reported missing after the Steinbergs had vacationed on Coronado Island in San Diego. Steve told her, "You must not have snapped it tight." In August 1980, the Steinbergs went to Lake Tahoe with the Goldfarbs. Elana told her friend Rhona Goldfarb that she didn't want to go, because the gambling was too tempting. Steve promised her that he wouldn't gamble on the trip, but one night in Reno he lost twelve hundred dollars in ten minutes. For the first time, Steve and Elana had an open quarrel in front of other people. The facade was beginning to crack.

After returning to Phoenix, Steve reported to his insurance agent that there had been a burglary at their hotel room at the MGM Grand on that trip, and that some of Elana's jewelry had been taken. Counting the watch that was reported stolen in Coronado, he was paid seventeen hundred dollars. This was the third theft report Steve had made on the jewelry over the years. It was amazing that Elana had anything left.

In the fall, Barney and Edith Singer's townhouse was burglarized while Edith was in the hospital having a heart bypass. The only signs of forced entry were in a bathroom window, the police said, but they didn't see how anyone could have gotten through such a small opening—it was mysterious.

There was a change in Elana. People who knew her well began to notice it. "She couldn't sit still," a neighbor said. "She would ask me over for coffee or something, and while I was there she would be constantly moving, walking around, putting things away. I said 'Elana, for God's sake, sit down.' She looked at me with those big eyes—she was very thin then—and she said, as if she were surprised, 'I can't.' "

Mitch had problems of his own by then, but he noticed the deterioration in his sister. He blamed it on Steve, whom Mitch was beginning to see as a loser. Mitch thought that Steve was making his sister a nervous wreck. It was hard to remember the uncomplicated and lighthearted Elana of Chicago days: the gambler's wife had taken over and the worry was eating deep.

From 1979 on, everything was frantic for Elana and Steve Steinberg. Steve was working long hours, their social pace was frenetic, and the gambling was spiraling. No one seemed to notice that there was a cloud forming over the Brass Derby. The steam was running out of the B. B. Singer's restaurant craze. When Mitchell had started, there were not many restaurants of this ambience in Phoenix and Scottsdale, at least not with the excellent food that B. B. Singer's served. But now competition was building. Restaurants are always subject to sudden changes in popularity. Summer in Phoenix is a terrible time for business. The corner of Central and Osborn, where the Brass Derby was located, was a graveyard, particularly on the weekend. Mitchell had spent money remodeling and redecorating the Derby, and there were horrendous cost overruns. No one seemed to know exactly what had happened or what had gone wrong to make the restaurants turn sour.

As usual, there was little or no capital, and the payback to the leaseholder and the restaurant-supply people was dependent on the expectations of business. Mitchell's debts were mounting. He had borrowed $100,000 from a supplier and had given the supplier a mortgage on his house. He had borrowed another large sum from a landlord. Everything at the Brass Derby was running at a deficit from the beginning—the restaurant that Steve Steinberg managed never had a profitable month. To compound the problems, Mitchell had been persuaded to take over a restaurant and bar operation at a hotel in Albuquerque. That turned out to be another disaster. If Steve and Elana thought there was money to be made in the restaurants at this point, they must have stubbornly closed their eyes to the reality of Mitchell's financial position. If Mitchell took on any partners, they would have had to put *in* money, not take it out. No one in the family seemed to be willing to analyze the problem and see that it was time for Steven Steinberg to go somewhere else —the golden ride of B. B. Singer's was coming to an end.

New Year's Eve in 1981 ushered in the end. It was a good party. The Singer and Steinberg clans were able to put everything behind them for the night, almost like the dancers at the ball in Brussels before Waterloo. I talked to the head chef about that night. He had a personal pride in his work—employees all down the line were proud of the Singer restaurants. Jason Parris remembered that New Year's Eve in a bittersweet commentary; it was one of the biggest nights of his life.

The restaurants were busy that night; all three restaurants were packed. Parris ran supply loads in his car out to Scottsdale and back, bringing shrimp and steak and lobster and champagne where it was needed. Barney, Edith, Elana, and Mitch and his wife were at the Brass Derby, and they made Jason sit with them. "This place couldn't go without you," they told him. It was almost dawn when the head chef went home, still laughing and exhilarated from the excitement of the night.

In March, Mitchell could see there was no going on. He asked Steve to call David Goldfarb and see if David could find a buyer. Goldfarb quickly found a prospect, Abe and Billy Platt, a father and son from New York who were in the deli and food brokerage business. In two days the Platts were in Phoenix to look over the operation, and an agreement of sorts was signed. The Platts were what Mitch described as typical New Yorkers: "very tough, smoking a big cigar." One of the Platts took a look at Steve behind the bar watching a basketball game and laid down the law to Mitch: "That's a gambler. You can't have a gambler working back there. I've seen them steal the fillings out of their mothers' teeth."

The Platts were going to buy into the restaurants, and they had different plans for Steve Steinberg. Billy Platt wanted Steve out in Scottsdale, and he was patronizing about it: Steve would have to give up the Mark II and work six days a week. Steve declined. It was a demotion he considered to be humiliating. He didn't like the Platts, and he could see that they didn't like him.

A week later Steve told Mitchell he was leaving and that Elana had agreed. Actually she wanted him to stay, even if he had to tolerate humiliation, until he had another job. Steve told Elana he wanted to go to real estate school and that he could always get a job with Goldfarb's business brokerage—he said an offer had already been made. He stayed for a few more weeks, then signed up for his unemployment checks and took a real estate course at night. Before he left the restaurant for good, there was a disturbing incident.

I had prodded Edith to tell me anything she remembered about Steve those last weeks. I thought there must have been something, some faint warning, that would foreshadow what came next. But Edith said no—there was nothing. Steve was quiet, but that was all, unless it was those two men that night, she told me. Edith and Elana were in the Scottsdale restaurant waiting for Steve to go home. He was supposed to be the front man that night, but he was engrossed in conversation with two men at a table.

Elana was worried, Edith told me. Billy Platt was there, and he was watching Steve and it looked as if Steve wasn't working. "When she asked him why he was talking to them," Edith said, "he turned on her and talked real hard. 'Goddammit, shut up! This is serious,' he told her." Afterward Edith said it left her with an uneasy feeling.

"I think they were pushing him for money. Elana never said another thing about it, though." This was a family that talked every day to each other, but at a critical time there were some things that weren't being said.

The two ominous-looking men that night at the restaurant were not the only problem. One of the banks was closing in and pressing Steve for payment; that loan was two thousand dollars behind. A balloon was coming due on another. Steve was ducking calls from First Federal. Elana answered the phone one time and put him on and he had to agree to meet with the manager to negotiate his problem. In May, Steinberg made his last big bet before Elana was killed. It was one of those sports spectaculars so irresistible to compulsive gamblers, when they believe they will recoup all their losses in one "get-out" bet— the championship series in the NBA between the Celtics and the Houston Rockets. It was Kevin McHale's first year in the NBA, and the Celtics looked unbeatable. The Rockets, led by Moses Malone, were a surprise that year and fought tenaciously. Steve made his get-out bet through Ira Gaines. When it was all over the Celtics had won in six games, and Steven Steinberg had lost four games in a row and owed Ira $6,200. On May 14, Larry Bird was photographed at a raucous victory celebration in the Celtic locker room smoking one of Red Auerbach's cigars. Steve and Elana were getting ready to go to California for his nephew's bar mitzvah. Disaster was approaching.

On the way to San Jose they stopped in Tahoe for the night, and a wild argument broke out when Steve started for the casino. Elana tried to stand in his way, and he threw her up against the wall. It was a glimpse of Steve that Elana had never seen before. She called Edith as soon as he left the room.

"Ma, what can I do? He's got all the money we have for our trip!" Edith was baffled and gave a feeble answer. "Call the police," she told her daughter. By the next day it was forgotten. Steve had come back to the room with the trip money essentially intact. In San Jose the bar mitzvah of Gloria's son went well. The week was upbeat for Elana.

Steve took photos of Elana and the girls that week in California, laughing and happy on a cable car in San Francisco. Elana called her mother from Gloria's house and told Edith wistfully that she loved California. "Maybe we could move here and start up all over again," she said. Steve said nothing about his precarious financial position to Gloria and her husband.

When they returned from San Jose, Steve's friend was pressing for the playoff money—Ira had to pay it himself to his New York contact. First Federal was calling and Steve was ducking. He was vague and preoccupied. On the 26th he met a neighbor in the front yard and asked him if he wanted to buy some chlorine for his pool. "I'm going to open a pool store," he told him.

On Wednesday, May 27, the skies were overcast. It looked as if it might rain. The morning paper arrived wrapped in plastic, as it was on those days. On page A-11 there was a story about the Supreme Court—the Court was taking up the appeal of Jeffrey MacDonald. The article described how the Green Beret doctor had told police that "hippies with long hair" had burst into his home and stabbed his wife and daughters as they slept. Elana put the paper on the coffee table in the den. That morning, Steve picked up his first unemployment check—a humiliating moment. In the evening he went to his softball game in Paradise Valley and took Shawn with him. Elana took Traci to a school concert and used her mother's car—the Mark II was gone. A friend recalls Steve at the baseball game.

"I've thought about it a lot—I've tried to look back and see if there was anything different about him that night," he told me. "He had his little girl with him. He seemed vague or preoccupied, but that's hindsight. I do remember this one thing. He played second base. There was this ground ball, and a man on first, and Steve fielded it and threw it to first. Everybody was yelling, 'Second, second!' That wasn't like Steve. He usually played with good instincts—now I think about that and I realize something was up."

When Steve got home that night it was quiet. The girls went to bed. Traci was working on cleaning up her school books —they had to be turned in the next day. Steve's stepbrother, Joel, called, and the conversation ended with Joel asking about the money Steve had borrowed from him six years earlier. "I expect to be paid, Steve," Joel said. Elana was irritated.

"Why is your brother bugging you about that now?" she said. She went to bed, and she called Edith Singer to say that she was home. It was beginning to rain, and there were lightning flashes in the southern sky. Steve Steinberg sat in the den, watching late-night TV and brooding. And then there were those screams.

CHAPTER SEVEN

THE MOURNERS OF JERUSALEM

It is in Jewish religious tradition that the dead should be buried as soon as possible—the day of death is the ideal, but that is not always practical. There is a kind of miracle, in summoning friends and relatives for a funeral on short notice. If the family is too distraught, the entire Jewish community is organized to do whatever is necessary for burial and for the period of ritual mourning. Burial is a time to reaffirm the continuity of Judaism. Even if the deceased was a newcomer to a city and knew no one yet, the local temple has a "mitzvah committee" that responds swiftly and surely to all of the demands of Jewish mourning. The temple will see that there is food for the mourners for the traditional meal of condolence and food for each of the seven days of *shiva*. No Jew has to die alone, and that is important to a beleaguered people who reaffirm their faith and their community with each other in the rituals of mourning.

It was not necessary to call upon any mitzvah committee to spread the news about Elana Steinberg's funeral. Everyone knew about it, either from the news or through a network of shocked friends calling each other. It seemed that everyone who had ever known Elana or the Singers came to the funeral. There were cooks and cocktail waitresses from the Singer restaurants, women from the exercise class Elana had taught, and all of the neighbors from the cul-de-sac on Via de Luz. The inner circle of Steve and Elana's friends came from north Scottsdale, the women visibly shaken and crying. It was the first time that death had entered the otherwise fortunate circle, and its very suddenness was shattering.

The chapel at the mortuary was packed. There were no flowers. Cut flowers are traditionally not sent to funerals, and there is no music. The effect is somewhat severe, but the essence of a Jewish funeral is simplicity. The ancient rabbis held that in death everyone should stand equal; displays of wealth at such a time were inappropriate. They prescribed plain white burial shrouds and simple coffins. The elaborate funeral that can bankrupt a bereaved family not able to withstand a funeral director's salesmanship is not acceptable in Jewish tradition.

The Singers and the little girls were in a side alcove separated by a gauzelike curtain. Edith was totally distraught. Traci clung to Bonnie Singer, Mitch's wife, who had been with the girls almost all the time since the murder. Bonnie was soft-voiced and pretty, a former third-grade teacher who was a favorite of the girls. Steve's relatives were in the chapel, but no one approached them—the situation was too awkward.

The rabbi was discreet in his eulogy, omitting traditional words about the bereaved husband. He spoke of the tragedy of a young woman cut off in the midst of her life. Suddenly Edith Singer cried out wildly, "Murderer! He murdered my daughter!" The atmosphere was electric. No one who was at the funeral has forgotten that moment.

Not everyone went to the grave at the cemetery in the desert wash, but it was still a large group. The rabbi pinned the black *k'raih* ribbons on the family—Traci's and Shawn's on the left side because children are closest to the heart. Then he cut *k'raih,* using the razor-edged knife to fray the ribbon and then ripping it with a tearing sound. To a Jew this is the most mournful sound in the world. It almost invariably moves everyone at the graveside to tears. Orthodox Jews tear their clothing or a lapel; the ribbon is a concession to Reform Judaism. The symbolism of *k'raih* as a sign of grief is universal—rending one's garments as Job and David did means utter misery. Everyone understands that.

The mourners shoveled earth in the grave to show the reality of death, but the shovel was turned upside down, to show reluctance. With the beautiful El Malei and the Mourner's Kaddish, Elana Steinberg's funeral was over. No one would return for eleven months, until the unveiling of the gravestone. Jews believe that it is best for the mourners not to sit by the grave at the cemetery, but to go on with their lives; the Talmud sets limits for every stage of mourning.

The mourning process was going to have to accomplish a lot, as far as Elana's parents were concerned, particularly Edith Singer. When the men came to the *shiva* house at sundown for Kaddish, Edith barricaded herself in her bedroom and cried hysterically. Edith Singer has a single-minded, almost childlike view of life—the situation was unbearable. She still believed in the bearded burglars to a certain extent, even though she had screamed out "Murderer!" in the midst of the funeral. No one could make sense of what had happened—the golden, beloved son-in-law had virtually butchered her daughter without warning. While Edith Singer was ambivalent, Steve's family knew better. There was going to be no room for accommodation from now on between the Singers and the Steinbergs—it was war.

Edith and Barney Singer sat *shiva,* the seven days of ritual mourning for the dead. For that week, the mourners do not work, not even to prepare food. Men do not shave; women abjure makeup. The mourners wear no shoes and sit on low stools. All the mirrors in the house are covered—a custom dating back to the twelfth century. The door to the *shiva* house is left ajar. Friends that call let themselves in and out, so that the family are not distracted by welcomes or goodbyes. There is a pitcher of water outside the door for callers to symbolically wash away the touch of death and the graveyard before they enter the *shiva* house.

Mourning is structured in precise time periods by the Talmud. The first three days are set aside for intense grief: they are "for weeping." Traditionally those days are considered too early even to give words of sympathy to the mourners, because it is too soon for them to comprehend that sort of thing. Those grieving are expected to move on to a new psychological stage for the remaining days of *shiva*. After that, for thirty days the mourners gradually reenter their lives, refusing social events and entertainment. The emphasis is always to go on, and not to lose oneself in misery. "If a person grieves excessively," the Talmud says, "he is really grieving for someone else."

One of Steve's friends broke the atmosphere of mourning at the *shiva* house with a discordant note when he came up to Mitch for help. "Mitch, he owes me sixty-five hundred dollars that he lost on the playoffs. I can't get the money when he's in jail. I can't see him. Mitch—can you talk to his lawyers and get the money for me? He promised me that night that I'd have it the next morning, he was going to get it from the bank in Christown. You know you can't mess around with these people."

Mitch brushed him off. "Talk to them yourself. I can't do anything about it, for God's sake. It's the last thing I've got on my mind whether you get sixty-five hundred dollars or not. The guy makes seven hundred a week, that's all. My sister's dead. What's the matter with you?" Mitch brushed him away. The man was stunned. "I always thought Steve made a lot of money —how could he make seven hundred a week and bet like he did?"

At the *shiva* house it was nearly dusk. The men began to gather for the *minyan* wearing their tallithim; the ancient strains of the Mourner's Kaddish were said by Elana's male relatives. With each saying of the Kaddish, mourners believe, the soul of the departed is elevated into paradise, but the Kaddish is really a hymn of praise to the God of Israel, a celebration of the primordial ties that bind all Jews together. They are mourning still the destruction of the Temple. As they leave the *shiva* house friends traditionally do not say goodbye, but affirm their loyalty to their common heritage by saying to the family, "May you be comforted among the mourners of Jerusalem and Zion."

The fabric of Jewish loyalty the friends were affirming in the *shiva* house was to be strained to the breaking point during Steve Steinberg's trial.

PART TWO

TRIAL BY PREJUDICE

CHAPTER EIGHT

FIND ME A MIRACLE WORKER

Steve Steinberg's world changed abruptly from the upscale life-style of McCormick Ranch to the subculture of the county jail in downtown Phoenix. When Steinberg was arrested, Maricopa County was still using the old jail on Madison Street. The supervisors had reluctantly agreed to build a new jail after inmates had filed a class-action lawsuit in federal district court, but the new building was not complete. The old facilities were overcrowded and grim. Sometimes there were eight men on stacked cots in a holding cell. Volatile, unpredictable prisoners were lumped together in dayrooms and cells. There was no exercise space or any provision for it; inmates who were not working as trusties around the courthouse literally never saw the sunlight unless they were on their way to court. A man who was not going to be out on bail before his trial quickly took on a sickly bluish pallor. Night in the jail is constant noise—doors slam, men shout, and bells ring. Jail is a terrible experience for everyone, and for someone as accustomed to sophisticated luxury as was Steve Steinberg, the contrast must have been extreme.

He adapted with surprising ease. Of course, he had many visitors. The first day after Elana was killed, eight people came to the jail to see Steve Steinberg. He even screened his visitors —Steinberg's brother-in-law Barry Levin left a message for the sheriff's deputies on the booking sheet: "Both Steve and the lawyers have requested that Mitchell Singer *not* be allowed to visit. Thank you." The lawyers he was referring to were the first that Steinberg called that night. They weren't permanent. Steinberg's business attorneys held the fort until a criminal defense attorney was lined up by the family, but they knew what Steve wanted.

That message is interesting on two levels. It indicates that Steven Steinberg had already attained a more favorable position in the jail—he was referred to as "Steve" and able to leave a message with his jailers at the desk almost as he would have in a Holiday Inn. The content of the message is also interesting, because it showed that battle lines were drawn between Elana's family and Steve the day after her murder. Steinberg was to tell everyone that he believed the hairy strangers had stabbed Elana until the truth was finally revealed to him weeks later by a succession of dreams. But he didn't want to face Elana's brother the day after she was killed and tell that bearded-stranger story again. The Singers had immediately become the enemy.

Steve's friends were welcome, though, and they found him marvelously resilient in jail. I got the impression afterward that the men in the Steinberg group were proud of themselves for hanging in there with Steve when he was in custody—there was a hint of excitement about it for them. For most, it was their first experience with a jail, and it made them feel daring and virtuous when they brought Steve cigarettes and magazines. One man told me he was amazed how many had been there before him. To his further amazement, Steinberg was doing very well.

"I thought he would be morose or scared as hell in that place. But you know, he was almost at home. I guess Steve was always flexible. He had taken on this kind of gangster air—he even talked differently. He had a cigarette hanging out of the side of his mouth, and he sounded kind of tough. He told me how he had one inmate get him this, and another do something else for him. It was like an old John Garfield movie. He was a wheeler-dealer in the jail, an operator—or at least he wanted me to think that he was."

Part of Steinberg's protection in the jail where he was to spend the next ten months was the reputation of the lawyer his family retained four days after the murder. No other group is more informed and critical of the quality of a lawyer than the population of the Maricopa County jail. An inmate who has a prominent lawyer gets instant respect. These fortunate ones are generally left alone by the jail deputies, who are also impressed —they seem to be able to make unlimited telephone calls from the jail lobby, and they enjoy a more favorable atmosphere than the other inmates.

Steve Steinberg's family had retained the very best. The criminal defense bar in Phoenix, like most big cities, is carefully stratified. At the top are a few, a very few, lawyers who have the big cases. They earn a good income. Their names are in the news regularly. The other criminal attorneys are often struggling, existing on poorly paid court appointments and drunk-driving cases. They add divorce cases to cover the monthly overhead. In criminal law, there is little in between. Ever since the courtly and handsome Phoenix attorney John Flynn had died of a heart attack on the ski slopes in Flagstaff, Arizona's leading criminal defense attorney was generally considered to be Robert Hirsh. Hirsh was in the model of Flynn, with prematurely white hair and an elegant, commanding presence. Hirsh was from Tucson—a hundred miles away from Phoenix, but his practice was really all of Arizona. He was not infallible and had had some losses in the past, but overall Bob Hirsh's trial record was impressive.

His specialty was the romantic homicide. In these killings, the victim is killed by a spouse or by a lover who has been rebuffed. Hirsh's technique in these cases was a "temporary insanity" defense that he had honed to perfection. He believed in it with an evangelist's fervor. One had to be a passionate believer in the defense to make it work, because romantic homicides for the most part have terrible facts for a criminal defense lawyer. The defendants are usually arrested holding the smoking gun, or the killer, like Steve Steinberg, calls the police to report the killing and waits for them to arrive. A conviction for some degree of homicide would seem certain, and the obvious strategy would be to approach the prosecutor and look for the best plea bargain one could get. Bob Hirsh had been brilliantly successful gaining acquittals in several romantic homicides by using an insanity defense, even though his clients had never had a hint of mental illness. Reporters called him "the miracle worker."

His first temporary insanity defense to catch public attention was a case in which he successfully defended a Tucson woman who shot her husband as he was getting ready to leave her with his graduate degree in hand. Usually, though, Hirsh's murder clients seemed to be men committing, as one reporter put it, "particularly vicious crimes against women." Hirsh demurred. "I've had women clients," he said. "They just don't come to mind." The stress of murder trials is intense, he told me, because he feels such responsibility to the client.

"I am all he has and I have to do everything I can. The weight of having that much responsibility is terrible, you can never relax. That's the worst thing about this job, stress, stress, stress." Hirsh was often criticized for his technique of trying everyone for the crime but his client, but he is never abashed. "It doesn't bother me. That's an essential tool in the defense attorney's arsenal, and you have to use everything available. The odds are really stacked in the other direction; the police have everything going for them and there is no limit to their resources. So if you are a defense attorney, it is your responsibility to pull out all the stops—would you want a defense attorney who didn't do that? Of course not. And then too, some people just ask for it, they cause their own deaths. They taunt somebody who is weak and sick and it's just bound to happen."

Steven Steinberg's trial and Robert Hirsh seemed to be made for each other, particularly since Steve's family could afford the fee that goes along with an attorney of Robert Hirsh's reputation. When it comes to fees, a criminal defense attorney faces a problem. In Arizona, once a lawyer has appeared for a defendant at his arraignment, the lawyer will not be permitted to withdraw from the case even if he hasn't been paid and never will be paid. Once in, a criminal defense lawyer is in for the duration. Any defense attorney who is naive enough to think that a criminal client can be trusted to pay in installments will learn the hard way. It is traditional for a defense attorney to estimate the worst that can happen—a long trial—and then require all the money up front before he makes an appearance. Bob Hirsh naturally does not discuss his fee in the Steinberg case, but it must have been substantial. The Steinberg family was able to pay it.

Hirsh told them that this would be a two-man trial. He needed help and a Phoenix base, and he wanted Mike Benchoff to be with him. Benchoff is a thin, intense former prosecutor with an unpleasant, driving technique of cross-examination. Like Hirsh, he is a prodigious worker who lets no details escape him. It was a formidable and very expensive combination— Steve Steinberg was going first class.

It took several days for Steve's family to settle on Robert Hirsh, and for the Tucson lawyer to agree. Until then, another firm of lawyers that Steinberg knew from business transactions held the fort, preserving Steve's position. One of them moved immediately to close off the house on Via de Luz. When Edith Singer came the day after the murder to get clothing for Traci and Shawn, all the locks had been changed. Steinberg's attorney was practical if not exactly gracious—things have a way of disappearing from the house in a domestic homicide. The attorney had done nothing wrong. By the law's own provisions, all of Elana's possessions, bank accounts, and real estate now belonged to her husband, and the title had passed directly to him at the time of Elana's death. Unless he was convicted of her murder, all of Elana's property was Steve's to keep, and he needed her assets now to finance his defense.

The real boost that Steve needed came from his sister, Gloria. Gloria and her husband came immediately from San Jose. The week before the murder, Elana, Steve, and the girls had gone to San Jose for the bar mitzvah of Gloria's son, and they had seemed happy. The disaster caught Steve's sister by surprise. Apparently Gloria and her husband hadn't known that there was trouble in Paradise Valley or that Steve's gambling was out of control.

After the murder, the family rallied to Steve's support. Gloria was the most important in the display of loyalty because she was willing to put up money for Steve's defense. Like everyone else connected with a murder trial, she was taking no chances. Five days after the murder, Steve signed and recorded a $75,000 deed of trust to his sister, secured by the house on Via de Luz. Theoretically the house belonged to Steve now and he could mortgage it as he saw fit. He might have raised the money from a bank, but under the circumstances that was uncertain. He needed the money immediately to retain the lawyers. Steve Steinberg's sister was not being foolish. She knew it was best to be cool and practical about lending money to Steve.

Steve's mother, Esther, and her second husband had moved to Scottsdale and lived in a retirement complex about a mile from McCormick Ranch. Over the years Steve had grown away from his mother, although Elana was always dutiful in keeping in touch with the Goodmans. From the beginning, when Steve had met Elana's parents in Skokie fifteen years earlier, he had adopted Barney and Edith Singer as parents, and they had reciprocated. Now that Steve was in trouble, his mother and stepfather rallied behind him. Steve was telling friends that he believed in the bushy-haired burglars, but his mother was more intuitive about what would have to be done. She told friends that Steve was the real victim, and that Elana had made her son's life miserable.

It must have been an excruciating time for Steve's mother. It could not be kept quiet; the pictures of her handsome son being arrested for the murder of his wife were all over the nightly television news and newspapers. For a Jewish mother the situation was particularly debilitating. After all, traditionally she is supposed to *kvell*, to speak with pride to the neighbors about her son and his accomplishments, traditional boasting that is part of the stereotype of Jewish women, cruel and comic at the same time. The sons are supposed to give their mothers who made sacrifices something to *kvell* about. Sociologists who have written about the development of the *Yiddishe mama* stereotype believe that these are vital, active women who have subordinated themselves to invest all of their considerable energies in their home and children. A child's failure becomes their failure. Not only this, but violence in the Jewish family is virtually unknown; a Jewish marriage and family are sanctified. The home is supposed to be a safe haven—a refuge from the blows of the outside world, not a battleground. Jewish feminists do not agree, but there is an idealized concept that Jewish men are incapable of violence in the family—Jewish men do not beat their wives, it is said, and homicide is unthinkable. The events of that rainy night were difficult for any family to absorb, but, culturally, even worse for Steven Steinberg's family. Still they rallied in an unbroken display of unity.

Hirsh and Benchoff were good judges of psychology, and they knew the nature of the Phoenix jury. They started to work as soon as the fee was paid, assembling the cast of characters that would be needed for what was to be a most unusual defense.

CHAPTER NINE

THE WAY TO WALK

Lawyers as successful as Bob Hirsh give the impression that they win cases because of their charisma. It is true that juries like the Shakespearean voices and carefully styled haircuts of these stars of the courtroom. A juror can usually describe the lawyers' performance after the trial with the toughness of a Broadway drama critic. But though style is important, every courtroom veteran will agree that the key to winning the big trial is not charisma, but painstaking work.

Witnesses must be found, then persuaded and interviewed over and over again. Obscure legal decisions must be located in the complicated way that lawyers look for such cases through digests and red books called "Shepards." One decision, no matter how bizarre, may catch the fancy of a momentarily bored judge and support the exclusion or admission of some devastating evidence. The lawyer must find his expert witnesses for ballistics or blood spots or whatever is needed, and that witness must be prepared so that he will not falter. Every chink in the enemy's case must be probed and catalogued for the right moment. It is slogging day-to-day work, and work that the trial lawyer usually does himself. Preparing for trial is something like packing a parachute—it is dangerous to delegate this job to someone who won't be on the line when things go wrong.

Successful trial lawyers, particularly criminal lawyers, don't take vacations. They work at night, on weekends, on holidays. They drive to obscure addresses in dark parts of town, they eat junk food. They fly in small planes and rent cars, and they buy innumerable drinks for strangers. The trial lawyer wears a perpetual look of preoccupation, because his mind and heart are always somewhere else.

It is not easy to be the wife of such a man—and the successful trial attorney is almost always a man. It is no coincidence that they tend to be married and divorced at an unusual rate. The trial lawyer is seldom home for dinner. The children's school play usually takes place without Daddy in the audience. When he is home, he can be a restless and irritable tyrant. It takes a very patient woman to survive marriage to a high-powered criminal defense attorney, and few do. Trial and preparing for trial can consume a man's whole life, and there is little left over for anyone else. This is work that cannot be done halfway.

In the summer of 1981, Bob Hirsh's problems were compounded. Hirsh had two murder trials to defend at the same time, and both of them were going to require some miracle working to save his clients. A month after Elana Steinberg was killed, a hard-drinking contractor named William Gorzenski shot and killed two people in the isolated Arizona town of Safford. The evidence was not exactly promising for a defense attorney. Gorzenski's pretty wife, Sandra, had filed for divorce. The jealous and frustrated Gorzenski had been stalking her for days, peering through windows where Sandra worked and drinking steadily and morosely. On the night of the murders, a trail of footprints showed that Gorzenski had first watched his estranged wife and her date through a window and then left to return with his gun. Sandra Gorzenski and a popular Safford public works director were literally blown to pieces with a shotgun as Sandra cowered against the wall trying to shield herself. Bill Gorzenski calmly helped himself to a beer from the murdered man's refrigerator while he waited for the sheriff. Graham County is so small and its revenues so slim that there is no full-time prosecutor. To the young attorney who did the state's work on contract, it seemed a clear conviction for the first degree murder, particularly in that law-abiding Mormon heartland. Gorzenski's lawyer in Safford knew that he had serious problems and called in Bob Hirsh. Gorzenski could afford it.

The Steinberg and Gorzenski cases would be tried back to back. Worst of all, both trials would have to be prepared for simultaneously. Bob Hirsh would have to learn about two completely different worlds, and learn quickly. Steven Steinberg was part of a sophisticated society that Hirsh could understand. Potential defense witnesses for Steinberg were given to the good life, vacations in La Jolla and Coronado Island. They drove luxury automobiles and had bar mitzvahs for five hundred close friends. Gorzenski was different.

William Gorzenski lived in a town isolated at the base of the rugged Pinaleno Mountains in southern Arizona. To get to Safford you had to want to go there—it is not on the way to anywhere else. Behind Mt. Graham is a wilderness area, accessible only on foot or horseback, a haven for rugged individualists, survivalists, and people who do not believe in paying federal income tax. The city of Safford is ruled by a few fundamentalist Mormon families coexisting in an uneasy truce with hard-drinking cowboys and the San Carlos Apaches. When Bob Hirsh and his staff drove the two hundred miles of mountain road through the copper towns from Phoenix to Graham County they were moving back in a Western time warp.

Both language and wardrobe would have to be changed to fit Safford society, so that William Gorzenski's witnesses would feel comfortable with a defense attorney who must have seemed exotic in that isolated town. Bob Hirsh would have to design the strategy of the Gorzenski trial for a town where Mormon patriarchs thundered against wrongdoing from their pews on Sundays and where no one had ever heard of a Jewish American

Princess. To prepare for both of these trials at once was a *tour de force;* to win both of them would be spectacular.

From the first, Bob Hirsh knew that both trials could not be successfully defended on the evidence. Under the circumstances, he would rely on his favorite and his most successful defense to the domestic murder—temporary insanity. There was a lean economy in having the two trials so close together, because Hirsh's favorite psychiatrist, Dr. Martin Blinder, could do his workup for both defendants in one trip from San Francisco. On August 31, Dr. Blinder came to Phoenix and saw Steven Steinberg in the jail. On the next day, Hirsh drove the psychiatrist to Safford to interview William Gorzenski in the Graham County jail. Blinder diagnosed the same condition for both men: "dissociative reaction," a cousin of the rare multiple-personality disorder. The insanity defense for both men was on track in two days.

For the Steinberg trial, the defense center was in Mike Benchoff's office in a Phoenix high-rise bank building. Since the strategy in the Steinberg case required a more delicate touch, Benchoff used an associate, fresh from law school, named Diane Lindstrom. A very tall and intelligent blonde, she made sure that no potential defense witness was neglected. Part of her job was to see Steve Steinberg on a regular basis in the jail, because he needed a lot of attention to keep his spirits up.

The most important function for Lindstrom and one that she performed superbly was to make the first contact with the Steinberg friends in Scottsdale. She came to their homes smiling and friendly, describing how Steve and the children would need their help. If a friend was receptive the next invitation was for a meeting with Bob Hirsh himself in Benchoff's office. This was heady stuff. Most people had heard of Hirsh's reputation and found it exciting to be a part of the defense project.

The defense began by having group meetings at night in Scottsdale in Diane Lindstrom's living room. The mass meetings were reinforcing and made the witnesses who were committing themselves to helping Steve feel more comfortable. Even the rabbi from the Reform congregation was at the first meeting, which almost made it seem as if God was in favor of what was happening. As an exercise in psychology, the group approach was impressive.

Downtown in the prosecutor's office, Jeff Hotham had no idea that the defense was successfully enlisting some of the Steinberg friends in a mass effort. Why would Hirsh want a mob of defense witnesses? Hotham thought that Steve Steinberg could call in a hundred friends as character witnesses and it wouldn't change anything. He viewed the crime as a clear case of murder. The police had interviewed all the people Steinberg called on the telephone that night—Mike Berkovitch, the Goldfarbs, Mitch Singer. They had Steinberg's fingerprints identified on the carving knife in blood. There just didn't seem to be any loose ends for anyone to worry about.

Hotham did interview one Steinberg friend. He called in Steinberg's betting companion, Ira Gaines, for a session in his office. Gaines brought his lawyer with him, which seemed to be a wise move under the circumstances in the event he needed immunity—bookmaking is against the law in Arizona. Gaines always said that he wasn't a bookie in the traditional sense, and at the trial, Steve Steinberg agreed. Gaines just placed bets for friends as a favor, and didn't take the bookie's traditional cut, or "juice." It was just a hobby for him, he said. He liked to gamble himself. Gaines's activities were not important to Jeff Hotham. He was only interested in talking to the man about Steve Steinberg's gambling losses.

Gaines got his promise of immunity. In return, he was to testify for the prosecution that Steinberg gambled heavily and had been losing big. As far as Gaines was concerned, that was certainly true. Ira was holding the bag for that with his contacts in New York.

Gaines and his attorney were both part of the Steinberg social circle. They had played in the softball game that night with Steve just hours before Elana was killed. After the interview in the prosecutor's office, Ira's attorney stopped to socialize with Hotham. He told me about it later. He said that he sensed what was coming and could see that Hotham wasn't going to be prepared for the onslaught.

"I knew Jeff—a hell of a nice guy. I used to be a prosecutor, I used to work in that office. I could see that he just wasn't in tune with what these people were like. I said to him, 'Listen, Jeff, this is a whole new kind of society for you and you've got to understand the culture. These are people who don't worry about paying the APS bill or the telephone bill, but they do worry about the Saks bill, because that is crucial. This is *different*, Jeff.' I could see that he wasn't really paying any attention to what I was saying. I left his offfice and I had this premonition —'My God, he's going to lose this trial.' "

Until Elana Steinberg was killed, the tight social circle that surrounded the Steinbergs in Scottsdale and Paradise Valley had never been disturbed by any ripples of discontent, nor did anyone guess that the ties that held the group together would be put to the test. When the news broke on the morning television that Steve had been arrested, the group was in a terrible dilemma. No one knew exactly what to do. For the men, the very thought of being in that jail on Madison Street was enough to send a thrill of fear through their trim stomachs. The old jail was crowded, dreary, and dangerous. Although the sheriff's office tried to do its best, it was not unusual to read in the *Arizona Republic* that a prisoner had hanged himself with his bedsheets, or that someone waiting for trial had been beaten up by other prisoners or, worst of all, sodomized. It was no place for a friend to be, particularly a Scottsdale businessman accustomed to the good life. For this if for nothing else the men who were friends of Steve Steinberg were willing to give an audience to his defense attorneys. It was the least you could do for a friend—you couldn't just abandon him.

Some of the group believed Steve's story about the bushy-haired strangers. They thought he must have been arrested in some terrible mistake—the Steve Steinberg they knew could never have killed anyone, much less Elana. Steve called his friends a lot from the jail. And when he did, or when the men visited him, his story was consistent. He didn't remember what happened that night, but he could still see the faces of the two men with bushy hair and beards. One of the wives, married to a friend who had stayed with Steve to the end, told me that she regrets her initial confidence in Steve's story.

"I guess I am very naive. I absolutely believed that he didn't kill Elana. He told everybody that he had these dreams every night and these people's beards were peeling away, little by little, until about September, I guess—when he said he saw that now it was his own face in the dream. When I heard that he was going to plead insanity, I was dumbfounded. Now that all sounds so silly about the beards peeling off like Velcro. I am really sort of bitter about it all."

When Bob Hirsh talked to Steve's friends he stressed the children, Shawn and Traci, and how they needed their father now because their mother was dead. When the insanity plea came out in the open and everyone began to realize that Steve actually had killed Elana, Hirsh spoke with eloquence of how Steve would get medical treatment if he was acquitted, and then they would all be together and the children wouldn't be orphans. These were people who gave enormous attention to their children, and the thought of Traci and Shawn as orphans was compelling. The children should have their father, some reasoned, no matter what had happened.

A few of Steve's friends were simply caught up in the excitement. And it was exciting. There was always something to talk about now, and impromptu meetings with Hirsh at the bar in Oscar Taylor's at the Biltmore. Not everyone joined the movement. Some of the Steinberg circle were resistant to overtures from the defense lawyers, even turning down a personal appeal from the charismatic Bob Hirsh himself. One man described his refusal to me. "Bob Hirsh talked to me a lot, and he was very charming and good at it—this is a guy that can charm the birds right out of the trees—but he knew instinctively that I would never be a good witness for Steve."

His wife went on to explain, "How could I say I felt sorry for Steve? He killed Elana, and she didn't deserve that. He took those children's mother away. I could tell what they wanted. It was to go in there and say Steve was wonderful, and he should get help, and Elana was not so nice. It didn't take a house to fall on us to see that."

The defense attorneys' handling of these potential witnesses was brilliant. It's not an exaggeration to say that it was critical for the outcome of the trial. The defense team picked and chose with discrimination. Hirsh would discard a witness he considered overeager and unpredictable. One man told me that he was disappointed that he was never called. He sat poised and waiting for two days for a telephone call from defense attorneys that never came. Hirsh's strategy was to polarize the friends who were approachable, and not erratic, into a cohesive group for Steve—a group so committed that they could disregard Elana's death in their zeal for Steve. Few who were active in that defense wanted to talk to me about their motivation when I approached them years later. It was as if I had the plague.

Those friends who hadn't gone along with Steve's defense told me that they didn't know what had happened. One woman said it is still a mystery in the remnants of the Steinberg social circle. "Why did some of the others do it? I don't know, because *nobody* ever talks about it now. It is just never mentioned. I think the rest of them were manipulated in a way—they just weren't paying attention to what was happening. I didn't know that Elana was the one who was going to need witnesses. Nobody told us that."

The men in the group tended to be more open about it when I interviewed them than did their wives. By and large, they did not have any illusions about why they were participating. One told me that he knew when he got to the first meeting that sides were going to be taken: he would have to choose between Steve and Elana. Some told me that they didn't go to Diane Lindstrom's voluntarily; that they had received a phone call from the defense office that didn't offer any options. Either they came in to talk voluntarily or they would receive a subpoena and have their deposition taken—the choice was theirs. Going to the meeting seemed less threatening at the time, although some of the friends have second thoughts now.

Once there, the lawyers were masterful in their handling of these semireluctant witnesses; they knew when to push and when to back off. One man told me about the personal attention he received.

"The lawyers went around—there were two of them. They talked one on one to everybody. And to me, it was Bob Hirsh. He asked me, 'Did Elana spend a lot of money and was Steve upset about it? Did she have a lot of clothes?' And I said, 'Hey, wait a minute, what does this have to do with anything? I'm not a witness for this.' And he backed away and said, 'Oh, no, don't worry.' But it was clear that was the focus, that was the main thing. I feel bad about it now, and I think, did I say things that sounded that way about Elana? I sure didn't mean to do that. I loved Elana."

Another man told me that he thought the defense attorneys were concentrating on the women in the group. "When you got there at this meeting you knew you were supposed to be on Steve's side, and I supposed that there would be a side somewhere for Elana too. Now, I'm not kidding myself—I know I was testifying for Steve and had chosen, so to speak. That was clear. But they really didn't say anything really bad about Elana. Now, maybe with some of the women they did. I know there were one or two of the girls they really worked with, they spent a lot of time with them separate from the others—I don't know. It's possible. Nobody will talk about it now."

There were no rules or guidelines for the friends of Steve and Elana Steinberg. None of the group, not even the rabbi, knew exactly what to do, for Jews just didn't murder their wives. The friends were on their own, and their natural reaction was to remain inconspicuous. It was a trying time for friendships. The parties stopped. The gourmet club met no more. No one said what was wrong, and no one criticized the ones who were working on Steve's defense. A few friends who were "on her side" were silent and worried. Not only was the trial silently tearing the group apart, it was also embarrassing—a *shonda,* a scandal for the *goyim.*

By some osmosis, the group had agreed on one thing, and that was to stay apart from Elana's family. After the funeral and after sitting *shiva,* Barney and Edith and the little girls were left alone. Some of this was Edith Singer's doing. The Singers were fearful that Steve would get to the girls and steal them away. The girls were seeing a psychologist. Traci once thought her father could come through the water pipes while she was taking a shower—she had heard him washing his hands that night. Edith was not easy to be with. She cried without stopping. She was consumed with anger and frustration and said terrible bitter things. It was an ordeal to talk to her, and most of the group didn't stay the course. As one, they decided to stay away. It made it easier to be remote from the grisly events of May 27.

The fact that Bob Hirsh and Mike Benchoff had called these group meetings was not improper. It's an economical use of lawyers' time. The only negative would be if Hotham had asked a witness about it at the trial, "Now, have you met with anyone to discuss your testimony for this trial?" If that had happened, it would have seemed that the witnesses had coordinated their stories. Then, too, there is something unattractive about the idea that these people, whom Elana considered her friends, met to put together critical stories about her. But this was never a problem. The prosecutor didn't interview any of these friends, and that critical question was never asked.

The actions of the friends who became a part of Steve Steinberg's defense are baffling to me, particularly since they were not particularly pleased with the outcome. They were so easy to channel into Steve's defense—there was little introspection. This may have originated in the self-isolation of the social group. Everything was internalized for them. They couldn't discuss the dilemma in which they found themselves with an objective outsider. They were locked in. Elana had made some enemies, it was clear, and they were unrelenting.

The Steinberg friends, particularly those who went to the group meetings and to the impromptu get-togethers with Bob Hirsh at the bar at Oscar Taylor's, don't like to talk about it now. They tend to have unlisted telephones, and they have security systems in the front of their adobe walls. Strangers are not welcome. A visitor must ring the bell and talk through a round black speaker in the wall, and is then answered by a disembodied voice from deep inside the house. Elana Steinberg's name makes a particularly hollow sound in the speaker of these adobe houses in the desert, and the voice that replies is not welcoming. For the group, it is a chapter closed.

CHAPTER TEN

THE PSYCHIATRIST FROM SAN FRANCISCO

It was time to get cracking on the insanity defense. There had already been one false move in this direction. Before Steve's family had retained Bob Hirsh they had talked to another attorney, but for some reason the representation did not mature. Court records indicate that this lawyer had brought in a Phoenix psychiatrist to examine Steinberg. If there was such an examination, no one ever heard the result. There is only one presumption: this was not a satisfactory psychiatric expedition for the defense. There are psychiatrists and psychiatrists, however, and one man's opinion is just that. The selection of forensic psychiatrists is a very delicate matter and must be done with a skillful touch. These doctors are the linchpin of the insanity defense. They must be able to convince a jury that they have the power to look into the past, to look into one moment in a man's mind that occurred months earlier, and to translate that moment into the language of medicine. The fact that forensic psychiatry has had such extraordinary success in this regard is a tribute to the skill and magnetism of its practitioners, and there are many.

There is no special body of knowledge or singular illnesses that makes up this specialty—forensic psychiatrists have no unique medical training. The difference between the forensic psychiatrist and any other is that "forensics" use psychiatry for a different purpose. The clinical psychiatrist practices in a medical setting or in a hospital; he has patients with diseases or illnesses that he has diagnosed, and his goal is to treat the patient—to make him well or more comfortable or to get him to stop some unacceptable behavior. The clinical psychiatrist's patients tell him things; this conversation between the doctor and his patient is confidential and can never be disclosed.

The forensic psychiatrist has a totally different function. His job is to examine a given individual and report to someone in a courtroom—either judge or jury. The word "forensic" comes from the Latin and means literally "suitable for the forum"—a perfect description. A forensic dispenses no medicine. He is not supposed to treat anyone or to be available for the midnight crisis call. His "patient" is not really a patient at all but more an interesting subject to be probed and squeezed and tested and reported, all for the courtroom. When the subject tells a forensic psychiatrist about his miserable marriage or his unhappy childhood, he does so not because he expects treatment, but because there is something happening in a courtroom that is going to affect him.

The word "forensic" conjures up the image of murder trials, but that is not accurate today. Forensic psychiatry has taken on a powerful role in all kinds of civil litigation. It is rare for there to be a child custody trial, the most bitter of all legal battles, without a forensic psychiatrist for each side giving an opinion on which is the better parent. A will contest is seldom without a forensic giving an opinion on whether or not the testator was in his right mind when he left his money to a second cousin in Cedar Rapids. In auto accidents and workmen's compensation cases, forensics will give opinions about injuries or give an opinion on whether the plaintiff is malingering.

Critics worry that these experts are becoming too powerful in the courtroom today and that their opinions may be wresting decision-making away from judge or jury. The most severe critics of forensics are psychiatrists themselves, like the highly respected Thomas Szasz of the State University of New York, or Lee Coleman, a well-known West Coast psychiatric rebel. These doctors write and testify that psychiatry is *not* a science suited to a medical model, and that the psychiatric opinions given so confidently by their colleagues in criminal courtrooms are little different from soothsaying. These critics are few in number but their voices are increasingly heard, particularly concerning the insanity defense. When a forensic psychiatrist testifies in a murder trial today it is not unusual for someone like Szasz or Lee Coleman to follow as an expert witness for the opposing attorney, debunking the whole idea of psychiatry as a science capable of giving an accurate opinion and urging the jury to disregard the testimony of his colleagues. The foundation of psychiatry in the courtroom is beginning to shake a bit.

Choosing experts in a high-level insanity trial like Steve Steinberg's had to be done carefully. Unlike Steve's first lawyer, Bob Hirsh was not in the habit of hiring a psychiatrist and then not hearing what he wanted to hear. A certain result was expected. Fortunately, a doctor's philosophical leanings are usually known, so selection doesn't have to be a guessing game.

Forensics generally fall into two categories, oriented toward the defense or toward the prosecution. Defense forensics, by far the larger group, believe that people commit crimes because they are sick, because they are depressed or stressed or were abused as children—all crime is mental illness to them. The prosecution psychiatrists go all the way in the opposite direction. The defendant can have a history of being in and out of mental hospitals for years and believe that he is the Angel Gabriel or that when he kills he is stopping earthquakes, but to these psychiatrists there is no problem. Everybody is sane.

If an attorney can get a forensic to alter his usual stance, it's a tremendous coup. Then the jury will see that the psychiatrist, because the attorney's case is so compelling, is testifying for a side that he normally opposes.

The doctors need credentials. Authorship of a textbook and a teaching position at a university hospital are best. Private practice is not as prestigious. All the forensics have *vitae* pages long; that is never a problem. Most attorneys prefer to find an out-of-town forensic, particularly in Phoenix, where it's traditional for experts to come from somewhere else. The out-of-town opinion is usually balanced with a second opinion by a psychiatrist from Arizona. This adds a hometown approach and cuts off the accusation "You'll notice my opponent couldn't find an Arizona doctor to say this—he had to go all the way to California to find one." It's a game of wits.

If your insanity defense is on shaky ground, it is essential to pick a forensic psychiatrist who testifies well. He shouldn't be stiff or cold or, worst of all, boring. He can't go over the jury's head. Jurors like psychiatry, but just a touch of it. If an expert gives the jury too much science or is too technical, jurors begin to fade. Trials as a spectator sport have not changed very much since the days when Christians were thrown to the lions in the Colosseum. There is still a certain measure of entertainment you have to provide, particularly in a murder trial. The lawyers are there to put on a show, to give the jury a chance to cry or to get mad. An insanity defense is the ideal stage for dramatic forensic testimony, because anything goes—there are virtually no limits to what a psychiatrist can say in this kind of trial.

Bob Hirsh chose Martin Blinder as his out-of-state expert for Steven Steinberg, and he chose him at a time when Blinder's reputation was sparkling. Hirsh had known the San Francisco psychiatrist for five years. He had testified for Hirsh in at least four big trials—Dr. Blinder told Jeff Hotham in a pretrial interview that he didn't really recall the outcome of those trials; Hirsh said they were all acquittals. In 1981, Dr. Blinder was the ideal choice for the unusual case, and the defense in *State* v. *Steinberg* was going to be unusual indeed.

Martin Blinder, M.D., has his San Francisco office in a trim brownstone in the Pacific Heights district and another office in Marin County, but his real home is in courtrooms all across America. Dr. Blinder is a forensic psychiatrist in great demand. He has all of the qualifications needed to rise to the top of his profession, including the first necessity for the courtroom: an impeccable academic background. Dr. Blinder graduated from Cornell and the University of Chicago, and had a residency and teaching position at San Francisco's Langley Porter Psychiatric Institute. He lectures on psychiatry and the law at the University of California's Hastings College of Law. His *vita* is eight pages long. He has written a textbook on psychiatry for lawyers which is in its sixth update. He appears at seminars throughout the West for the toughest of all audiences—the trial lawyers. If there was one cloud on the academic horizon for Martin Blinder in 1981, it was that he had never passed the examination to be board-certified in psychiatry, a lack that is usually made to look more significant in a trial than it really is. Most opponents seized on this supposed flaw at trial, but the tactic was usually a mistake. Dr. Blinder's testimony about his lack of board certification was so engaging that jurors usually liked him all the more—it showed that the doctor was human and not just a cold academic. "I'm no good in neurology," he would admit cheerfully.

Martin Blinder's most sterling quality was his charm and control on the witness stand. The doctor is round-faced and good-natured and never at a loss for words. To the irritation of some of his colleagues, Dr. Blinder tends to dispense with technical psychiatric language in trial. He seldom uses phrases like "somatoform dissociated hysteria" when he is testifying. Martin Blinder's clients "snap," they "do not have their wits about them," they are "discombobulated" or are "at war with themselves." A Tucson prosecutor remembers one trial at which Martin Blinder described the defendant as "looking at the world through manure-covered glasses."

It's not that the doctor does not have the clinical vocabulary. In his writings for lawyers, Dr. Blinder says that he believes that the proper role of the psychiatrist in the criminal trial is to draw a psychological "portrait" of the defendant in lay language—to tell a story the jury can appreciate and warm to. In Dr. Blinder's medical reports his subjects are struggling deep in human passions. They love and are rejected by the ones they love; they are abused by parents, lovers, or bosses; they are cruelly taunted with provocative sex or led astray by their victims. Women are generally typecast as either madonna or whore—there is little neutral ground. Jurors love it. Psychiatry seems close and intimate to them after hearing from Dr. Blinder in his vivid language. The defendant becomes easy to identify with and less frightening.

Sometimes a single case will catapult a forensic psychiatrist into the limelight. For Martin Blinder his testimony in two murder trials brought him prominence. *People* v. *Berry* and the murder trial of Dan White have become California criminal law folklore. These are trials that lawyers remember by name, because each represents a turning point in law and psychiatry.

In 1974 the defense attorney for a man named Albert Berry asked the doctor to examine his client. Berry was on trial in San Francisco for first degree murder. The facts were dismal. Mr. Berry had long displayed a hair-trigger reaction to any frustration in his life, particularly imposed by women. Some years earlier he had stabbed his first wife eleven times—"she was a bad woman," Berry explained to a jury later. After this incident, Berry had miraculously slipstreamed through the overcrowded California justice system with a minimum penalty considering the severity of the offense. After a short stay at Vacaville, Berry was out on parole.

Almost at once he met and married a young woman from Israel named Rachel. Albert was soon overwhelmed with jealousy, and shortly after the wedding he confronted Rachel with his suspicions about her infidelity and choked her into unconsciousness. Rachel survived the attack and lodged a criminal complaint against her husband, who had disappeared. When she returned from the hospital three days later, Albert was waiting at the Berry apartment. He had made himself a cup of tea while he waited and had a telephone cord ready in his hand. "All I wanted to do was talk," he told police later, and he told Rachel he didn't know whether he would kill her or not. She began to scream.

The screams apparently tipped some fragile balance for Albert, who then strangled Rachel (this time successfully) with the telephone cord and wandered out into the street. Berry was charged with the two attacks on his wife—one count of attempted murder for the first assault, and one count of first degree murder for the last.

It looked like an impossible case for his defense attorney. Berry had tried twice in three days to strangle Rachel, the second time lying in wait with the telephone cord. The two attempts and the ambush in the apartment showed premeditation, the essential element of first degree murder. When things are that bad, an insanity defense is always a potential, but to make a successful insanity run Albert Berry would probably have to take the stand and testify himself. That would be a disaster, because then it would be disclosed that Albert had tried to murder his first wife—miraculously she had lived, although Albert had stabbed her eleven times—certainly not a disclosure that would endear Berry to the jury.

Martin Blinder was called in to examine Berry in preparation for what was known as a "diminished capacity" defense. His approach was spectacular. According to Dr. Blinder, the dead Rachel Berry was not only a sadistic and cruel woman given to tormenting Albert, but had also been strongly inclined to commit suicide. Dr. Blinder testified that because Rachel did not have the strength of purpose to kill herself, she had deliberately provoked Albert into fits of jealousy, hoping that he would do the job for her. Finally, according to the psychiatrist, "She achieved her unconscious desire and was strangled."

By Dr. Blinder's analysis, Albert Berry was not criminally culpable, but was really doing the mixed-up Rachel a favor when he killed her. Throughout the trial Berry appeared disheveled and sad, weeping whenever Rachel's name was mentioned. At one session he appeared in court without his shoes, crying pitifully, a pathetic figure.

The criminal defense technique of attributing character and conduct to the dead person in a "psychiatric autopsy" of the murder victim was not the brainchild of Martin Blinder, but *People* v. *Berry* was its apogee. Gerry Winkler, the young assistant district attorney, was infuriated. California had no pretrial discovery in criminal trials, so the Blinder attack on

Rachel Berry came as a surprise. Working at night, he was able to locate and subpoena relatives and a neighbor of the dead woman and bring them in for rebuttal. They said the young woman was upbeat and kind, and terrified of Albert Berry. Incredibly, Berry's attorney tried to keep these witnesses from testifying—Rachel's character wasn't relevant, he told the judge, and she couldn't be rehabilitated at the trial.

By this time Winkler was almost apoplectic. His closing argument to the jury sizzles on the paper. Most of it is directed at the San Francisco psychiatrist; it is filled with sarcasm and ridicule when he talks about Dr. Blinder's view of the helpless Albert Berry and the "sadistic and cruel" Rachel. The jury was out only a short time before it returned with a first degree murder verdict.

The supreme court of California was more receptive to Dr. Blinder's medical opinion that Rachel Berry had really wanted to be murdered when it reversed Berry's conviction. Blinder's psychiatric autopsy of Rachel was printed, without comment, as if it were the undisputed facts of the case. The Blinder theory had little to do with the reversal, but merely by being printed in the supreme court's opinion as a viable medical diagnosis and method, the Blinder autopsy gained credence—it became respectable. The eventual outcome in *People* v. *Berry* was not significantly different—on the eve of his second trial Albert Berry pled guilty to second degree murder.

The real significance of *Berry* was that the California supreme court had accepted two revolutionary ideas without question—that a victim's psyche could be analyzed, after death, by a psychiatrist in a murder trial; and that a victim of a homicide could somehow provoke her own murder. No case had ever gone so far in forensic history to spotlight the person who had been killed rather than the individual on trial—*Berry* opened new vistas. Martin Blinder's name was displayed in the lawbooks for everyone who read the case to see. His reputation as a forensic rose like a rocket.

Dr. Blinder's next showcase trial received mixed reviews. The controversy is still alive in the city of San Francisco. The psychiatrist is both proud and defensive when he writes about his testimony in the murder trial of Dan White.

In 1978, San Francisco had voted to change its form of city government. The city's supervisors (the equivalent of councilmen) were going to be elected by district instead of at large. A boyish, good-looking city fireman named Dan White was elected from a conservative working district. The Castro district elected Harvey Milk, an avowed homosexual who represented the Castro's growing gay population. There was a newly elected mayor, the popular and flamboyant George Moscone.

The neophyte White had trouble adjusting to the political art of compromise. In an impulsive moment of frustration, White resigned. His supporters were horrified. White changed his mind under this pressure and asked Moscone to let him withdraw his letter of resignation, but it was too late for White to reverse what he had done so hastily.

On a rainy morning White heard a news report that Moscone had decided not to reappoint him as a supervisor. He took his service revolver (he had once been a San Francisco policeman) and a load of extra ammunition and drove to City Hall. White did not use the public entrance with the metal detector but crawled through an open back window, ending up in a boiler room. He went directly to Moscone's office and fired four shots at the mayor, emptying the revolver. While the mayor's staff stared in shock, White walked down the hall to Harvey Milk's office, reloading the gun with the ammunition in his pocket as he went. "Why are you trying to cheat me out of my job?" he shouted. Before Milk could answer he died in a barrage of five shots.

From a prosecutor's viewpoint, the case was clear enough. The mayor of San Francisco and a popular supervisor had been assassinated. There was incontrovertible evidence from White's activity that morning that the killings were premeditated, which made it first degree murder. To assistant district attorney Tom Norman, a veteran of numerous murder trials, the outcome was never in doubt—how could it be?

Defense attorney Dan Schmidt drew in his troops for a

diminished capacity defense, which in California would reduce the crime to manslaughter. Diminished capacity was a watered-down insanity defense then possible in California, and it, too, needed some good psychiatrists. Martin Blinder was not the leading light of the defense team, but to Mike Weiss, a reporter covering the White trial, in the end he was by far the most effective. It was Blinder's testimony that the jurors asked to have read back to them in the jury room while they were deliberating.

Dr. Blinder used homey and simple terms to describe White's mental state at the time of the murders, in contrast to the tortured psychiatric language of the other experts. White was "discombobulated" and "didn't have his wits about him," he said. To the health-conscious, jogging California public, Dr. Blinder added an intriguing theory to help explain the lethal episode at City Hall. When Dan White was depressed, said Blinder, he would gorge himself on Twinkies, Coca-Cola, and junk food. Sugar had triggered violence in some people— clearly Dr. Blinder thought White was one of these. Dr. Blinder told the jury that there were even some studies in which they had "taken criminals off their junk food, put them on milk and meat and potatoes, and their criminal records immediately evaporate."

In legal seminars and writings, Blinder repeats his *People v. White* testimony as an example of the best of forensic psychiatry, but he bristles when his name is coupled with the word "Twinkie." He sees his theory as scholarly and well supported.

In the aftermath, the public reaction to the White psychiatric defense was largely negative. The idea that the ingestion of sweets like Twinkies and junk food could trigger such lethal violence seemed to make the killings of the mayor of San Francisco and Harvey Milk appear trivial. Dr. Blinder gained fame and visibility on a national scale after the White trial, but ironically that publicity actually narrowed his forensic territory in California. He was perceived for years as being vulnerable in cross-examination to the very mention of the word "Twinkie." Everyone in the Bay Area knew what that meant. One prosecutor was rebuked by the court of appeals for referring to Blinder as "Dr. Twinkie" throughout a trial. Regardless of the criticism of the Twinkie defense, the litmus test for success was met in Dan White's defense strategy—the desired result was obtained.

Mike Weiss believed that Dr. Blinder's testimony was effective not so much because of the Twinkie defense but because he succeeded in making Dan White human to the jury. The Blinder report described White sympathetically—he was a white knight, somewhat naive, fighting against a changing San Francisco landscape that he did not understand. The humanizing of Dan White was particularly compelling because it came through the mouth of a doctor—when Dr. Blinder described White's good qualities it became a medical fact, like a broken arm. There were villains. Dr. Blinder testified that White told him that City Hall was "rife with corruption" and that the supervisors "didn't give a damn about the voters." An unattractive picture of the supervisors and city government wafted through the medical report—Moscone and Milk were not the most sympathetic of victims after this testimony, and there was a hint of justification for their killer. The two-pronged strategy of the defense is summed up by Mike Weiss in his book *Double Play*. "They had it coming, and besides, he couldn't help himself."

The jury agreed. On May 21, 1979, it returned a verdict. Dan White was convicted of two counts of manslaughter on the diminished capacity theory. The verdict was a shock to the prosecution, particularly as to the Milk homicide, in which premeditation had seemed so clear. San Francisco exploded that night as the gay population of the city broke windows and set fires in an unheard-of show of violence—now it is called "White Night."

When surprise verdicts like Dan White's occur, there is an inevitable backlash. California immediately reacted—the voters passed a statewide initiative to eliminate the diminished capacity defense. The city abandoned district elections, the district attorney was defeated in the next election, and the police chief resigned. Prosecutor Tom Norman was never quite the same again, everyone agreed.

White was sentenced to the maximum for manslaughter

under California law, which amounted to five years in Soledad in real time. In prison he kept fit and took up running. His wife remained loyal. A year after his release from Soledad on parole, Dan White closed himself in his garage, hooked up a garden hose to the exhaust pipe of his 1970 LeSabre, and started the engine. He was imposing the ultimate penalty on himself. There was no way to tell if Twinkies or junk food had played any part in the last act of this tragedy. Martin Blinder saw the ending as a vindication for him. "White killed out of a depressive despair," said Blinder to the *Chronicle*. "The suicide is entirely consistent with my diagnosis seven years ago."

This is not the way one of Martin Blinder's persistent critics sees it. Dr. Thomas Szasz, in his book *Insanity: The Idea and Its Consequences,* thought that Dan White might have been harmed, not saved, by the success of his defense:

"Thanks to the 'Twinkie defense' White was convicted of voluntary manslaughter instead of murder. . . . how did White benefit from this great courtroom victory? He received a shorter prison sentence that he would have. . . . perhaps a longer, more appropriate prison sentence would have enabled White to atone for his sins and, by saving his soul, might have saved his life. . . . Like anyone not completely duped by psychiatry, White too must have felt that his defense was as phony as a three-dollar bill; he must have known . . . that his crime constituted a carefully orchestrated performance."

Like many psychiatric innovations in the criminal courtroom, the sugar or Twinkie defense had a short life-span. It was probably used successfully only one time—for Dan White. But since Dr. Blinder's performance on the witness stand had been so skillful, his reputation now took on national dimension. In 1981 when he came to Arizona to examine Steven Steinberg and William Gorzenski, he was nationally acclaimed and supremely confident.

The psychiatrist met with Steven Steinberg for two hours in a room made available in the Maricopa County courthouse. The basis for a psychiatric diagnosis is usually the interview, although there may be some psychological testing to back it up. When the subject has no history of mental illness, like

Steven Steinberg and William Gorzenski, the interview and his-
tory-taking are really the only clinical tool available. Dr. Blinder's report on Steven Steinberg after their meeting in the jail
now became a medical document with almost the same impact
as a report of the biopsy of a tumor, or a blood test. It was
intended as medical fact.

Unlike other medical reports, this one was a story, sixteen
pages of scathing denunciation of the dead Elana Steinberg and
of her family. In Dr. Blinder's report, Steven Steinberg was a
helpless and innocent victim to the materialism of the Singers;
a henpecked husband mired in a loveless marriage to a shrewish
and demanding woman. Every bad quality is Elana's—she
shops, she spends, she nags, she withholds sex and drives her
husband to gambling. Steinberg's father-in-law, Barney Singer,
is corrupt and dissolute, a stupid man. Edith Singer embodies
the worst of mother-in-law jokes. By contrast, members of
Steve's family are religious, simple, and unostentatious,
"pushed aside because Steinberg is consumed by the Singers'
prejudices." The personae on the stage are set in absolutes—
they are good versus evil, black versus white. If Dr. Blinder
questions the objectivity of his subject in weaving this tale,
there is no sign of it in his medical report.

On the afternoon after he finished with Steinberg, Dr.
Blinder went to Scottsdale to interview Barney and Edith
Singer and the two little girls. The emphasis in this trial had
shifted already. Elana Steinberg, not her husband, was in the
psychiatric spotlight. Hotham did not accompany Dr. Blinder,
although he had the right to do so. He was leaving the Singers
to fend for themselves. Edith told me when I interviewed her
that she didn't even know the doctor was working on Steve's
behalf.

"It didn't occur to me then that he was against me, or
Elana. I guess I wasn't thinking of who was on what side or
anything like that, I was still too upset.

"He asked me if he could use the bathroom. He came in a
taxi, he said he had been driving and out of the office for a
while. I said of course. We have two bathrooms, one for the
girls' room and one off the master bedroom where Barney and

I sleep. He went in there, and I heard the door to the medicine cabinet open and close. I thought he wanted an aspirin or something, but I thought it was strange. Now I think that he really wanted to see what medicine we were taking, or if we were on drugs or something.

"We were so stupid. Barney even offered to drive him back downtown, and we tried to help him—I thought he was a doctor, you know. I didn't know what he was going to say about us, and Elana, and how terrible we were."

Traci was more astute than her grandmother—she realized that it was best to be wary of the psychiatrist from San Francisco. After he had talked to her and the twelve-year-old's bitterness about her father had come out, Blinder asked, "Does your grandma tell you what to say?" Traci was quick to reply, "No, *I* tell *her.*"

By day's end, Martin Blinder was finished in Phoenix and ready to go to Safford the next day for the examination of William Gorzenski. The doctor from San Francisco had performed his psychiatric autopsy on Elana Steinberg, and it was time to move on.

CHAPTER ELEVEN

A WALK WITH DANIEL
M'NAGHTEN

By July, Steinberg had been in the county jail for six weeks, and he was restive. Most suspects in Arizona are out on their own recognizance, "OR," if they have roots in the community. For the rest, putting up 10 percent of the bail is enough to buy them daylight. The big exception is for capital crimes, and first degree murder is the only capital crime. In Steinberg's case, the commissioner had refused to set bail. Bob Hirsh's first order of business was to get his client out. Then Steve could be more relaxed, help prepare his defense, and avoid the terrible jail pallor which looks so bad in the courtroom.

The case had been assigned to Judge Marilyn Riddel, a statuesque, handsome woman in her forties with a crown of prematurely white hair and an unfailingly cheerful air. The judge's gracious manner could not be interpreted as a softness for criminal defendants—the judge was the scourge of defense attorneys, who usually avoided Division Five, exercising their one free "strike" of a judge as soon as they learned that Riddel was assigned to a trial. She was considered a hanging judge. While she would bake cookies every night for the jurors and speak graciously to defendants, she was known for imposing the harshest sentences in the county, smiling all the time. In 1975, Judge Riddel single-handedly enforced the state's welfare rules when she sentenced the mother of nine children to three years in jail—stacked sentences—for food-stamp and welfare fraud. In the following weeks, lines of people appeared at welfare offices all over the state to confess outside income so that the same wouldn't happen to them. In 1986 a man whose offense originally started with a traffic ticket and a failure to appear spent over a year in the Maricopa County jail after a Riddel sentence. The Arizona court of appeals found the sentence unjustified, but too late to benefit the defendant, who had already served his time.

Hirsh and Benchoff held a conference—should they stay in Judge Riddel's court for the trial? There were factors in favor of this, rather than opting for their one free change of judge. Steinberg was appealing, with his good looks and tragic air. The two lawyers were charming, and Mike Benchoff had years of prosecution experience known to Marilyn Riddel—he was respected. They decided to chance it and stay in Division Five, the first of many astute judgments they were to make.

The bond motion was set for July 13. Bob Hirsh's theory was that the Steinberg murder wasn't a capital crime, because it was highly unlikely a death penalty would be imposed. In addition to his legal position, Hirsh had mobilized some of the friends who had been meeting in Diane Lindstrom's house for their first task. They were to write letters to the judge, telling her that their friend Steve Steinberg had an exemplary character. The letters that they wrote are in the court file—they have the ring of sincerity and a certain innocence, although they were obviously written at the request of the defense attorneys.

In the bail letters the friends say that the Steinberg family life was idyllic; Elana Steinberg was a wonderful wife and mother. No one saw Elana as unusual, nor did anyone pity Steve for working to provide for her. The contents of the bail letters indicate that the group believed that being a good provider was an asset, not a liability, and something that a good Jewish husband should do. "He was a workaholic," wrote David Goldfarb in his letter. "A fifteen-hour workday for him was the rule and not the exception. He simply wanted to provide his wife and children with the best." The Waldmans were equally positive about the role of husband as provider. "Steve seemed to fit the pattern of a 'family man,' as he frequently gave gifts to his wife, treating her kindly, and spent much time with his two daughters." Living well was the expectation of these families. They saw nothing unusual about the Steinbergs, at least not when they wrote these letters in July.

Cecil Kirk was the police witness at the bail hearing. He was to tell the police theory of the crime and identify the fingerprints on the knife. Outside the courtroom, the prosecutor discovered something that made his heart sink. On the day of the hearing, Kirk was still struggling to match the fingerprints on the knife with Steinberg's, although Hotham had already filed his response to the bail motion saying that the prints had been identified. The problem wasn't serious. The prints on the knife had been made in blood, and were "reversals"—all that was needed was to have a reverse-color negative made to make the prints appear in their normal configuration. The real problem was that Kirk hadn't picked up on that, and now the defense attorneys were aware that he hadn't. The prints were sent out to the state lab for damage control, but Hotham could see that Mike Benchoff had filed the incident away for future reference. The slip-up meant that Hotham couldn't use Kirk for anything substantial after that—no testimony about blood splatters or matching the knife slits; nothing about the victim's position at the time of the attack. Once a police witness can be made to seem like a bungler, he is fair game for a good defense attorney. Everything else he says will be ridiculed. Hotham sighed. He had just lost any police expertise from Scottsdale.

Some of Steve's friends were in the room waiting to give character evidence. Mitch Singer was there—he wanted to be sure Steve was staying in jail. The prosecutor argued vigorously. This was a heinous crime, he said, and met the standard for death-penalty cases, so it was inappropriate to set bail. Mitch

Singer thought that the judge was obviously angered by the photographs of Elana's body. "I could see her expression change. I felt relieved. They were taking it seriously, I thought."

The judge was decisive. She ruled from the bench that there would be no bail; the crime was sufficiently "cruel" to meet the standards of a capital crime. Steve Steinberg put his head down on the table and wept. Jeff Hotham had won, but he felt unexpectedly gloomy. Bob Hirsh had lost, but he had scored two important points. The judge had been desensitized to the gruesome evidence of Elana's death; those pictures would not be so shocking the next time. More important, Hirsh had found a sensitive nerve in the prosecutor's case; Jeff Hotham had little confidence in his police officers. The shadow of the Crane murder was still there.

By August the defense strategy was beginning to gel. Hirsh changed the plea of not guilty to an insanity defense. He was not relying solely on the celebrated psychiatrist from San Francisco. He had retained a second psychiatrist for Steve Steinberg. In the beginning of September, some three months after Elana Steinberg was killed, Dr. Donald Holmes arrived in Phoenix to examine Hirsh's client. Holmes was the director of a community mental health clinic in Casa Grande, a small cotton town in the center of the state. Dr. Holmes has had a distinguished background in psychiatry. He was a professor at the University of Michigan, had written a textbook which is still in print after many years, and had graduated *summa cum laude* from medical school. Unlike Martin Blinder, Dr. Holmes seems to have written exclusively for medical readers; his subspecialty is adolescent psychiatry. Holmes has apparently not crossed over to the world of lawyers and the courtroom. He is not a true forensic. Though Martin Blinder would seem to be on the cutting edge of any new approach to the insanity defense, Holmes was the defense psychiatrist who was going to break new ground.

After Dr. Holmes talked to Steven Steinberg, he said firmly that Hirsh's client had been in a deep sleep when he got the carving knife from the Steinberg kitchen and when he killed his wife. He was a sleepwalker, and a homicidal sleepwalker to boot. After the trial, I read Holmes's report and his interview with the prosecutor before trial, and I was intrigued. Deep in my memory was something unforgettable that happened to me one evening years ago. My husband and I watched in astonishment as our six-year-old daughter walked down the stairs and into the living room, obviously sound asleep. We walked her back to bed with no problem. It was an experience she was never to repeat, but nonetheless it left an eerie feeling. I had always read that sleepwalkers were clumsy and uncoordinated in their movements; they could fall down the stairs or stumble into a wall. I had never believed that sleepwalkers could kill, and so brutally as Steven Steinberg had that night. Could this be so? Or was this to be one of those one-time psychiatric defenses that burst upon the scene in criminal law and then disappear as did Dr. Blinder's Twinkie defense?

One day in the fall almost four years after the Steinberg trial I drove up to Oak Creek Canyon to see Donald Holmes. The doctor had moved his practice to the red-rock paradise of Sedona, surely one of the most pleasant places in the world to live. At the base of a fortress of spectacular red pinnacles Donald Holmes now practices in a small community mental health office in a trailerlike building. It is a quiet setting, very much out of the mainstream of psychiatry. Dr. Holmes had been kind enough to provide a copy of his *vita*. Typical of the relaxed air of this mental health office and of the Verde Valley in general, the copier is an old one and the *vita* is faint and hard to read.

Dr. Holmes is a very large man, tall and heavy-boned, in his late fifties. He has a kind face and looks like a country doctor on a television series; he is gentle and exceedingly polite. I could see that a patient would not hesitate to tell this psychiatrist troubling, secret thoughts. I came away from Sedona liking Dr. Holmes; he seemed to be an extremely pleasant man with no ego to bruise and no feathers to ruffle. The jury must have liked him too.

Although Donald Holmes described Steinberg's state as sleepwalking, both Holmes and Blinder found that Steven Steinberg was in a dissociative reaction when he killed Elana, what they both called an "altered state of consciousness." There wasn't any significant difference between the two opinions;

sleepwalking was just a refinement. Dissociation is one of the hysterical neuroses, defined as a sudden alteration in mental functioning, almost a trancelike state. If it lasts long enough, it is a "fugue." A person in a fugue state can leave home for months, assuming a new identity and forgetting who he is. The consummate hysterical neurosis is the multiple personality, that unique individual whose body is inhabited by two or more distinct personalities.

The last time a man had been tried for murder in Arizona and had claimed that he was in an "altered state of consciousness," the Arizona supreme court had said that this diagnosis was not enough to be considered insanity under the *M'Naghten* rule. The law hadn't changed: Arizona still used the *M'Naghten* test of insanity in criminal trials. A jury was supposed to decide whether a defendant "knew the nature and quality of his act," or if he did, whether he "knew it was wrong."

M'Naghten has never been a satisfactory test, because no one ever has been able successfully to explain what it means. Some psychiatrists can find the test met with every defendant they examine, and others will never find it. In the long run, juries do what they wish. The confusion all began in 1843 with a modest Scottish woodcutter named Daniel M'Naghten who believed that the Prime Minister of England, Sir Robert Peel, was trying to persecute him. M'Naghten came to London for the express purpose of killing that gentleman. He purchased a gun and then waited on a street where he knew the Prime Minister's carriage would pass. In one of those freakish occurrences which make history, Sir Robert was not in his carriage on that day; he had given his place to his private secretary, and that unfortunate gentleman was killed instead.

Daniel M'Naghten had the good sense to have the services of a man who must have been the outstanding criminal lawyer of the century, Sir Alexander Cockburn. His counsel relied on new and trend-setting evidence derived from the just-beginning study of the human mind. Cockburn was able to convince the judge and the jury that M'Naghten's delusions of being persecuted spilled over into the other areas of his consciousness, making it impossible for him to refrain from killing that day.

The trial judge was so impressed with this advanced presenta-
tion that he came very close to directing an acquittal for
M'Naghten without even submitting the case to the jury. The
jury had no difficulty in finding M'Naghten not guilty by reason
of insanity. If nothing else, the acquittal demonstrated the persuasive power of a brilliant trial lawyer working in tandem with
a medical expert. Daniel M'Naghten spent the remaining
twenty-two years of his life in a grim hospital for the criminally
insane. His victory was a hollow one.

Queen Victoria was understandably incensed with the outcome of the M'Naghten trial. It was the fourth attempt at political assassination in forty years and the second in which the
assailant had been acquitted by reason of insanity. When the
Queen's chancellor spoke to the House of Lords about the verdict, it was clear that he was furious as well and he wanted
something done about it.

The Queen decided to act with—what else?—a fact-finding commission. She called together the most renowned judges
in England, the fifteen justices of the common law courts, and
asked them to answer five hypothetical questions about insanity
and criminal responsibility. The commission was operating in a
politically charged atmosphere, which is a bad way to make law.

In 1843, just as today, an English or American court was
not supposed to give what are called "advisory opinions." These
are opinions which are not based on any particular set of facts;
they are opinions in which there is no contest or adversary
proceeding before the court, opinions in the abstract. When a
court does anything it is supposed to be based on an actual case
or controversy, and that is the way the "common law" is made.
In the next case, the next trial, there will be a different set of
facts and the law can go forward building case law on top of
case law, as bricks build a wall. The adversary system has some
drawbacks—it has helped to give lawyers the bad reputation
they have had since the days of Shakespeare and earlier. It
makes them contentious, because that is what lawyers are supposed to be, but the adversary system makes the English law
work as no other system does.

The Queen's commission in 1843 didn't have any facts or

controversy before it. Daniel M'Naghten had been acquitted and could not be tried again, so his verdict could not be appealed. The justices replied to Queen Victoria with two vague sentences which have survived to live on in almost every state in America: a defendant is not criminally culpable if "he does not know the nature and quality of his act" or if "he does not know that the act is wrong." It is an unsatisfying formula which does not give the jury any real guidelines.

Jurors listen politely to the two opposing groups of psychiatrists in an insanity trial. In the long run, they will decide whether the crime is one that the community can tolerate or even sympathize with, and whether this defendant would ever be a danger to themselves if let loose. Some killers are obviously feared by jurors, and they will choose punishment for this kind of person in the face of all psychiatric testimony to the contrary because they want protection. Unlike Daniel M'Naghten, no one will stay for long in a mental institution, and the jury knows it. Some crimes are more acceptable than others, and some defendants are more attractive. It is the job of the forensic psychiatrist to bring this to the attention of the jury. That's *M'Naghten* in action today.

M'Naghten in Arizona has never included an "altered state of consciousness"—the Arizona supreme court said so with no equivocation. Either defense attorneys had found a new approach or psychiatry had learned a new language since Joseph Alvin Schantz killed his wife in 1965 in a quiet Phoenix neighborhood. Schantz was a mild-mannered husband with no history of violence, much like Steven Steinberg. One May night he erupted with a furious attack on his wife, Matilda, stabbing the middle-aged woman repeatedly with a butcher knife in the Schantz kitchen while she screamed to the neighbors for help, and finally beating her over the head with an iron skillet so forcefully that the skillet shattered into pieces.

By the time the police arrived, Mrs. Schantz was dead. Schantz had amnesia, just like Steve Steinberg, and had no explanation for what had occurred. The sole psychiatrist to testify said that Schantz was in an altered state of consciousness, which was the exact diagnosis the defense doctors had for

Steinberg. The facts of the two cases were identical. *State* v. *Schantz* is a case that lawyers call "on all fours" with Steinberg's, which means that there should be the same legal result. Unfortunately for Mr. Schantz, his defense attorney was not as forward-looking as was Robert Hirsh. His attorney took it for granted that an "altered state" was not insanity under Arizona law. He urged the court to create a new mental illness category that would fit this situation. Both the trial judge and the supreme court of Arizona rejected his idea—an altered state of consciousness in 1965 was not insanity nor anything else that would excuse Schantz from criminal responsibility. Clearly something must have happened to *M'Naghten* in the seventeen years since Matilda Schantz was stabbed and beaten over the head with the skillet by her mild-mannered husband.

Probably neither Hirsh nor the prosecutor thought of *State* v. *Schantz*. If Bob Hirsh did, he wasn't talking about it. After *Schantz*, dissociative reactions had fallen into a decline for seventeen years, but they were now back. The jurors in the Steinberg trial were going to be treated to a polished performance, which is probably what Joseph Alvin Schantz's defense had lacked.

CHAPTER TWELVE

VOIR DIRE

Jurors . . . introduce into their verdicts a certain amount—a very large amount, so far as I have observed, of popular prejudice and this keeps the administration of the law in accord with the wishes and feelings of the community.

— *OLIVER WENDELL HOLMES, JR.*

It was February, nine months after Elana Steinberg's death. The judicial process was lumbering to its conclusion. Steve was still in jail. Each side had exchanged lists of witnesses— Hirsh, in a lawyer's game of "find the real witness," gave Hotham a list with fifty names on it. Hirsh had interviewed all of Hotham's witnesses and had transcripts made; Hotham had interviewed only the two defense psychiatrists and Ira Gaines, and his investigator had talked to a few more. Hirsh offered a plea—he would advise his client to plead to manslaughter, with no jail time. Hotham laughed.

On February 2, 1982, the delicate and frustrating business of jury selection was beginning. Forty-five people would be sent to Judge Riddel's courtroom, to be questioned in a general way by the judge. In this process, some of those questioned will be excused for various reasons—a potential juror may know one of the witnesses; he may feel he can't be a fair juror on a drunk-driving case; he may be ill, or hard-of-hearing; he may need his wages and be unable to take time off. The first thirty-four that remain of the original forty-five are the panel, the venire, and the rest are dismissed. Then each of the lawyers in a murder trial take their ten peremptory challenges. Peremptories can be exercised for any reason that an attorney chooses. He may just have vague misgivings about a particular juror. He may strike a juror because of the stereotypes about what certain occupations and age types are likely to do—"Women tend to be prejudiced against other women, particularly if the other woman is pretty"; "Avoid engineers and accountants if you're a defense attorney." The lawyers can also observe the jurors' appearance and attitudes as they sit in the courtroom and respond to the judge's questions. Some psychologists deem themselves expert in picking jurors in this way and will make a study of body language and gestures; Martin Blinder has done this often. The way a woman juror holds her purse will label her as either "submissive" or "a leader." Folded arms, a facial tic, the way a man crosses his legs, the wearing of a certain lapel pin—supposedly all of these are clues to a juror's personality. In his textbook for lawyers, Dr. Blinder even theorized that the condition of a juror's teeth might be significant—poor dental work might signify that a potential juror would be a good defense juror in a civil case.

It's a very unsatisfying procedure. In a big-money case, the attorneys will go so far as to commission a public opinion poll, so they can analyze the answers with the background of the persons polled. It's all done by hunches; there is no science to it. There is never any good feedback—no lawyer knows with certainty what works and what doesn't. A lawyer can talk to the jury in the chaos of the courtroom after the trial is over and the verdict is in, of course. Unfortunately, no one ever knows whether what the jurors say then is accurate, sometimes not even the jurors themselves. Hidden deep inside each juror may be prejudices and predispositions that no one will ever know about. It was pure chance to find the twelve people who would be just the right combination for Steve Steinberg. It was a mixture of computer science, a judge's rigidity, and human guesswork that put it all together.

First there was the machine. In the basement of the oldest

building in the county complex there is a mechanical marvel, kept carefully cooled and tended, always dust-free. The marvel is the computer system for the business of the County of Maricopa. Properly programmed, the computer can do just about anything. In 1982 one of its jobs was to select the venire for all of the courts in Maricopa County, to find the cross section of the community that would be prospective jurors—the peers that the Sixth Amendment requires. Picking jurors at random should be a simple matter, but it is not necessarily so. A formula for random selection is as esoteric as anything could ever be in mathematics, and it is for masters of problematical statistics. Things happen along the way of random selection that will skew the accuracy of the jury panel. Purists will say that no technique can make a perfect demographic match for the community. In Phoenix, especially, there are too many transients who will fall out of the jury pool because they don't settle long enough to have a firm address; low-income groups are generally underrepresented. The million people who make up the pool are selected originally from a "motor/voter" list—licensed drivers and registered voters. It's the best that can be done.

Since the court system in Phoenix has always been forward-looking, the jury commissioner uses the most modern methods and software. The pool of one million is narrowed three different times before forty-five prospective jurors ever reach a courtroom. The last two cuts are done using a process that few but the most brilliant could comprehend. It is a system that generates random numbers by computer according to a formula conceived by a Stanford mathematician. The formula is known as the Donald Knuth Congruential Method of Randomization. The Congruential Method distills chance. To a gambler it would be the equivalent of a mammoth and perfect game of roulette, with no odds to the casino. Steve Steinberg is a gambler, but he has never really liked roulette. He was never lucky at the game. But this was the opening day of Steven Steinberg's trial for murder, the most important day in his life, and the gods of probability and the Congruential Method of Randomization were smiling on him.

Three hundred prospective jurors were milling around in

the big jury assembly room on the first floor of the courthouse. This was the pool for five jury trials that were expected to start that day. It was an oddly assorted group—all ages and races were represented here. There were a few young mothers with babies in strollers; if they were chosen, the babies would be a problem. A number of the veniremen were retired, soberly dressed and serious about their responsibility. There was a sprinkling of cowboys in the crowd and some young people in jeans and T-shirts with wild messages on the fronts. Random selection can bring together a mixture of social classes and ages seldom seen together in one room—the occasion and the mixing are unique. Now the computer had one more choice to make to pluck out forty-five names for each courtroom that needs a jury. The program was plugged in again.

State v. *Steinberg,* CR 119983, was third in line on that day, and forty-five names were called out—not alphabetically, for that would go against all principles of randomization. The forty-five filed out to the elevators, looking self-conscious and solemn. On the ninth floor, they filled the back of the courtroom and were told to sit in rows of seats much like church pews; the first names pulled were put in the jury box at the side of the room. Now the Knuth Congruential Method had done its job, and from this point humans, not the computer, were in charge.

The lawyers were already seated at their tables in the front of the courtroom. Everyone looked up to size up the panel. Steve Steinberg was sandwiched between Hirsh and Benchoff. He was not looking his best. Steinberg had lost twenty pounds in the jail, and he was definitely pale. The clothes he was wearing on that day would have surprised anyone who knew him. He wore an inexpensive business suit in a preppy style, a button-down oxford shirt, and a knit tie. These are not the kind of clothes that Steve Steinberg liked. He is normally given to silk shirts open at the throat and gold chains, generally a style associated with the entertainment business or Las Vegas.

Edith Singer said that Steve loved clothes. "He had a velvet jacket, royal blue, and he was wearing it one day in July when I was over there. It was one hundred and eight that day, and I said, 'Steve, aren't you hot in that?' He told me he loved it and was going to wear it and he didn't care how hot it was. He loved clothes, silk shirts, he had drawers full. It was like he was starved for those things." One of the defense team told me that Bob Hirsh was horrified by the wardrobe. "There is no *way* you are going to walk into a courtroom dressed like that," he told Steve.

Steve blamed Elana for the offending clothes. "She bought all my clothes, she picked them out, I didn't have anything to do with it." Someone was sent to Sears to buy two outfits so that Steinberg could alternate at the trial. The clothes struck just the right note; they were conservative, almost humble. Elana Steinberg was going to be pictured in this trial as a professional shopper at Saks and I. Magnin, but her husband's clothes were going to proclaim that the shopping she did was never for him.

Bob Hirsh, tall and restless, was wearing an olive gabardine suit and a light blue shirt. Defense attorneys do not hold back on their clothes. Modest dress at a criminal trial is not considered to be an asset for them. Dressing down wouldn't have worked anyway, since Hirsh and Benchoff could never pass unnoticed in a crowd. Mike Benchoff is not tall, like Hirsh, but he is thin and has a flair for clothes. He wore a beautifully tailored banker's pinstripe and a red tie. Benchoff's bald head gleamed in the spotlight; he looked like a severe professor of art. He seldom smiled. The levity was all reserved for the mobile face of Bob Hirsh, whose expression could change in an instant.

The lawyers are like actors, and this courtroom was theater-in-the-round. The lighting was particularly dramatic, with recessed spots at the front where the drama would be played, and dimming lights at the rear of the courtroom, back of the rail. The judge's bench and the witness stand were high above the floor; behind the bench was a gray marble panel up to the ceiling, with Arizona's "Ditat Deus" seal embossed on it: "God Enriches," a particularly apt motto for the courtroom. Diane Lindstrom took a seat behind the rail instead of in the front at the counsel table. She gave the impression of being a sympathetic friend rather than an attorney. Throughout the trial she was seen talking in a friendly way to Steve Steinberg at recesses. It was a good idea to split the forces. Three lawyers arrayed against the prosecutor might make Hotham look like the underdog in the trial, and this is the role that should be reserved for the defendant, if anybody.

At the prosecutor's table, Frank Hylton was the police officer designated to assist the state. The Scottsdale detective was uneasy, and with good reason. Hylton hadn't worked on the case since early August of 1981, seven months earlier. Just weeks after Elana was killed, Jeff Hotham transferred the case file to Mike Vest, an investigator in the prosecutor's office. Hylton was amazed when he learned a month before trial that he, not Vest, was going to be the trial officer.

"I'd never had a strategy meeting with Jeff Hotham," he told me when I interviewed him later. "I thought I was off the case. For a long time I didn't even know there was an insanity defense; I'd never seen any psychiatric report, never saw any of Vest's notes—I felt like what am I doing here?"

It was Hylton's first murder trial. There was no experienced homicide section to be relied on back in the plaza with the reflecting pool but he instinctively knew enough to feel gloomy about what was going on.

Hirsh and Benchoff, working together, were very intimidating. When they were interviewing Scottsdale policemen in January, Hylton had watched the prosecutor and Hirsh in a contest. He thought that Hotham was tentative and seemed to be out of his depth. Hylton had tried to talk to Marc Budoff at the County Attorney's Office about it and had been told firmly and not very politely to mind his own business and that Jeff was fully capable of handling the situation. Hylton felt rebuffed. He thought part of it was the low esteem for the Scottsdale police just then, since the Crane murder. He was not optimistic as he watched the forty-five people find their seats for voir dire.

Voir dire is the process of questioning prospective jurors to see if they are competent to be jurors, to see if they can be fair and impartial at the outset of the trial. "Voir dire" means "to speak the truth." Like everything else connected with the origin of trial by jury, the words are French. They come from the Norman conquerors of England, who were disenchanted with the more primitive Anglo-Saxon fact-finding methods, such as trial by ordeal, in which a defendant was deemed innocent if he or she sank to the bottom of a pool instead of floating, or if a burn inflicted with a hot iron did not fester within three days. There were some things, like their landholdings, that the Normans did not choose to leave entirely to this kind of divine intervention, and so the idea of a fact-finding jury was conceived.

Voir dire can be done by the judge, the attorneys, or a combination of both. In Arizona, the voir dire is generally done by the judge. Marilyn Riddel takes a very strict position on this. She had permitted the attorneys to submit questions to her in advance of the trial. Although Hirsh had drafted a long list, Judge Riddel was not very cooperative in asking those questions. Generally, only the barest of biographical information is all that the judge will permit. Any questions about a prospective juror's attitudes are out. "We won't get into attitudinal questions," the judge told the lawyers in chambers. This was a severe blow for both sides: inquiring into attitudes, looking for potential bias, is the heart of voir dire. That kind of restriction hits the defense attorneys hardest. Voir dire is a critical stage where trials are won and lost for them. Most trial lawyers believe that it is essential that they question the prospective jurors themselves, rather than have the judge do it all. It is the only one-on-one contact a lawyer is going to have with a juror. The lawyer can probe for hidden prejudices that fit the strategy of his case, and best of all, he may be able to begin to educate the jury about his client and his theory.

It was surprising that Bob Hirsh accepted this state of affairs in Judge Riddel's court so gracefully, but he did. His list of questions got short shrift. The judge's voir dire questions were such that they could be answered in platitudes. Questions like "Can you be a fair and impartial juror in this case?" yield nothing. For the Steinberg trial, even observing the body language of the panel had to be done in a hurry. Judge Riddel believes in firm control of her courtroom. She moved through voir dire at a breakneck pace for a murder trial. There was a lunchtime recess, and a few questions afterward—the lawyers knew it would be the last of voir dire. In chambers, Mike Benchoff made a last request—would the judge ask which jurors had been to college, and if anyone on the panel was familiar with sleepwalking? The judge agreed.

The panel of forty-five was a good cross section of Phoenix; the Knuth Congruential Method had worked well so far. There were office workers, a credit manager, a social worker, an attorney, five engineers, four Air Force men, a gospel singer, a high school teacher, and a reporter for the *Phoenix Gazette*. The rest of the panel were housewives, whose background would remain virtually unknown as far as the voir dire was concerned. "I am married, I have three children, ages ten, eight, and four, and my husband is a mechanic" was the extent of the knowledge about most of these women. Two members of the panel were acquainted with each other. It was a virtual certainty that one or both of them would be struck by the attorneys. No one wants two people who know each other on a jury; that is part of the folklore of voir dire. Five prospective jurors said that they had seen sleepwalking children at some time in their lives. A fourth of the panel were college graduates. Some had master's degrees.

Judge Riddel asked if there were any prospective jurors who would find it difficult to serve for two weeks. A number responded. One cared for a child in a body cast, one had had a coronary bypass and severe angina, there was a sister's wedding that would have been missed by one juror, and one woman breast-fed her infant at noon. For many judges, these would be strong reasons to dismiss these panel members, but Judge Riddel was unrelenting. None of these reasons moved her to excuse anyone. A man who said he was hard of hearing was told that he could sit in the front row if he was selected. Only two people were excused by the judge, one a probation officer and the other an attorney who knew one of the witnesses. Two women moved up to take their places. A panel of thirty-four was now in place. At the end no one knew much about these people other than bits and pieces of simple biographical information, the equivalent, perhaps, of the military's name, rank, and serial number.

The attorneys took their ten peremptory challenges to cut

the jury to fourteen—twelve jurors and two alternates. An intelligent decision based on this narrow questioning in voir dire would have been virtually impossible. When I interviewed the two attorneys years afterward about this, they agreed that it was like flying blind. Bob Hirsh told me that he always looked for "eye contact" and "smart people," and then he laughed, leaving me to wonder whether he was being serious or not. Jeff Hotham said he thought it was a good jury for him—"That shows how much I knew about it." He told me that he struck all the jurors who had experience with psychology—he thought they would accept the defense psychiatrists too easily.

At the end all of the people who had said that they had seen a sleepwalker were gone. All but one of the nine jurors who had been to college were gone as well. The result was a group that broke up the demographic pattern generated by the computer when the forty-five first walked in the courtroom. For the most part, businessmen, professionals, decision-makers, were missing. The panel was bland and innocuous by occupation, consisting of housewives, retired military personnel, and workers for large institutional businesses like the electric and phone companies. From the standpoint of the professional jury selector, it was the best of all worlds. Naive and nonassertive jurors are generally preferred. No one wants a highly visible, self-confident juror; they are usually shunned lest they dominate the jury. There was comfort for both sides in the stereotypes. There were nine women. By tradition, women would tend to sympathize with or mother the handsome Steinberg and to be critical of his dead wife. On the other hand, there were three military men, and they were supposed to be prosecution-minded, according to the books. The final panel was modestly dressed, neat, and well groomed; an unexceptional panel by all standards. The fourteen were issued notebooks and pencils and yellow badges with "Juror" imprinted on them so that no one would speak to them by mistake in the halls or the courthouse cafeteria. Jurors are told to keep to themselves and, most important, to discuss the case with no one.

When I interviewed these jurors, at least as many of them as I could find after four years, I discovered that they were all intensely interested in the voir dire. For the most part they were amazed that they had been chosen. In those interviews I found something startling. I couldn't help concluding that it really set the tone of the Steinberg verdict. Two of the jurors had experienced a divine visitation in the courtroom, and the trial for them was now a religious mission. They had talked to God. "The minute I walked in the room, I heard from Him. He said, 'You were meant to be on this jury,' and I prayed and of course I was chosen just like He said I would be," one woman told me. Another made virtually the same comment: I never knew whether they had compared notes about it. I don't think they had. It was just an everyday experience for these women, I think.

After any trial I have been involved with has ended, I've talked to the jurors, and sometimes I have been astounded by how they functioned. They often decide the case on a little thing that really didn't have anything to do with the case in my mind. Sometimes a jury that I thought was very unsophisticated will have applied really high-level reasoning and seen through a complicated matter. I've tried to think about picking a jury in the Steinberg case and what I would have been looking for if I had been the prosecutor. The defense was mainly that Steinberg was a poor slob with a nagging wife who bought expensive things and drove him crazy—which I think is a ridiculous premise in the first place. If I had been trying this case I would have liked to know if there were bitter divorce experiences on this panel, particularly among the men.

For example, there were four military men on the original panel. In my experience, military men are very prone to divorce, probably because they move around so much. It has also been my experience that military men are incredibly possessive about their retirement pension. The law now says that the wife owns half of the pension if she and her husband get divorced, but a military man just goes up the wall when he hears that. Normally you would think that military men would be good jurors for the prosecution, but in this case it might be entirely different, particularly if any of them had been divorced or had an unhappy marriage. I certainly would have wanted to probe that on voir dire; but whether a judge will allow this kind of personal question is never certain.

One remarkable factor in the final selection was that all the people who held upper-level or decision-making jobs and all the people who had been to college were gone, with one exception. This was a bad break for the prosecution, because Jeff Hotham was not dealing with a true insanity defense on a medical model, but a kind of emotional soap opera. For this defense to succeed, malleable, impressionable people were needed.

Though there is no way to know who was responsible for striking all the college-educated people from this panel, I'm sure the prosecutor must have used some of his peremptories on these nine people—Bob Hirsh couldn't have done it all. I appreciate Hotham's theory that he didn't want jurors who had been exposed to counseling, but it might have been a mistake. A person who has experienced counseling might have looked more pragmatically on Steinberg's excuses. It took a degree of naiveté and simplistic thinking to bring about this verdict.

The absence of a strong person is typical of most juries. No one seemed to dominate. Usually that's good. Neither lawyer wants a strong, opinionated, domineering juror unless he is certain the juror will be on his side—otherwise this kind of person will take over the jury and will explain everything to everybody else and it will be, in effect, a one-man jury. A trial lawyer wants followers, not leaders, on a jury.

I don't think anyone could have guessed that the trial was going to pivot on religious prejudice. If the prosecutor had seen that coming, he might have picked a more sophisticated panel. There are occasions when questions concerning religion can be asked on voir dire, but it would be difficult to anticipate that this was going to be one of those occasions. Any judge, and particularly Marilyn Riddel, would be cautious about asking a juror his religious beliefs.

One of the things that a lawyer can do to get a bit of information when the judge won't do very much voir dire is to try to hold the final selection over—to stall until the next morning. Every good lawyer knows how to stall; that's no problem. That night the lawyer, or his investigator, can go out and look at the neighborhood where each prospective juror lives to see what the house looks like. Is it run-down? Are there wrecked cars? What kind of bumper stickers do they have? A rule of thumb is that the poorer and more run-down the neighborhood is, the better the person would be as a defense juror, and vice versa. Generally, this kind of sophisticated jury selection is for the defense, and prosecutors don't bother with it. I don't know if Bob Hirsh did anything like this. When I talked to him years later about the serendipity of finding these particular jurors, he left me with the impression that he chose them by instinct. One of the reporters told me that she saw the defense attorneys huddling with a local psychologist while they were marking their choices on the jury form, but that man would not confirm it to me when I called him about it.

There are just some juries that are different, and this was one of them. Some groups have a symbiosis when they are together—there is a certain dynamic process by which each member's strengths and weaknesses are intensified and reinforced. No one can predict what a jury will do, and that's one of the excitements, one of the risks, of being a trial attorney. A jury is always a mystery. In the Steinberg trial the jurors were chosen by chance, pure chance, without a meaningful voir dire. One person could have changed the outcome of the trial. Steve Steinberg was very lucky.

CHAPTER THIRTEEN

DAY ONE: THE CURTAIN OPENS

In 80 percent of all trials, it is said, the jurors have made up their minds by the end of opening arguments. No one knows if this is really true, of course, for all jury research is pure speculation. What jurors say to reporters after a verdict is in and what jurors actually do in the jury room are not necessarily the same. It is not hard to believe that minds could be set quickly, because the opening statements give the jury a capsule version of the crime. They have an instant opportunity to see whether they like the appearance of the defendant sitting at the table. For the first time, they can observe the lawyers in action. That combination of emotions and show business is potent. Not much more can happen in a trial to change the balance of sentiment.

Most attorneys are extremely cautious in opening statements. They must take care not to promise evidence that they won't be able to deliver—that will not go unnoticed or be forgiven and can be a fatal mistake. At the same time, the opening is an opportunity to point out your strengths and the flaws in the opposing side, and to "draw the sting" by telling the jury in advance about problems you have in your own case so that there won't be shock when the problem is revealed. The opening statement is the opportunity to prepare the stage psychologically.

Jeff Hotham had the jurors in his hand, ready to direct their attention, but where? The prosecutor had been given the Holmes and Blinder reports months earlier. He should have known the strategy that the reports revealed. His plan of attack was to show how brutal the crime was and that the insanity defense was a fraud. But Elana Steinberg was going to be the focus of this trial—she was going to be pictured as a nagging, extravagant shrew, and her husband was to be a long-suffering saintly figure, irresistibly compelled to kill because of her spending. Hotham had opportunity to spike this notion for the first time by saying in his opening argument to the attentive jury, in effect, "Now keep your eye out for some cynical ploy to try to abuse this dead woman so that the killer can escape responsiblity." But in order to counter the obvious defense strategy, Hotham would have had to know something about Elana Steinberg and her husband as well. The truth was that he knew nothing about Elana and very little about Steven Steinberg. There was no sensitivity to the defense that was to crush him.

Jeff Hotham has a good voice, beautifully modulated. He is not a fire-eating prosecutor, ready to do battle at any time with a pugnacious defense attorney. Hotham is polite, gentlemanly, and serious. His argument is on a high plane, almost businesslike.

"This case is really quite simple and at the same time it is very tragic and ugly," he began. "Shortly before midnight on May 27, the defendant took a knife with a nine-and-a-half-inch blade from a drawer in the kitchen, went into the bedroom, and brutally butchered the beautiful body of his young wife as she lay sleeping in her bed. He stabbed her at least twenty-five times. He stabbed her in the head, he stabbed her in the chest, he stabbed her in the back. He cut into her liver, her spleen, her stomach, her lungs, and her brain."

Hotham paused. The jury looked alarmed, particularly when they heard that Elana had cried for help to her children.

"They'll bring in a couple of doctors," Hotham said, "who will tell you that the defendant stabbed and killed his wife while he was sleepwalking or something to that effect." Hotham promised that he would have different psychiatric testimony— that the defendant was completely sane when he killed his wife. As to any motive, the prosecutor was silent.

"Slowly but surely you will come to the realization that the defendant planned to kill his wife and blame it on these fictitious burglars. He opened the arcadia door so that he wouldn't have to prove that the burglars broke it. He opened a dresser drawer and threw various articles of his wife's clothing on the floor to make it appear that the burglars had ransacked the home. And he also moved all of his wife's jewelry so that he would later be able to claim that the burglars took the family jewelry.

"But he made one fatal mistake. When he was stabbing his wife, his hand slid down the knife and cut himself, and just about at the same time, Traci started yelling, so having a bleeding hand and his daughter screaming he panicked and he made the one fatal mistake that I am now mentioning to you, and that was that he put the knife underneath the bed. . . . So the defendant, being a creative individual, switched from Plan A, which was the burglars, to Plan B, which is the temporary insanity defense."

So far, so good for the prosecution. But there was a gap here. Hotham did not offer the jurors a suggestion of Steinberg's motive. If he had planned to kill Elana, as Hotham said, why? Was it rage or hatred for her after fifteen years of marriage? Was it because Elana was standing in the way of his gambling, or had she confronted him with the question of the disappearance of the money from the safe at B. B. Singer's? Was the killing the cold act of a sociopath to solve his money problems? The prosecutor was not prepared to speculate about any of these motives. In contrast to Bob Hirsh's groundwork, the prosecution's investigation had been primitive. The unanswered question "Why?" was to plague Jeff Hotham for the next five years.

Next it was Bob Hirsh's turn for the defense. Other lawyers who have watched him in trial say that Hirsh has a charismatic ability to communicate with a jury as if he were saying, "Let's all find out the truth together." He talks to jurors as if they were his partners in the search. Hirsh moves and walks back and forth so all can see him, slumped over the counsel table at one moment, nervous and pacing at another moment—it is impossible to doze while this man is on his feet. He looks directly at first one juror, then another. There is a feeling of camaraderie, a shared excitement between Hirsh and the jury: the curtain is going up.

In his opening statement, Hirsh spun a story that was a cross between Balzac and the *Ladies' Home Journal.* The jurors sat back, entranced, because they sensed that they were now going to hear a tale that would be fun, intriguing. It was going to be a story about nagging wives and credit cards and stores which these jurors seldom, if ever, saw. It was going to be a story about restaurants in Scottsdale, and decorator wallpaper and bronzed faucets, and gambling in Las Vegas, and meddling mothers-in-law who call on the telephone at night. There were going to be villains that everyone could understand, bitchy wives and brothers-in-law who call the shots at work. There was going to be a hero—a simple man who put his humble background and widowed mother behind him for the fleshpots of Scottsdale and Paradise Valley. It was a story of good and evil that was almost biblical. On this jury were people who thought in biblical terms, people who had never set foot in I. Magnin's or hired an interior decorator. The way Bob Hirsh told it, it all made perfect sense. Steven Steinberg was a man pushed to the wall by forces beyond his control, a man just like them.

Hirsh began.

"The first thing you are going to hear about is his character, and I'll tell you, there will simply be no disagreement; he was loved by the community. He worked ten, fourteen hours a day to support his wife and his family. Everybody will tell you that."

Bob Hirsh was sure of his witnesses when he said this. The people that had met together on those evenings in Diane Lindstrom's living room were tight and cohesive; there was nothing to worry about there. Hirsh need have no qualms about their testimony—there would be no backsliding or second thoughts.

"And this man also was a man who loved his family and he was very close to his family as a young man. And he got married—he was from Chicago, came out here in 1975, and he got married to a woman, his wife, Elana. Similarly, Elana also came from a family that was very close, just like Steve Steinberg's family.

"There was a little difference in the Singer family that you will not find in most families, and that difference is that it was a family run by the mother, Edith Singer. . . . She ran the show. Barney's role was to go out and work and provide the money for Edith, and Edith would manage the household affairs. Elana was very much like that. And Elana's function and responsibility in the marriage was to take the paycheck. In fact, she would take Steve's paycheck every month or week, whenever it came out, and her responsibility was to run the family. And I'm not telling you this for reasons of judgment. This is simply so. This is the way it was."

Hirsh went on in the indictment of Elana and her mother.

"And the other family trait that Elana and Edith both had was that their life was devoted to show for others. Elana's house was the most beautiful house. Everything was in order. You will hear testimony that Elana got up at two in the morning to clean the house. It was important for her to purchase things that were new, things everybody would admire. She was insulted if you went into her house and didn't say, 'Elana, this is beautiful; this is gorgeous.' It was important for Elana to have the right clothes, and to have all the clothes that you had to have in order to have some stature in the company, and she did. She bought clothes, and this relationship worked fine.

"Elana was a rather dominating, persuasive woman. Not

Midwesterners found a new life-style in the Arizona desert on McCormick Ranch in
Scottsdale. The Steinbergs moved here in 1975.

The Steinberg house on Via de Luz. The master bedroom is at the rear of the right wing of
the house. To the left, behind the garage, is the kitchen. The judge and jury interpreted
the distance between these two rooms differently.

A classic World War II wedding picture of Elana's parents, Edith and Barney Singer, at an army base in Washington State. The photograph was taken just before Barney Singer shipped out with his battalion for the South Pacific. (Courtesy of Edith and Barney Singer)

Nineteen-year-old Elana dances with Steve in Chicago. (Courtesy of Edith and Barney Singer)

The Steinbergs were a handsome and happy couple when they were married at the Blackstone in Chicago in 1966, before Steve's compulsive gambling clouded their lives. (Courtesy of Edith and Barney Singer)

A self-confident Steve adjusts his tie before the wedding. Elana's friends thought he looked like a young Tony Curtis. (Courtesy of Edith and Barney Singer)

Elana was vivacious and funny, a facet of her personality that was unknown to the jurors at the trial, who heard her described only in negatives by defense witnesses. Here she dances with her father at a party in Scottsdale in 1981. (Photograph by Tom Story. Reprinted with permission of *The Arizona Republic*. Permission does not imply endorsement by the newspaper.)

The last happy time—Elana, Traci, and Shawn on a cable car in San Francisco after the trip to San Jose for the bar mitzvah. The photograph was taken ten days before Elana was killed. Steve said nothing to his family about the crisis facing him when he went back to Phoenix or about the money he owed for his last NBA bet. (Courtesy of Edith and Barney Singer)

Detective Frank Hylton fills out a report. The Scottsdale police officer was astounded by the jury's verdict. "It's almost like I'm in a dissociative state," he told reporters with irony.

Deputy County Attorney Jeffrey Hotham had a string of death penalty convictions as a prosecutor. He had seen the carnage at the Steinberg house, and it never occurred to him that there would be a problem obtaining a conviction in the homicide. (Alfred Jacobs, Scottsdale, Arizona)

torneys in Tucson call criminal defense attorney Robert rsh a miracle worker, particularly in romantic omicides. He is acknowledged as the master of the efense known as temporary insanity. (*The Arizona Daily* *ar*)

The Honorable Marilyn Riddel, Maricopa County Superior Court Judge, maintains her cheerfulness in the face of criticism after the Steinberg verdict. Her instructions gave the jury two options—first degree murder or acquittal. (Photograph by Earl McCartney. Reprinted with permission of *The Arizona Republic*. Permission does not imply endorsement by the newspaper.)

Noted forensic psychiatrist Martin Blinder in his San Francisco office. He is best known for his psychiatric theory (a theory that some have dubbed the "Twinkie" defense) in the defense of Dan White, when White was tried for the murders of Harvey Milk and the mayor of San Francisco. (*San Francisco Examiner,* photograph by Chris Hardy)

Steven Steinberg, still in his conservative trial clothing, leaves the courtroom in a walk to freedom after the verdict in February 1982. His celebration of his deliverance from danger later caused bitter controversy in Scottsdale. (Photograph by Nancy Engebretson. Reprinted with permisison of *The Phoenix Gazette*. Permission does not imply endorsement by the newspaper.)

As reporters wait outside the police property room, Steinberg picks up the evidence, his late wife's jewelry, after the trial. Although police talked about an insurance fraud investigation, it never materialized and the case was closed. (Photograph by Ed Gray. Reprinted with permission of *The Phoenix Gazette*. Permission does not imply endorsement by the newspaper.)

only this, but rather demanding, because in order to give, in order to sustain the values that we're talking about, in order to have fine clothes and a nice house, it takes money. These things don't come about free, I can assure you. And Steve Steinberg is going to work over at Singer's, and he is going to get six hundred dollars a week, which sounds like a lot of money, but I can tell you it was simply not enough money for Elana to run their household and for them to go out to dinners a couple of nights a week with high-status people and nice restaurants, to have the clothes that are purchased at Saks, at I. Magnin, and there was pressure from April of 1979."

Now Bob Hirsh drew the sting—a concept that trial lawyers are familiar with. Steinberg's gambling losses, should they come up, had to be explained. Hirsh would have been walking on shaky ground here if Jeff Hotham had known anything about Steinberg's background, but he felt secure. His client's gambling was of recent origin, Hirsh told the jury, and was merely Steinberg's way to earn money for his grasping wife.

"And a tragedy occurred. Steve Steinberg, in order to get more money to provide for the house and his family, not for himself, started to gamble. Everybody knew Steve gambled, and when Steve won, it was great. He was encouraged to win and bring home the money. The procedure was that he would give it to Elana. 'Steve, thanks, guy. You're a great guy.' Nobody liked Steve when he lost. So the gambling became a rather furtive secret activity—when he lost, he told no one. And when he couldn't get relief from Mitch, he started to gamble. And the gambling got worse and worse and worse. And I tell you these people had a relationship: they couldn't talk. And Elana, despite the complaints of not having enough money, continued to go to the department store, continued to spend, had the house carpeted, she had the house wallpapered, continued to look at new houses, continued to look at automobiles, continued this pressure overlay that increased on this man as we go through the spring of 1981."

Hirsh went on to the climax. "In early May he doesn't have a job. He starts drawing unemployment. Steve Steinberg—to whom it was as important as it was to the Singers for him to be a self-respecting fellow—who has been successful, now finds himself without a job, with the bills piling up. And I tell you this was essentially the setting on May 27 when this man was strangled, suffocating in this tension that has all but enveloped him when he awoke on May 27. He wakes up and Elana has twenty-six stab wounds."

So much for the murder. One sentence, structured so that Steven Steinberg does not take action, disposed of the crime. Now for the psychiatry.

"Dr. Blinder is a man who has been a psychiatrist for twenty years, who has examined and evaluated hundreds of people who have been in situations where they've crumpled under stress. And he'll tell you this man broke under all this pressure; that he dissociated, where there was a breakdown of the integration of motor behavior, of consciousness and identity, and he went into an altered state. And he will tell you that he has no question that that was Steve Steinberg's condition on May 27, and he will tell you his conclusions; that he was in an altered state, that he did not know right from wrong."

Bob Hirsh had written out an outline of his opening statement the night before. While it seemed spontaneous and he used no notes, the statement was well planned and organized, but he was still able to pick up on a fatal flaw of the prosecutor and incorporate it.

"In fact, you'll notice there was a complete absence of any statement by Jeff of any potential motive in this case. A man who, every witness says, went out of his way to help others, went out of his way to be a good person."

The flaw was noted. In a murder trial the state is not required to find a motive and prove it—the jury is given an instruction to that effect. The reality of a murder trial is somewhat different. If the prosecution does not at least suggest some semblance of a motive, it is not going to get a conviction. The gauntlet had been thrown down, and it was a masterful job by Robert Hirsh. Now those witnesses, Steve's friends, had to deliver for him—and they would.

*   *   *

The day was not yet over; there was still time for one witness before five o'clock. The speed of this trial was amazing —picking a jury had barely consumed three hours, with time out for lunch. The insanity diagnosis that Steinberg's psychiatrists had made was a rare disorder, complex and difficult; one would expect this trial to be slow and deliberate. But *State* v. *Steinberg* was running on its own momentum and was on a very fast track.

Since Jeff Hotham was accustomed to quick trials, he had his first witness ready and waiting in one of the anterooms. The prosecution usually begins with a bang—a strong, interesting witness to catch the jury's attention. The boring, but necessary, witnesses can follow, the fingerprint and crime-scene people and a host of police witnesses who tend to make the jury restless with their repetition but cannot be omitted. After this, Hotham's witness plan grew weaker and seemed to lose punch.

The prosecutor began with the witness who was really his trump card—the sweet, devastatingly appealing Traci, who loved her mother dearly and had somehow survived emotionally intact. The twelve-year-old had been through a crucible for the nine months after her mother's death and had emerged poised and composed. She had not been to the jail to see her father, nor did she want to go—her smoldering resentment toward him had grown. The two girls had been away a lot that first summer after Elana's death. They went to the beach in San Diego with Edith Singer and then to Chicago to stay with Edith's relatives, where they were treated with enormous attention and care. When Mitchell and Bonnie went to Denver to start a new restaurant after the B. B. Singer's disaster in August, they took the girls with them. The travel must have been helpful. Traci survived and was even mothering six-year-old Shawn and calming her. She was intelligent and had a fiercely independent mind, as her testimony was to show.

Jeff Hotham led the little girl carefully through the events of the night of May 27, how she had started to clean up the pages of her school books and had fallen asleep, how her mother and father were spending a normal evening. She told how she awoke in the middle of the night to hear her mother screaming, "Traci, Shawn, Steve!" "After she screamed everything went quiet. And I yelled, 'Mom!' I yelled it twice."

> Q. And what happened when you yelled out to your mother?
> A. My father said, "Shut your door right now." And I said, "Why?"
> Q. And what was the reply?
> A. Well, he said a bad word.
> Q. What did he say?
> A. He said, "God damn it, shut your door right now"—I was going to get up and go to my Mom's room to see if everything was all right, and he goes, "Stay in your room and shut your door, the god damn door, right now." I shut my door, and then I went back and laid in my bed.

There was a silence in the courtroom. The image of the little girl lying in her bed after the screams was disturbing.

Traci had been interviewed by a lot of people since Elana's murder, but none of the interviews had been very thorough, because everyone was afraid to probe too much. After all, this was a twelve-year-old who had been through a horrible experience. Before the trial, Benchoff and Hirsh had wanted to interview her. Edith Singer had refused to allow her granddaughter to meet with the lawyers unless she was present herself. Edith was beginning to doubt the skills of Hotham and the Scottsdale police. Barney had heard rumbling in Scottsdale that some people were mobilizing in Steve's defense, which Edith Singer was perceptive enough to realize meant nothing good for her daughter's memory and which she bitterly resented.

They all met in the County Attorney's Office for Hirsh's interview. Traci told them that her father had washed his hands that night, a detail that had not previously appeared in any of the police reports. Edith said that Mike Benchoff seemed paralyzed when he heard this, and Frank Hylton grabbed Hotham's arm and said, "Did you hear that, Jeff?"

Traci had also been interviewed by Mike Vest of the County Attorney's Office when he was doing the investigative workup for the prosecutor. In that interview Traci told Vest a different version of the "bad word" her father had said to her that night —she told Vest that Steve had said, "Shut your fucking door."

The handwashing and the "fucking door" were details that had fallen out along the way to the trial. The prosecution never pursued them and no one ever mentioned them again. Both had disastrous potential for the defense, particularly the phrase "Shut your fucking door." The language was so *wrong* for the moment and for the image Hirsh was presenting to the jury of the mild-mannered Steinberg in a deep sleep. Steve swore a lot. It was the way of the restaurant business to talk that way. That was no problem. Steinberg could have said this to Elana and it would not have bothered the jurors, but not to the little girl that night, that way. The image was wrong. Did it happen? Was the language sanitized because no one, even the prosecutor, wanted this word to come out of the little girl's mouth? No one knows, and now it is buried in long-lost memory.

When it was Hirsh's turn to cross-examine Traci, he was very cautious, as any attorney would be with a twelve-year-old child. Overkill or badgering here would be a terrible mistake. The few small things that Hirsh did want to accomplish with Traci were sidetracked by the child. Of all the witnesses who knew Steven Steinberg, Traci was the only one who seemed to understand the strategy of Hirsh's defense. She was adamant, and she couldn't be led.

Hirsh wanted Traci to say that her father had kissed her and tucked her into bed on that night, and that he did it all the time. It was a small sentimental touch for the jury—the loving father who could hardly be thinking of murder when he put the children to bed with a kiss. Traci was not cooperative. "I told you he just did that sometimes, and didn't do it that night."

Hirsh would have liked to shorten the time during which Steinberg was in the bedroom with Elana after she stopped screaming. This was important, because the prosecution could claim that Steinberg had set up the scenario for the burglary then—hiding the knife under the bed, throwing the underpants around, moving the jewelry, opening the arcadia door. When Traci testified that it had been forty-five seconds before her father came out of the room, that was not what the defense attorney wanted to hear.

> Q. Do you remember telling me it was about ten seconds that afternoon we talked over at the County Attorney's Office? Does that help your memory at all as to how much time it might have been?
> A. Well, I know it was like forty-five seconds, because I remember I got back in the bed. I was thinking—why would he tell me to shut my door? I was just thinking about what was happening.
> Q. So you mean it's pretty much what you're thinking about, it seems like forty-five seconds?
> A. Well, it *was* forty-five seconds.

When Hirsh's emphasis shifted to arguments between her mother and father about money, the twelve-year-old grasped what Hirsh was trying to do and was not sympathetic.

> Q. Would they argue that he didn't have a job or that she thought he ought to have a job?
> A. Well, of course he needs to have a job.
> Q. Yeah, I'm sure, but was your mom mad at him because he didn't have a job?
> A. Well, he was mad, too.

The close of Traci's cross-examination was no more productive. It was obvious that Hirsh would have liked the little girl to end with a sentimental outburst of affection for her father despite what had happened. It was the stuff that jurors are fond of, the implication that all was or would be forgiven and that there was not so much devastation caused by the killing of Traci's mother that it could not be mended. The child saw this as an attack on her love for Elana, and she was having none of it.

> Q. Let me ask you one last thing, Traci, and I think we are going to let you go. You and your dad were always pretty close, weren't you?
> A. I was just as close to my mom, maybe a little closer to my mom.
> Q. And your dad was awfully close to Shawn, too?
> A. Uh-huh. But I think Shawn—we were both a little closer to my mom.

After the court session was over for the day and the jury had been dismissed, there was an emotional scene. I spoke with Pat Sabo, the *Gazette* crime reporter, about it. She told me that it was probably the most dramatic moment she had ever witnessed in years of following trials.

"Everyone had gone. I was the only one there besides the judge," she told me. "He—Steinberg—asked if he could see the little girl, because he hadn't seen her for nine months. And he asked if he could meet her in the courtroom. He was crying. The judge said it was okay if the child wanted to. They met sitting in some of the seats. At first she couldn't talk. Tears were just running down her face, and her expression when she looked at him was just tragic. She said, 'Daddy, why did you do this to us?' He tried to hold her, but she kept saying, 'Daddy, why?' Then she sat down and they talked a short time. I wrote about it in the paper. It was one of the most emotional things I've ever seen in a courtroom, ever, and I remember it still."

For Traci and Steve Steinberg it was goodbye. She has not seen him since.

CHAPTER FOURTEEN

DAY TWO: EXEUNT BUSHY-HAIRED BURGLARS

The public is generally aroused when it reads about a successful insanity defense. It sounds so easy to achieve, particularly in the hands of clever lawyers like Bob Hirsh. That's not exactly true. It is a hard and double-edged defense, and the situation has to be grim before insanity will be raised. This defense exacts a very stiff price from a defendant; he must virtually give up on the first part of the trial—that part in which a prosecutor has to prove his case. In effect, Steven Steinberg had to say, "I did it. I killed my wife; you can forget about those bushy-haired burglars with the fake beards and plastic gloves." The average juror has enough practical good sense to realize that Steinberg cannot say two things at the same time: "It was those two other men with bushy beards who killed Elana, but anyway, I was insane and I didn't know what I was doing." This simply does not play.

At the beginning of this trial, Jeff Hotham was somewhat relieved from the normal burden of prosecution. The bushy-haired burglars were going to be gone, and another defensive favorite, the bungling and inept police, was not going to be a factor in the trial. Bob Hirsh had conceded that in his opening argument; the real fireworks would not begin until the defense began its case and the psychiatrists entered center stage. The prosecutor's task in this part of the trial was to showcase the setting of the murder, to show the body and the brutality of the attack, the knife with its bloody fingerprints, the attempts at concealment. There could be no opposition to this testimony. For some reason, Hotham was unexpectedly gloomy. One of the state's technical witnesses thought that the prosecutor was depressed about the trial from the beginning: "I got the impression he just didn't want to try it—he wasn't himself."

Apparently something had happened before the trial began that had destroyed Jeff Hotham's usual self-confidence and verve. Up to now, he had never lost a trial in the five years he had been in the County Attorney's Office. The death penalty had been imposed in five of the murder convictions he had obtained. He was a winner, but this was Hotham's first exposure to an attorney like Robert Hirsh. Hirsh's driving, slashing questioning of the state's witnesses in interviews before the trial was a new and unpleasant experience for the prosecutor. Hirsh and Benchoff had spared nothing in their preparation. They had interviewed each of the witnesses on the state's witness list and had transcripts made. The interviews were intimidating and almost frightening; what was worse, they showed what was to come.

Bob Hirsh is the consummate cross-examiner. Some Arizona attorneys think he is the best in the country. It all begins with the interview he has with the witnesses before the trial, a rarity in criminal trials in other states but permissible in Arizona. The interview is often a psychological ploy to intimidate or lessen the strength of a witness. After they have been through this, witnesses are not anxious to come to trial and go through it again; they have lost confidence in the prosecutor's ability to protect them.

Hirsh tries to get a simple yes or no answer to his question, and it is invariably a question which doesn't lend itself to that. He gets angry if he doesn't get what he wants and keeps on trying—poking and yelling, wording the question in different ways until the witness gets exhausted and says, "Oh, all right, yes." Then it's over—he will take that answer and run with it at trial.

This, then, was what Jeff Hotham was facing. Hotham had spent little time preparing his witnesses for Hirsh's pretrial interviews, or, for that matter, for the trial itself. "Someone told me just to go on in there, tell the truth, and don't volunteer anything," one police officer told me. The Scottsdale policemen and the technical witnesses from the Department of Public Safety created no major problems for Jeff Hotham, mainly because their evidence was noncontroversial and because the policemen were well-spoken and intelligent, characteristic of the Scottsdale force. But there was to be one slip, and it was costly.

In his pretrial interview with Bob Hirsh, Hylton's partner, detective Chris Bingham, had been enticed into giving a yes answer to one of those tortured questions that Hirsh was so skillful in framing, a triumph of semantics. His response made it seem as if Bingham were vouching for the truth of Steinberg's claim that he actually saw bushy-haired burglars. Hirsh began immediately to showcase this little gem at the trial by making Bingham seem like a masterful interviewer.

> Q. Mr. Bingham, your job as an interviewer or someone that interviews people to get historical information is part of detective work, is it not?
> A. Yes, it is.
> Q. And I guess that's one of the primary things that detectives do; is that right?
> A. That's one, yes . . .
> Q. And that's really what you are trained in, and that's what your experience was in, when you became a detective?
> A. Yes, it is.

Bingham was built up as a twelve-year police veteran, "a student of human nature to a certain extent" with a "pretty good feel for people when they believe they are telling the truth." Now for the kill. Hirsh asked the detective about the questioning of Steinberg at the police station on the night of the murder.

"It appeared that he was trying to tell it the way it happened, the way he remembered it; isn't that so?"

"All I can say is the story is basically the same story," said Bingham.

"But didn't you tell me in an interview that he was trying to tell it the way he remembered it?" Hirsh pressed.

Bingham was cautious—he didn't like the way this was going. "I don't know if that's what I said in my interview with you." Then the defense attorney whipped out the transcript of the interview. He approached Bingham with the papers in his hand so the jury could see that he had the Scottsdale detective in a bind.

"Let me ask you," said Hirsh, "if these questions were asked and these answers were given down at the bottom of page twenty-six:

Q: Didn't he appear to be trying to tell the truth,
    to tell it the way he remembered it?
A: At that time, other than the fantastic story, I
    had no other indication he was lying to me.
Q: That's what I mean. I mean, he appeared to
    be telling it the way he remembered it?
A: Yes, yes.

"Were those questions asked by me and—"
Bingham surrendered. "Yes, they were."
Hirsh pressed on. "And were those answers given, sir?"
"Yes, they were."
After Bob Hirsh was through with the cross-examination of Bingham, the prosecutor said nothing to correct the impres-

sion that Bingham vouched for Steinberg's honesty. The implication remained unaltered and unchallenged. Hirsh was going to use it to the fullest extent. In reality, Chris Bingham had no intention of making it seem that Steinberg was telling the truth. No one believed Steve Steinberg's story, as evidenced by his arrest the same night. It was a matter of semantics or misinterpretation that could have been corrected on the spot. Since Jeff Hotham never corrected the implication, it was going to burn a small, deep hole in the state's case. To the jurors, Bingham had been placed in the position of vouching for the honesty of Steven Steinberg, and that is certainly not what the Scottsdale detective ever meant to do.

Five years later I asked Chris Bingham about his testimony. Sergeant Bingham is fatalistic; he has been a policeman for a long time and he accepts things as they come. He told me that it was a little depressing for him to read his testimony now.

"There was a level of sophistication in Hirsh's questioning that we were just not quite used to. I never meant to say, certainly, that I believed Steven Steinberg was truthful. And, in fact, I knew that he was not because we arrested him that night. I meant that when he told that story he was believable in the way he talked, for whatever weight that has. Accomplished liars sound believable, too."

Sergeant Bingham said there was a problem with testifying. "You answer in a sparse way and you think that someone will correct it if it leads to a misleading impression. In this case, no one did."

Four other Scottsdale police officers testified. They were all crime-scene witnesses—testifying about how Steinberg looked when they arrived. Chadwick and Kasieta recounted how they had approached the door with guns drawn; Barnett described Steinberg in the street that night, including the "You asshole, that's my wife!" remark. The officers' testimony was repetitive, but it had to be done. Hirsh was angry and pugnacious in his cross-examination of the officers, but there was little to be gleaned for the defense.

Perhaps one of the reasons that the prosecutor seemed gloomy at the outset of the trial was that he knew he could not count on one witness who should have been a solid ally, the assistant medical examiner of Maricopa County. Generally, one of the strong points for the prosecution in an especially brutal killing is the testimony of the coroner and the effect of the autopsy photographs that he will introduce. Anyone who has never seen these frozen images of sudden death cannot imagine their impact. The color pictures are large and of excellent quality. The death wounds are seen close-up, and they look terrible, for it is characteristic for blood to flow to the surface after death. What would be a minor bruise or abrasion in a living person becomes a dark, purplish-black spreading mark on a dead body. The victim's eyes are open or frighteningly rolled back. Sometimes the bodies are nude, with clothing disarrayed. Bodies of dead children are particularly sad and heartwrenching. The photographs of Elana in death are notable because they show the tawny healthy skin of the young woman, her pretty hands, her pale blue cotton nightie pushed awry, and the awkward position of one leg doubled underneath her. The stab wounds are terrible. A close-up of her fingernails broken to the quick shows a desperate struggle for life. Normally, a defense attorney will put up a fight to keep the crime-scene and autopsy photographs out; he will say they are too inflammatory. This is a token fight which is seldom successful. Hirsh didn't try.

The medical examiner's testimony about the cause of death should be a prosecutor's strength, not because the coroner is an employee of the county in league with the police, but because he is an expert on death by violence who will not mince words. In cities with full-time medical examiners, though, it is not unusual to find a certain peculiar tension between these doctors and the police.

Hotham's difficulty in working with the medical examiner is not unusual. It's a fact of life for many prosecutors, and not anything sinister. These are both very independent groups. Both of them say, "I want it my way and no other," and they don't want to give an inch. The tension between police and prosecutors on one side and medical examiners on the other side exists all over the country. It takes considerable diplomatic skill to avoid friction. In Phoenix there has been a running feud between the two medical examiners and the police, and a more subtle rift with the prosecutor's office. At the time of the Steinberg trial, prosecutors were given to understand that they must use the medical examiner assigned to each murder. For an outside medical examiner to be brought in, extreme reasons had to be present. Turf could not be violated. For Hotham, it was a stroke of bad luck, one totally out of his control, when he drew Dr. Thomas Jarvis for this autopsy.

Tom Jarvis is a longtime veteran of the Medical Examiner's Office, a man in his sixties, with a curly white beard and a curly white head of hair like Santa's. He has a prickly nature, not surprising for a man who has been working on cadavers in a secluded medical atmosphere for many years. He is eccentric and outspoken. Jarvis and the chief medical examiner in Phoenix have sometimes exasperated the Phoenix police. He doesn't hesitate to assert his independence. "They don't own me," says Jarvis. "I have to be free to do what is right. I have to be free." Dr. Jarvis was indeed free in his testimony at the Steinberg murder trial.

The pathologist testified that of the twenty-six stab wounds, four were potentially fatal. One penetrated the lung and the interior vena cava, the large vein leading into the heart; Jarvis said this was instantly fatal. Another went through the spleen and stomach; a third was inflicted through the back and went in through the kidney; and the fourth was thrust down through the diaphragm and into the liver. Any one, or a combination of the four, could have been fatal. Dr. Jarvis referred to the rest of the wounds as being "superficial," a word which apparently had a greatly different meaning to the medical examiner than it was to have to this jury. To Dr. Jarvis, "superficial" meant that the stab wound terminated in fat or ended on bone, without penetrating a body organ. As Dr. Jarvis said about the remaining twenty-two stab wounds, "they generally terminated on bone; that's what stopped them."

The last of the stabs had gone through the skull and penetrated the right temporal lobe of the brain. That wound was potentially fatal too, said Dr. Jarvis, but by this time, Elana Steinberg's blood pressure had dropped and she was either dead or near dead. The police theory was that Steinberg's hand slid down the knife when it hit the victim's skull, and it was at this point that the palm of his hand was cut. The print of an index finger was on the handle of the knife and a palm print was on the blade, both in blood. Jarvis's testimony was sketchy and quick. Hotham didn't ask him to describe the force that it must have taken for that thrust through the hard plate of the skull and into the brain.

When I interviewed the jurors later, none of them had the slightest idea that the skull had to be penetrated to reach the brain. I got the impression that some of the jurors couldn't accept that premise. "The stab wounds were all superficial, the doctors said so," they all told me. The ferocity of this blow was difficult to fit with the idea of trancelike sleepwalking. Since Elana was dead or near death when this last thrust was made, it must have been inflicted *after* Traci was awakened by Elana's screaming—after the child had cried out, "What's wrong, Daddy?"

It takes a masterful attorney to turn this last terrible wound into an advantage, but Bob Hirsh had been working on a theory to do just that for several months. He argued that Steven Steinberg had grasped the carving knife by the *blade* instead of the handle throughout the attack because he was in an "altered state of consciousness." It is a brilliant strategy— Hirsh turned the knife into evidence of insanity. "No one in their right mind would grasp a knife like this," Hirsh argued.

Hotham was concerned about this strategy and attempted to discuss it with Jarvis before the trial, but he had no cooperation from the pathologist. Hotham knew that he was about to be torpedoed by the coroner. To discount the testimony the prosecutor needed a medical witness to testify that it was ridiculous to think that Steinberg held the knife by the blade while he was stabbing his wife. The blade on the knife was almost ten inches long and razor-sharp. If he had made twenty-six stab wounds, most of them stopped by bone, with his hand wrapped around the blade while someone was fighting him off, his hand would have been cut to ribbons, shredded. Instead, Steinberg had a single, simple cut on his palm.

Dr. Jarvis had seen eight hundred stabbings, but inexplicably, he equivocated when Hotham posed the question. It was all that Robert Hirsh needed.

Q. Doctor, that laceration on the hand that we looked at could also be consistent with the person grasping the knife down on the blade and then hitting the body or some object, would it not?

A. Surely. Either way.

Q. It could have been either that the hand was on the handle of the blade and when it hit the body it slipped down, is that right?

A. Yes, sir.

Q. Or the hand was grasping on the bottom of the blade and then causing the wounds, is that right, sir?

A. That's possible, yes.

Hirsh tried for the ultimate then—a double play. He wanted to have the coroner say the wounds were "shallow," and fit that in with the blade theory. "And in fact, the shallowness of those wounds, the shallowness of the depth, would suggest that these wounds are consistent with somebody grasping the bottom portion of the blade, would it not, sir?"

Dr. Jarvis had gone as far as he could go on this, but it was an enormous boost: "Consistent, I suppose. I don't like the theory very much, frankly. But it's possible. And the physical evidence is consistent with it."

Dr. Jarvis had helped to destroy the prosecution. I have never heard of a prosecutor who could not get an outside expert if he really wanted one. I have to assume that the prosecutor thought that there was no need for this, that the knife theory was just so outlandish that no one would give it serious consideration. In hindsight, he could have used a plastic surgeon specializing in the hand, a highly specialized surgical field, because working with the hand is so complex and delicate. Dr.

Jarvis probably would have deferred to a hand surgeon on that point, but no one could be completely certain with this medical examiner.

After this head start from Dr. Jarvis, Bob Hirsh worked magic with the knife and its bloody prints. When I talked to the jurors years later, I was amazed at how persuasive this testimony was to them. Some jurors were totally convinced that Steinberg held it by the blade. One man told me that he believed that Steinberg's hand was not cut more deeply because he was in a trance—he had been like a Hindu fakir who can walk barefoot across burning coals and afterward display that there are no burns on his feet. After the trial Frank Hylton told a Scottsdale reporter that he was dumbfounded by one juror's remark that Steinberg had held the blade, not the hilt. He still feels that way. "It is absolutely impossible to look at that blade and imagine that anyone could inflict those wounds holding the knife that way—simply nonsensical."

After this body blow, Hotham decided to forgo asking medical questions that would normally be asked of a forensic pathologist. For example, no one helped the jury comprehend just how the wallpaper above Elana's bed came to be stained with blood. Everyone knew that the blood splatters were there; they were in the photographs. Everyone realized that stabbing was a bloody affair. After all, Elana Steinberg had bled to death. But no one explained how the wallpaper was stained. To do so would have given the jury a graphic and chilling sense of the ferocity of the attack. Droplets of blood flew through the air from the blade of the knife when Steve Steinberg raised his arm behind his head to make the downward thrusts—that was how splatters stained the wall. Would Dr. Jarvis have testified to this if he had been asked? No one knows. The coroner was not helpful, although he had seen eight hundred stabbings. In his testimony, the wounds were underplayed. His continual references to "superficial" stabs were misunderstood.

Several jurors told me afterward that Steinberg had just been playing with Elana, just making little pinpricks, and hadn't meant to hurt her, because of the Jarvis testimony. I got the impression that this was a way for some of the jurors to rationalize their sympathy for Steve Steinberg because the testimony downplayed the violence of the attack.

Two of the wounds, one on the cheek and one in the back, were S-shaped or irregular in form, what pathologists call "scrimmage" wounds. They are the result of the twisting of the knife in the victim, or the victim's twisting movements while the knife is inserted. Dr. Jarvis defused the unattractive aspects of this when Hirsh asked him, "Now, you didn't find any specific evidence that there had been any twisting of the knife in any of these wounds, did you?"

"No, it was only suggested in two of them; the one on the right cheek and the one on the back."

Hirsh asked, "And was that wound on the back and that wound on the cheek fully consistent with the knife being extended on withdrawal?"

"That's true," said Jarvis.

Hotham didn't pursue this; it was obviously best not to ask anything more, since for all intents and purposes the coroner was a hostile witness. It would have been risky for the prosecutor to press on—Jarvis could have done more damage.

After the Steinberg trial, Dr. Jarvis traveled to Safford, where he testified for Bob Hirsh in the Gorzenski murder trial, opposing and demolishing the Graham County coroner. It is perfectly acceptable for a medical examiner to accept outside work. Had he known Dr. Jarvis was going to work for Hirsh the next week, Hotham could have had a window of opportunity to ask for an additional medical examiner without offending the political realities in the county. And too, Dr. Jarvis is Mike Benchoff's father-in-law, a fact that is known throughout the county and is not considered particularly significant. In other days and in other trials, Jarvis had been known to dismantle Benchoff's cases for him, much as he had just dismantled Jeff Hotham's. The Jarvis-Benchoff relationship presented another opportunity for Hotham to obtain a more amenable pathologist. He could have said, 'I just don't want to put you in an awkward position because you're the defense attorney's father-in-law, Doctor,' and there would have been no problem with turf. In the end, the jurors really never comprehended the ferocity of the attack on Elana Steinberg in her bed that night. The medical examiner's testimony was a disaster.

At the end of day two, it was score one for Hotham; the Scottsdale police witnesses had all looked intelligent and respectable, which is always a major accomplishment, and there were no major gaffes. It was score two for the defense: the foundation had been laid for the argument that Steve Steinberg had actually held the carving knife by the blade. It turned the gore into craziness. Then, too, Chris Bingham was depicted as a walking lie detector who believed on the night of the murder that Steven Steinberg was telling the truth.

CHAPTER FIFTEEN

THERE GOES FIFTEEN YEARS DOWN THE DRAIN

Mitchell Singer did not make a particularly good impression on the jury. Mitchell likes to work out. He has muscular shoulders and looks like a weight lifter. He is good-looking in a rough, sultry way; there is a great resemblance to the pictures of his father when Barney Singer was in New Guinea in 1944, but without Barney's gleam of good humor. Mitchell's wraparound glasses were a mistake. Perhaps it would have helped if he had had a wardrobe change from Sears as did Steven Steinberg, but Mitchell Singer would never have held still for this. Elana's brother is not the type to submit to cosmetic changes. Mitchell's testimony on day three of the trial gave the distinct impression that he was bluntly honest, as well as totally unprepared for any artifice. He had obviously not been coached. On cross-examination, Mitchell said things that Bob Hirsh wanted to hear and he did not understand that what he was saying could be damaging. Neither Mitch nor his sister was humble and self-effacing, it seemed. Hirsh's questions were all about

Elana—no one seemed concerned about the relevancy of this. There were no objections from Jeff Hotham.

> **Q.** In fact your sister was very demanding about money, was she not?
>
> **A.** She wanted nice things and she wanted success just like everybody—just like I do, you do, or somebody else does.
>
> **Q.** And, as a matter of fact, she did have nice things, didn't she? The house was always very well—
>
> **A.** The house meant a lot to her . . . to keep it clean and nice, that was very important to her.
>
> **Q.** And it was very important that she have nice clothes and be well dressed and the children be nicely dressed?
>
> **A.** Yes, that was important to her.
>
> **Q.** And she was very much concerned about the appearance of things, was she not?
>
> **A.** That's correct.
>
> **Q.** Isn't it true, sir, that if she didn't have money to spend she would get in a crummy mood and that's the thing that would create pressure for her?
>
> **A.** That would be a pressure for her, yes. I mean it would be for anybody, though, if they had no money.

Elana was aggressive, said Mitchell. "She's like myself," and Steve was "more the passive type." Mitchell was not apologetic. To him, having an aggressive personality and wanting nice things were normal and he saw no reason to dissemble. Mitch may have been a good restaurateur, but he was naive when it came to understanding the dynamics of the trial. Twelve-year-old Traci was more intuitive. If there was an ambush for Mitchell Singer when he answered questions, no one pointed it out to him.

Hotham led him through the night of May 27, when he

and Bonnie and the baby arrived on Via de Luz. He told the jury about the moment with Steve in the kitchen that night, when Steve emptied the glass of water and said, "There goes fifteen years down the drain."

Mitchell told the jury that a month before his sister's murder, he recognized that his brother-in-law was a pathological gambler.

"Do you remember a gambling trip in April of 1981, when you and the defendant went to Las Vegas?" Hotham asked.

"We were at Caesars Palace, Steve and me, for a blackjack tournament. We were having a terrific time." Mitchell said he had gone to bed around one, and tried to coax Steve up, but Steve wanted to stay. Steve had won a lot of money playing blackjack—thousands of dollars, he said. Mitch had put some of it in a safe-deposit box at the hotel; it was his share of the winnings.

"Did anything happen to change that terrific time?"

Mitch gave the fascinated jurors a glimpse of Steve's gambling at the end. "I went to sleep and about an hour later the pit boss called me in my room.

" 'You better get down here immediately because your brother-in-law has signed your name to vouchers—or whatever they call them—for nine thousand dollars.' I thought, how can that be? Steve was up quite a bit when I went to bed and it hadn't been that long, but I ran down.

"He had lost everything he had and then he signed my name to the nine-thousand-dollar marker, I think that's what it's called. So, I got out the hotel's safe-deposit box and I gave the pit boss the forty-five hundred dollars that I had put in it earlier. That wasn't enough, and then I had to sign a line of credit for five thousand. I told the casino guy I would have to make it up as soon as I got home and I would send him a check. Fortunately, he let me do that."

When Mitch was taking the money out of the safe-deposit box to pay the pit boss, Steve tried to knock it out of his hand. "He started shouting, 'Let me have it, Mitch, I'll get it back, I swear I will, I'm going to win.'

"He was like a wild man, an animal. He had this leather

coat on and the sweat had come clear through the front of it. It was all wet. I thought, this is a sickness."

Mitch had to write out a check for five thousand dollars to Caesars Palace when they got back to Phoenix, he told the jury. There had been an argument about it between Steve and Elana. Although Steve made Mitch promise that he wouldn't tell Elana, she had found out some way, he said. "They argued about his gambling, particularly after we got back," Mitch said. "He told me once, 'If she doesn't stop, I'm going to walk.' "

Mitchell told me that when he got back he told his mother that Elana should leave Steve. "I called up Elana and told her, I remember my exact words, 'It would behoove you to leave him.' She hung up on me. She always stood up for Steve."

The sweating man in the casino was a new view of his brother-in-law for Mitchell. Elana's interference with Steve's gambling was a potential motive for her murder, but the prosecutor didn't pursue it. On cross, Bob Hirsh made it seem that Steinberg was wild that night because he had called Elana first, in the flush of winning, and then lost it all after she was expecting it.

"Didn't he call and tell her he'd won a lot of money and everything was great and he was happy?" Hirsh was pointing his finger now, angry.

"He told me he was going to call Elana and tell her he was ahead. I don't know what's part of his happiness," Mitch said.

On cross-examination, Hirsh asked Mitchell, "When you were growing up, Mr. Singer, I think you told me that you considered Steve Steinberg like a big brother, isn't that so?" Mitch said that was true, he liked Steve very much.

"But at the restaurant you said you were angry with him a lot and you gave him a lot of grief, is that right?"

"That's right. I'm a very difficult person to work for. I have a different personality at the office—then it's work. The restaurant business is a very hard business, very demanding. If you don't give the customers what they want, they won't ever come back and there goes your whole life, and it was my whole life. I was a very strict boss. I gave Steve grief, so much grief I thought sometimes, why does he still stay around? A lot of times I couldn't understand why he even wanted to be in the business, he really wasn't suited to it. I was always trying to shift things around and find the right spot for him, where he would be good at it. I gave him grief, but no more than everyone else who worked for me. I'm different at home."

Hirsh asked if Mitch had led Steve on with promises that he would be a partner in the restaurant business, but Mitchell denied this.

"Well, I already had a partner, one for the first restaurant and then I had one for the Brass Derby and the business was in a funny spot then, things could have gone either way. If things go right, which sometimes they weren't, I told him then it would go right for him because he would go along with us. He was family, you understand, but I don't think he was interested in being a part owner. I think he just liked a good salary and running the restaurant. That's what made him feel good," Mitch said.

The next witness was Bonnie Singer, Mitchell's pretty wife. Bonnie described how she had gone to the house on Via de Luz that evening at dinnertime to return a television set; the whole family had come out to talk to her in the driveway, the last time they were all together.

"I said to Steve, 'How is everything going, how's your real estate exam,' because I know from other people that have taken the exam that it is not the easiest thing. But he said, 'It was a breeze,' he was sort of cocky, everything seemed to be all right.

"The next I heard was when I answered the phone in the middle of the night and I heard this moaning, 'Give me Mitch!' I gave the phone to Mitchell and he just froze. He said, 'My God, my God.' Then he told me to get dressed, and I said, 'No, I'm not going,' and he said, 'Yes, you are, and bring Todd.'

"When we got over there, my husband said to Steve, 'What were you doing when they were killing my sister?' Steve held up his hand, do you want me to tell you what he said? He said the F-word, 'How do you think I got this?'

"One thing that sticks out in my mind is when my mother-in-law, Edith, went to hug him. She said, 'Steve, come here, my Stevie,' and he pulled away from her."

Hotham asked Bonnie if she had an opinion as to whether Steve was "truthful." Hirsh exploded; he was not going to put on any evidence about Steinberg's honesty, he said—it wasn't an issue in this trial. The prosecutor let it go. Theoretically, from this point on there should have been no testimony about whether Steinberg was "telling the truth" about anything.

By this time, Bob Hirsh was in complete command of the trial. Modestly but firmly, he was taking over rulings on the evidence—"Pardon me, Jeff, that is hearsay." Sometimes the judge didn't even intervene, almost a spectator. The prosecutor generally gave ground when Hirsh objected. Many times Hotham did not even return to the line of questioning, abandoning whole areas, as he did now with the "truthfulness" issue. Hotham did not seem to have the spirit for a confrontation with Hirsh and Benchoff. Hirsh was the object of everyone's eyes—he slouched back in his chair, arms behind his head, twisting and squirming, in constant nervous movement. Even the judge watched the defense attorney, not the witnesses, at times.

It's not unusual for the dramatics to come from the defense attorney in a criminal trial. Prosecutors, by contrast, fill a different role. While some prosecutors are fire-eaters, most are like Jeff Hotham—cool, deliberate, polite. While eyes were on Bob Hirsh, it was because he was brash and outrageous, sarcastic and angry. Hotham was different, but his style had always served him well before.

An observer told me later, when I asked what Hotham was like in trial, "I would say he reminded me of Steve Garvey— you know, clean-cut, handsome, a gentlemen—sort of the ultimate Midwestern role model, Mr. Clean. He gave the impression of being well organized. The questions came rolling out smooth and in sequence. Anywhere else it would have been fine, but Hotham needed something else here, and he was gradually falling behind. He was accustomed to this buddy-buddy interaction with the public defenders, not dealing with tigers as he was in this trial."

The state's part of the trial drew to a close; the blood on the knife had been identified as Steven Steinberg's, and the blood everywhere else was Elana's—on the walls, the floor, the bedding, and even her husband's brown bathrobe. Cecil Kirk introduced most of the evidence. The knife was wrapped in plastic, with bloody smudges still visible. There was a chilling note—the blade of the knife was bent at the tip, Kirk said. The fingerprints were identified by Bill Watling of the state lab. Hotham was comfortable with this part of the evidence. He liked to work with technical evidence, and he spoke quickly and confidently with the experts.

Two of the witnesses called by the prosecution were members of the Steinbergs' social circle—the only friends who were witnesses for the state. They were not there to say good things about Elana Steinberg, because Hotham was oblivious to the need for that. Mike Berkovitch and Elana's closest friend in Arizona, Rhona Goldfarb, were called as crime-scene witnesses. Since Steinberg had called both of them that night, they had had the opportunity to observe him.

Mike Berkovitch said that Steve was screaming when he called him the night of the murder. When he got there, Steve was subdued, sitting on the floor in the hall. Steinberg tried to get past the police to get in the bedroom, Berkovitch said, and he had interpreted that as "wanting to be alone with her out of love—to be with her one more time."

Later I met Berkovitch, a handsome manufacturer's representative in his forties. He was one of the group who didn't go to the defense meetings. I could see why Hirsh had given up on him—he seemed like an independent and analytical man. "Bob Hirsh had talked to me about an hour, I think, but I believe he was perceptive enough to see that I was not a soft touch, so to speak, and he was really kind of wary of me. Hirsh certainly gave me the impression that if Steve were acquitted he would go into a hospital and have a lot of treatment; I was amazed to find out later on that didn't happen.

"You'll be interested in this," he told me. "Right before I stepped into the courtroom to testify, Hirsh asked me to come into this little anteroom, a little room where lawyers meet, I suppose. And there was Steve sitting there. He cried and put his arm around me and said, 'Mike, Mike.' It was very emotional and effective to do that just when you are walking in to be a witness."

Rhona Goldfarb would have been the best equipped to speak for Elana's character had she been asked, since she and Elana were so close. Mrs. Goldfarb is thin, small-boned, elegantly dressed, and somewhat aloof. The prosecutor had never met her before. Mike Vest, his investigator, had interviewed her a few weeks earlier, but she was a resource that was never really used. She was never asked at the trial about any of Elana's worries or confidences or about the character of her dead friend. Jeff Hotham wanted her to testify about the argument between the Steinbergs on that vacation trip to Tahoe, but it wasn't showcased to full effect. Bob Hirsh was cautious in his cross-examination—this, also, was a witness of whom he was unsure. Rhona Goldfarb was obviously not in the fold; she hadn't been to the jail to visit Steinberg, and she told the jury that she did not welcome his telephone calls. Bob Hirsh asked a few surface questions about Elana's character, and the victim emerged unscathed—true, Elana liked money, but again didn't everyone? Obviously no one in the Steinberg circle had taken a vow of poverty, and the well-dressed Rhona Goldfarb was no exception. The most that a friend would say for Elana Steinberg in this trial was a brief segment of Rhona Goldfarb's direct testimony:

> Q. What type of woman was she?
> A. She was my friend.
> Q. Did she appear to live for and love her children?
> A. Very much.
> Q. Did she appear to care for and love her husband?
> A. Yes.

Through Mrs. Goldfarb, the prosecutor introduced a photograph of Elana and the two little girls on a cable car taken in San Francisco the week before the murder. They are all laughing and happy. Elana's hair blows in the wind. It is a charming picture.

The Goldfarbs had seen the Steinbergs on May 25 at a party, Rhona said. Steve seemed happy. He told her he wanted to leave early so he could show Elana a car in a showroom—they were looking for one. Hirsh didn't like that.

"Wasn't it Elana that said she was looking for a car?" he asked. "Elana wanted a car, did she not?"

"No, it was Steve."

Hirsh wouldn't let up. He wanted to show that Elana was still buying in a moment of financial disaster, when Steve was out of work, and this doesn't fit the scenario.

"But she approved, didn't she?" he asked Mrs. Goldfarb. It was the most he could make of it. Mrs. Goldfarb was tight-lipped and not particularly friendly to the defense. She hadn't been at any of the group meetings, and she was staying out of the fray. The witness related the open argument about Steve's gambling at Lake Tahoe. "She was very upset. He had promised her he wouldn't gamble. She told me he was lying to her, it was a sickness."

On cross-examination, Bob Hirsh wanted to be sure that the jury knew that Steinberg hadn't seen his children. "When he called you from the jail all those times he was concerned about their welfare because they were with Edith, was he not, ma'am?" Hirsh is stern.

"He told me he was having a hard time getting to them and there was a custody battle going on, yes," Rhona admitted. It was a touch of sentimentality for the jury. If he lost this trial, Steve Steinberg would also lose his children, Hirsh wanted them to know—to Edith Singer.

The state's case was over and the prosecutor was reasonably satisfied. There were some sleeping land mines here, chief among them the absence of good medical testimony for the state. The jurors had no idea of the fierceness of the attack on Elana; they had not been told that multiple stab wounds are characteristic of rage and that what appears to be overkill is the rule, not the exception, in domestic stabbings. It had been a mistake to introduce the murder weapon shrouded in a plastic bag. The jurors needed to be able to touch it, to wrap their own hands around that razor-sharp blade, to look closely at how the blade was ominously bent at the tip. The plastic packaging made the knife too remote.

Technically, everything was complete. It was an insanity defense, and all the state had to do in the first part of the case was to show that the crime was done and that the defendant did it. The next step was for the defense. It would have been good to have a motive. The gambling motif was pretty thin so far—Hotham hadn't really pursued it, but it wasn't too late to do that. The problem was that Hotham knew little about Steven Steinberg or Elana. Unfortunately for him, it was too late to correct that problem.

Meanwhile the defense was settling in. Judge Riddel customarily permitted defendants who were in custody to set up headquarters with their attorneys in a small room off the courtroom, rather than go back to the holding tank down the hall where prisoners are generally kept. Steve and his lawyers had settled in there; meals were catered in, his family and friends visited, there was a bustle and hum of activity around the room. The sheriff's deputy who was regularly assigned to convey Steve to and from the jail became his friend, rather than his jailer, an indication of the remarkable Steinberg charm. I talked to that deputy later and he told me that he had never had that kind of friendly feeling toward a defendant before or since.

"I saw him in every court appearance, because I had to sit or stand real near him," he told me. "He was very polite, very considerate. They used to get food in there all the time— Chinese food or other things. Steve would always ask me if I wanted some. After it was all over, he called me several times, he wanted to sell me some furniture. My wife wasn't crazy about that; she didn't like the way things turned out. Even though Elana was so terrible, Steve said he didn't hate her."

The deputy still seemed surprised at himself for having had such rapport with a defendant in custody. Part of it might have been the experience of being close to the flamboyant Hirsh on those noontime recesses. It's a much tighter ship in the Maricopa County courthouse now, because there have been some dangerous courtroom incidents. The loose atmosphere that prevailed in the hall during the Steinberg trial might be considered risky. But this trial was always different.

CHAPTER SIXTEEN

JUST WALKING IN
MY SLEEP

Bob Hirsh's choice to lead off for the defense was a surprise—
Dr. Donald Holmes. Martin Blinder had examined hundreds
of criminal defendants. He was an old hand in the courtroom.
But Holmes was a novice—he told the jury that this was the
first time he had ever testified in a trial. The Casa Grande
psychiatrist had worked for Bob Hirsh before, but the cases had
never gone to a jury.

Dr. Holmes set the villains on the stage immediately so
that there would be no mistake. His testimony attacked Elana
and her parents mercilessly. After his interview with Steinberg
in the jail in August 1981, Dr. Holmes wrote a devastating
report in which it was easy to distinguish the good guys from
the bad. Steven Steinberg had a happy "warm" childhood; his
mother was "warm and loving"; his sister, Gloria, was "wonderful"; his stepbrother and sister, said Steinberg, "were right here
when I need them." Steinberg cried whenever he mentioned

his family to Dr. Holmes in the jail, and he did it again in court when the doctor retold his story on the witness stand.

"He told me that he had a close, warm, and loving relationship with his mother. He never realized until now how much he cared for her, he told me, and he wept when he spoke of his feelings for her," Holmes said. By now several of the women jurors were crying too. Steve's tears were usually contagious.

Esther Goodman wasn't in the courtroom to hear how much her son cared for her. She, like all the witnesses, had been excluded by the court rule that says that witnesses can be in court only when they are testifying themselves. Barney and Edith Singer were not there either, to hear Steve's psychiatrists destroy their daughter and themselves. Exclusion of witnesses during a trial has never been questioned until recent years. It's always been considered a good thing. If witnesses were in the courtroom, it might be tempting for them to tailor their own testimony to fit the gaps.

But there is a problem with this when it comes to victims, and Barney and Edith Singer were victims in this trial, if only by proxy. Victims have a greater stake in what goes on in a criminal trial than do other witnesses. They are the ones who have been hurt, and they feel frustrated and impotent when they are shut out. Some crusaders want to change the witness rule for them—there is even a proposal now in Arizona called the victim's "Bill of Rights" that would allow them in the courtroom at every stage. While it would have been painful for Barney and Edith Singer to be there when the defense witnesses flayed their daughter, it would seem more just for the Singers at least to see her accusers.

Dr. Holmes testified from his report, elaborating and explaining it in a free flow of narrative. All of Steven Steinberg's assessments of people and events appeared to be those of Dr. Holmes. The posture of the doctor as a critical observer had evaporated. The possibility that a man in jail awaiting trial might be speaking in self-interest, to avoid blame, never crossed the doctor's mind, or, if it had, the idea had been immediately dismissed. Somewhere along the way the psychiatrist dropped descriptive words like "he told me" and the jury was left with the impression that the doctor had adopted as his own Steinberg's descriptions of Elana and the Singers; they had become medical truth. He had accepted everything that Steinberg told him because Steve was honest, Holmes said. He knew this, he told the jury, because he was a doctor. "As a psychiatrist, I've had thirty years of experience in talking with thousands of people, and you do become computerized and sensitive and pretty accurate in your appraisal of when people are telling the truth and when they are not," he said.

"Elana was a lavish spender, and Steve gambled to liquidate his debts which she incurred with her credit cards—Steve did not use them," Holmes said. "She was oblivious or utterly uncaring about their financial realities. When he asked for discretion in her spending she responded with angry, redoubled demands that he make more money," the doctor said.

Steinberg loved his own family dearly, said Dr. Holmes, until he was seduced away from them by his wife and in-laws, "who are all very materialistic" and who called his mother and stepfather "stingy and cheap." Although Steinberg had joined the Singers in their materialism, Holmes said that now Steve wanted to return to the simple life of his parents. He knew that he had made a mistake. Elana Steinberg was "an absolutely uncaring spendthrift who paid no attention to financial realities." When Steve tried to explain to her that they didn't have money for one thing or another, said Dr. Holmes, she would go out and "shop for a new car and a new house or new clothing, running up heavy bills on credit cards."

Dr. Holmes was horrified himself. He said that he asked Steinberg why he didn't "either stop her or separate her or divorce her." Steinberg replied with a picture of his own ineffectiveness. He tried, he said, but he couldn't control Elana's spending; divorce was unthinkable. Dr. Holmes testified in a sentence that made it clear what he thought about Steve's options: "I don't think Steve ever could have earned enough money to make Elana content."

In this story, everyone else did bad things or manipulated the helpless and hapless Steven Steinberg. The pool and patio business in Phoenix was "ruined by Barney Singer's skimming, and because of this, Steve was forced to sell it," Dr. Holmes told the jury. Steinberg claimed that it was his father-in-law who cleaned out the safe at the restaurant the day Elana was killed. "It was Mitchell's father. I've seen him do it. I told him not to do it, and so did Mitchell. I never did that." Steinberg told the psychiatrist that he was not a drug user but had tried cocaine several times. It had really been cocaine that had caused Steinberg to gamble during the wild March trip to Caesars Palace, and the cocaine had been supplied, of course, by someone else. The doctor relayed Steve's explanation of the whole episode. "Mitch bought a gram of it, and I went back five or six times for more. I was a schmuck, letting him talk me into it. I lost all that money because I was high on coke."

Holmes told the jury that Steve gambled only to "liquidate his debts." The gambling was, in Holmes's opinion, "sometimes out of hand. Toward the end I think it became increasingly compulsive—the gambling was a desperate effort to obtain enough money to resolve family problems too."

Finally the invective against the dead woman and her family became a little too much for the psychiatrist. "There may be a misapprehension, I talked only with Steve Steinberg. Obviously, I could not talk with Elana. I do not accept the picture of Elana as the total villain in this relationship. Mr. Steinberg is a grown man, and he was responsible for accepting the role that she assigned. . . . She had her way a good deal more than he had his way, and he accepted those terms by remaining with her."

Dr. Holmes described Steinberg as being incredibly patient in dealing with Elana. "She would associate only with important, affluent people. Most of their disputes centered around her demands for more and more money, her bitter criticism of his failure to make more, her endlessly invasive demands on his time and energy—she just screamed and yelled. I asked him if he were henpecked, and he said that he was not, that if he wanted to go out, 'I had to get Elana's permission, but she almost always let me go.' "

Now, for the first time, the phrase "Jewish American Princess" was heard. It came from Donald Holmes, or more accurately, from Steve Steinberg as reported by Dr. Holmes. The doctor is not Jewish, and he seemed somewhat mystified by the fact that Steinberg would use that phrase for his wife.

"Steve was dispassionate, without apparent rancor, when he described his wife to me as a 'spoiled, overindulged brat—the stereotypical Jewish American Princess,' " said the doctor. His commentary is puzzling. Did the psychiatrist find it unusual that "rancor" didn't go along with calling someone a Jewish American Princess? Or was he just amazed that Steve Steinberg didn't hate his wife despite her terrible qualities?

Not only was Elana a princess, but even Traci was a stereotype. Traci was a good student, but a PIT—a "Princess in Training." The psychiatrist said that Steve was worried that the girls were living with the Singers, "who will spoil her, bring her up the way they did Elana."

Holmes said that he was positive, beyond any medical doubt, that Steinberg was completely asleep and unconscious when he walked to the kitchen to get the carving knife and then came back and stabbed his wife twenty-six times. According to the psychiatrist, the defendant was probably awakened by Elana's screams. He was in a confused state, much like awakening from a deep sleep, when he hid the knife under the box spring and threw the underwear out of the drawer. The attempts to clean up the scene and create a fake burglary, said Holmes, were "denial"—a psychotic, not a guilty, reaction.

Now was the time for a dramatic piece of evidence. Hirsh played the tape of the telephone call made by Traci to the police that night. At the beginning of the tape, Steinberg is heard screaming hysterically:

"Hurry! My wife was just murdered and he walked in the house, my God, please. We were just robbed, and my wife was killed—hurry. I'm bleeding. I'm trying to stop the bleeding. My God, will you get here!"

"What is your name, sir?"

"Steinberg. Don't fucking ask me questions, get here! . . . They threw me on the floor, and I told them where to get the jewelry and they left, and my wife has died!"

Then Traci comes on the line, somewhat calmer, and stays on until the police arrive. It is an intensely dramatic recording. Dr. Holmes said that during this call Steinberg was still in the process of awakening from the sleep state—it was a transition period, said the doctor, that could take a good deal longer than a matter of seconds. The call was genuine, the doctor said, not contrived. He could tell that, he said, because he was an experienced psychiatrist and could evaluate such things.

The doctor told the jury that he had determined that there are genetic factors which indicate that somnambulism runs in families and that the Steinberg family was riddled with it. "Both Traci and Shawn are known to be somnambulistic," he said, "and just this morning I had an opportunity to talk with Mr. Steinberg's mother, who told me that her aunt, that would be Steve's great-aunt, was somnambulistic even in adult life. She said one time after the aunt was married that she got out of bed, came downstairs to the living room, took down an extensive array of heavy velvet drapes, folded them together, stacked them, and went back to bed."

The homicidal sleepwalking was Dr. Holmes's baby, and he liked it. He told the jury that there was a large body of technical literature reporting homicidal violence during sleep.

"But, Doctor," Hirsh asked, "when someone is in that state and there was stabbing and screaming and Mr. Steinberg cut his hand, wouldn't he by necessity wake up?"

Not so, said Holmes. Not only did sleepwalkers typically engage in complicated acts while they were unconscious, they were impervious to the kind of scene that took place that night on Via de Luz. "Somnambulists are not even awakened by pain. One patient in the literature was dreaming of being assaulted, and stabbed himself in the chest four times without waking up; another man shot his wife and was not awakened by the report of the gun."

There was no need even to discuss the *M'Naghten* test in regard to Steve Steinberg, according to Dr. Holmes, because the defendant was totally unconscious while he was killing Elana, and was not in a position to know right from wrong, or the nature of his act. When the prosecutor asked what particular evidence made him so certain that Steinberg was sleepwalking, Dr. Holmes had an interesting, if not particularly scientific, answer. "First is the well-established character of Steve Steinberg as a nonviolent person dominated by his wife, who never struck her once in fifteen years of a stormy marriage. And secondly, there is a great deal of significance in the wound pattern. It is aimless, with a 'stitching' pattern that didn't aim to inflict any fatal wound, totally superficial, in fact, I'm not even satisfied as to what the cause of death was in Elana Steinberg's case."

Dr. Holmes was on unfamiliar ground here, particularly since this was his first testimony in a murder case. He was testifying now as would a pathologist familiar with stabbings. "If he had the intention of 'finishing her off,' why not do it with the first blow?" asked Holmes. "Strike maybe once or twice, or maybe three times if he were really in a rage. But why go 'punch, punch, punch'? I can see myself and any other healthy male making a very successful single thrust."

There was an essential problem with the defense as set forth by Donald Holmes: either Steinberg was asleep and unconscious, or his wife was a terrible person who made him kill. Normally, you can't have it both ways. Was Steinberg walking aimlessly in his sleep? Could he have stabbed a pillow or the family dog or anything that wandered in the way? Or did the defendant hate Elana so much that he was trying to kill her? According to Dr. Holmes, there was no problem. It could be both—it was possible to be aimlessly sleepwalking going 'punch, punch, punch' *and* aim at the hated Elana at the same time—it was sleepwalking with a purpose.

Jeff Hotham had decided to use a scientific approach with Dr. Holmes and had prepared a set of medical questions, heavily influenced by a legal "how-to" book. The book, *Coping with Psychiatric Testimony,* is in every trial lawyer's library and is the jumping-off place for examining psychiatrists. It is a book for debunkers and intended to shock. The author, Jay Ziskin, is both an attorney and a clinical psychologist; his writings are harshly critical of forensic psychiatry. He is particularly bitter about his fellow practitioners who do not hesitate to go to court and diagnose a defendant's state of mind months after the fact. To Ziskin this is nothing but "fanciful speculation"; he sees psychiatric evidence in a criminal trial as useless and a waste of the court's time and would bar it completely. The only evidence that should count, Ziskin writes, is observations of the defendant made at or near the time of the offense. An insane person would be so plainly psychotic then that anyone, even a lay person, would recognize it. "I know it when I see it" makes perfect sense to him.

Being a sensible man, Ziskin knows that the forensic psychiatrists are here to stay, and that their expertise is still deferred to in court. His book is a manual designed to create as much jury doubt as possible in the ability of a forensic psychiatrist to know what he is doing. The book lists sets of questions, gives probable answers, and tells the lawyer what to do next— "If he answers 'no' to this, then ask him about the research on validity listed in Chapter Three."

Cross-examination is an intensely personal matter. Hirsh is a master of it and has made it his own. Hotham was not able to add enough of himself or to follow through on the lines of questioning that are suggested in Ziskin's book—when a point was scored, he failed to follow it up or to bring it out in other ways. He was hamstrung; the effect was flat. In addition, the psychiatrist from Casa Grande was not playing dead. He had obviously been made aware of this line of questioning, and he answered in a cheerful way. It was like hitting a pillow.

> Q. Doctor, sometimes people charged with crimes are less than honest, wouldn't you agree?
> A. I certainly would.
> Q. And sometimes they succeed in fooling the psychiatrists; isn't that correct?
> A. It's possible, yes.
> Q. And is it possible that the defendant was fooling you as to his symptoms in this particular case?
> A. In my opinion, it's not possible, no.

Q. Well, if a person was successful in fooling you, you wouldn't know that you were fooled, would you?

A. You have answered your own question, Mr. Hotham.

Q. You would agree with that, wouldn't you?

A. I can't deny it.

Q. So at this very moment, looking at this defendant you don't even know whether you've been fooled?

A. I know to my satisfaction, but you don't.

The key areas where Dr. Holmes was vulnerable were not to be found in Ziskin's book. First, Holmes had applied little or no critical analysis to Steinberg's account of his life story, and there were a lot of "incidents" in his life that were not mentioned. Holmes seemed to accept everything and anything he was told without question. Never having testified in a murder trial before nor seen a stabbing homicide, the psychiatrist was nonetheless willing to testify about what a knife murderer would do: "He would just pick one good thrust and get it done." In actuality, it is difficult for a nonprofessional to stab someone to death, and there is seldom "one good thrust." Stabbing deaths are usually characterized by multiple wounds, symbolic of rage—sometimes a victim is stabbed as many as a hundred times.

Holmes also testified mysteriously that he "wasn't even sure of the cause of death," disputing the findings of the coroner for some unknown reason, and leaving everyone to wonder what the psychiatrist would ascribe as the true cause of Elana's death. Hotham let all of this stand unrefuted, but calling Dr. Jarvis back on rebuttal would have been a frightening prospect for the prosecutor.

By the kindliness of his face alone, Holmes made a strong impression on the jury. He did not appear to be what is known in the legal profession as a "whore," a psychiatrist so committed to the adversarial process that he will testify to virtually anything. The jury saw him as a country doctor, honest and true. Today, Dr. Holmes says that he remains totally convinced of his original theory—Steinberg was in a deep sleep when he walked into the kitchen to get the knife and when he killed Elana.

I asked Dr. Holmes about the homicidal sleepwalking that he had diagnosed when I met him four years later. At the trial the doctor had testified that there was a "wealth of scholarly articles" about homicidal violence in sleepwalkers. I had searched but as yet I had been unable to find them. Holmes told me he had not kept the articles but that he had used the AMA computer to find them—presumably I could do the same.

Since the doctor was so enthusiastic about his diagnosis of somnambulism I was surprised when he told me that he had not written about the Steinberg case in a medical journal. He seemed anxious to let me know that he didn't do forensic work anymore after his brush with the limelight in the Steinberg and Gorzenski trials. I'd heard that Bob Hirsh sometimes referred to this team of psychiatrists as his "traveling circus," and I asked Holmes how he felt about that. He laughed. "That's just Bob talking," he said. "It doesn't bother me—he is just so nice a guy and it's the way he talks."

I got the impression that Dr. Holmes was greatly relieved to be away from the courtroom. He does not appear to be a man who enjoys combat or even the limelight, but he does enjoy talking about his Steinberg diagnosis and the verdict. There is a difference and a very closed reaction when I ask him about the Gorzenski trial in Safford and his testimony there. "I don't want to talk about that," he told me. I had read his report, and it was a blistering attack on the dead Sandra Gorzenski—the technique was the same, the diagnosis was the same, and the final result was the same. But for some reason Donald Holmes felt comfortable with one trial, but not the other. He has never repeated the sleepwalking idea again, he told me. Somnambulism seems destined for a short life in Arizona criminal law.

After I came back from seeing Dr. Holmes in Sedona, I was able to crack the computer system for medical research, with some help from a doctor friend. I found the articles about homicidal sleepwalkers that the doctor had been talking about.

The form of these case histories came as somewhat of a shock to me, but it was probably because I wasn't familiar with the form of psychiatric research. There were no scientific studies as such, which was what I was expecting. The research consisted of case histories of several paragraphs. Doctors apparently write cases up in the form of a letter to a psychiatric journal and they are reprinted there. Most of the sleepwalking homicide cases had appeared in foreign journals—the English were especially prone to this unusual problem, it appeared. The articles were the kind of vivid anecdotes that could have headlines like those in the *National Enquirer*—they had the same flavor. I amused myself with making up some headlines for them: "Australian mother murders nineteen-year-old daughter with an ax while sleepwalking, says she was 'dreaming of ghosts who had come to take Pattie.' " "Young Dane kills mother with hammer, as a child the defendant had been known to sleepwalk, crime committed while under the influence of a dream, says his psychiatrist." "French detective missing one toe walks in his sleep and kills midnight swimmer on the beach and then solves the case himself: 'It was I who killed André Monet, I can see it by the footprint missing one toe—but I have no motive, I was walking in my sleep,' says detective."

In the ten case histories on record, the conclusion that these individuals were somnambulistic seems to be based on two considerations. First, the defendants were acquitted, and second, the murders didn't seem to make much sense otherwise. As to scientific testing of this conclusion, there was nothing. My search for hard data was disappointing.

I decided to try to find an expert on sleep. It was not difficult—there are clinics all across the country for the treatment of sleep disorders, and one of these is at the medical school at the University of Arizona in Tucson. The clinics are staffed by medical doctors who specialize in internal medicine. I found a young and enthusiastic doctor affiliated with the clinic who agreed to talk to me about the subject—he seemed somewhat baffled by the story of the Steinberg verdict. He told me that the clinic had very few sleepwalkers as patients; he couldn't remember even one. Their patients were mainly suffering from sleep apnea (transient failure to breathe while asleep), insomnia, or narcolepsy.

I showed him the little pack of articles I had found in the English journals. "What do you think of these? Can people really do all these things—walk around and shoot and stab people in their sleep? I thought sleepwalkers were docile and just wandered around. The way that this stuff is written seems frivolous to me," I complained.

"That kind of research is traditional," he told me. "A doctor will see something in his practice and write it up in the form of a letter, and then someone else will read it in a journal and he will say, 'That's like my case,' and he will send it in. That means the phenomenon is observed, but perhaps nothing else will ever happen from this point—no studies, or anything else. I think you are being too critical—that's the way medical things are.

"But you're right. If the doctor testified in your trial that there was a wealth of material on homicidal sleepwalking, I would tend to disagree. There's no scientific study of somnambulism that I know of. Generally, sleepwalkers move slowly, stumble, walk into things, and would tend to harm themselves rather than kill someone. They're noncoordinated and they can be directed very easily. The reason we never see them here, I think, is because sleepwalking is just not a problem." The doctor was intrigued, I could tell.

He told me that sleepwalking is common in children, but rare in adults because it is something that occurs in "slow-wave" sleep. In lay language, that's a mixture of being both awake and asleep simultaneously. The human sleep pattern evolves and matures as a person grows older. A child's sleep might be as much as 25 percent slow-wave. Since an adult experiences very little slow-wave sleep, there is little sleepwalking after childhood.

I thought it would have been interesting to have a doctor like this come in on rebuttal, after Holmes had testified. This doctor was so serious and skilled—no nonsense here. I asked what he would have said if he had been retained to be an expert witness on sleep disorders. He was nervous, as all doctors are with lawyers, but he finally warmed to the idea.

"I don't want to commit myself without being totally knowledgeable of all the facts, but based on what you've told me I would testify generally about the nature of slow-wave sleep, and what little we do know scientifically about the capacities of the sleepwalker. I would have to say that I would be highly suspicious of a unique and isolated instance of sleepwalking in an adult aged thirty-seven. I would ask myself, 'What's to be gained from telling this story?' Because all these cases seem to be about murder and people on trial. Is it some kind of legal defense theory? But then, that's psychiatry."

The jurors never truly bought the theory that Steve Steinberg was in a deep sleep when he killed his wife that night, or at least that was what they told me afterward. Perhaps the theory was too fanciful for them. They were impressed, though, with the sweet-faced kindly doctor from a small Arizona town and with his sincerity when he described for them the bad character of Elana Steinberg. If Steven Steinberg had been forced to be the first one to say those things about his wife in the courtroom it might not have been so effective; it would sound like a defendant trying to save his own skin at the expense of someone else. But when Dr. Holmes described Elana Steinberg as a nagging, spending, "stereotypic Jewish American Princess" it was different—that was science.

Dr. Holmes told me that he had never intended to convey through his testimony the impression that it was acceptable to kill Elana Steinberg and that he would never have done so. The jury didn't quite grasp that.

CHAPTER SEVENTEEN

THROUGH THE THICKETS OF THE HEARSAY RULE

Now it was Martin Blinder's turn for the defense. The doctor is tweedy and round-faced, with a cherubic countenance. He seems bathed in cheerfulness and bustling energy. From the minute he took the witness stand, the jury could tell that the man loved this arena. He was so clearly at home, speaking in vivid colloquial language that anyone could understand. Dr. Blinder is a storyteller by nature, and his psychiatric reports have a storylike quality. In fact, Dr. Blinder wrote an article for a women's magazine called "When Loved Ones Become Killers" some years after the trial. Save for the names of the characters, who are called Solly, Morris, and Roselyn, his Steinberg medical report and the vignette in the magazine are interchangeable.

Hirsh began with the psychiatrist's credentials, and they are impressive. Dr. Blinder is not shy about describing the myriad activities in which he has been engaged. It is difficult to see how one man could do so many things. Blinder said that in addition to teaching, lecturing, and writing, he had done "thousands" of forensic examinations in half of the states in the United States, forty counties in California, and even territories as far away as Guam, where he has had twenty-five forensic cases. The man is amazingly energetic. Dr. Blinder said he doesn't care for whom he works, it just doesn't register—"I suppose I have testified for prosecutors outside of California, but it's not significant to me who calls me."

Of all of the witnesses involved in *State* v. *Steinberg*, Martin Blinder would probably be the first to agree that the trial is a carefully crafted play with characters who are to represent good and evil. In the popular textbook Dr. Blinder has written for lawyers, he is totally frank about the trial strategy that was being used in the Steinberg case. According to Blinder's book, juries will surprisingly acquit certain individuals in crimes of violence even though there is overwhelming evidence against them. Blinder explains the tactics employed to obtain these strange verdicts. "The successful defense attorney conveys to the jury that his client is very much like them (obviously more difficult to do when twelve white, elderly middle-class jurors are sitting in judgment on a young ghetto black). . . . The attorney persuades the juror that the offense resulted from singular events not likely to be repeated, and that his client is no threat to *them*."

Blinder writes, "Finally, the successful defense attorney's prosecution of the *victim* is often as vigorous as the State's attack on the defendant. In the classical domestic homicide the defense attorney will use the 'try the victim' defense, bring out how the decedent was a self-indulgent, intolerable philanderer while the surviving spouse, his client, was a long-suffering, hardworking person whose coping mechanisms were suddenly exceeded after twenty years of abuse. He suggests that anyone would 'snap' under such circumstances. . . . Now that the wayward spouse has been dispatched, however, and not a moment too soon, the defendant is no longer a danger to anyone."

Dr. Blinder is equally frank about the role of the psychiatrist in such a trial. In another part of his book he describes the psychiatric autopsy, when a psychiatrist can help to make the jury more "forgiving" to the defendant: "When a woman kills her husband, it often can be shown through the psychiatric autopsy that the victim was an abusive, hard-drinking man who threatened her and assaulted her psychologically until she snapped." The word "snap" appears frequently in Dr. Blinder's writings—it is apparently his shorthand word to communicate to the jury what Hirsh calls "temporary insanity." It has a popular appeal for the layman—all the jurors told me later that Steve Steinberg "snapped."

Dr. Blinder tells lawyers that there is another helpful tool to build sympathy for the defendant and "distaste" for the victim, and that is the defendant's history—the mainspring of a psychiatrist's report. That history, says the doctor, contains "incidents" upon which distaste and sympathies can be formed, and which the forensic psychiatrist can repeat. "These incidents are usually an integral part of the defendant's history, and thus a legitimate basis for the psychiatrist's conclusion," he writes.

In his textbook, Martin Blinder has described what was about to happen in *State* v. *Steinberg.* When he was finished with his testimony, there would certainly be sympathy for Steve Steinberg, and a virulent "distaste" for his victim. The medical report that he had prepared, and that he repeated to the jury, was in reality a series of "incidents" in which Elana Steinberg was tried, as the law so neatly puts it, *in absentia.*

Dr. Blinder's ability to spin a tale was far superior to that of the doctor from Casa Grande. His language and similes were delightful for the jury; at times they smiled. Steven Steinberg's dissociative condition, for example, was just like a pressure cooker with a blocked valve. "Now, I think it's been years since anyone has used pressure cookers anymore, but I understand it lets out a little pressure at a time. If that doesn't happen, it can explode with your brisket gristle all over the kitchen ceiling, and we find that happens in real life, where individuals will explode with a disastrous effect."

How did Steven Steinberg hallucinate those two bushy-haired burglars in the room? Simple, said Dr. Blinder; hallucinations happen all the time. "For example, a man might dream that he always wanted to be a bed partner of Raquel Welch. Now that's not likely to happen and so he just has a dream about doing that and his dream enables him to have what he cannot have in real life . . . ."

Who could resist this fascinating testimony? The jurors were intrigued, obviously. They were leaning forward, spellbound; they smiled at the right points.

Blinder introduced a new criticism of Elana Steinberg, that she fitted another stereotype of the Jewish American Princess. He implied that she was cold and frigid in matters of sex. JAP jokes are often sexual and based on this idea. Steve Steinberg was a pressure cooker, at least in part, because his wife "put a damper on their sex life." There was mild disapproval in the doctor's testimony about this, although he acknowledged that in 1979 Elana had cancer of the cervix and then valley fever, a fatiguing fungus disease of the lung common in Arizona. Elana thought her cervical cancer was related to sexual intercourse, a crazy idea put into her head by Edith, said Dr. Blinder. It was no problem anyway, he told the jury, because her cancer had "no sequelae." The source for his diagnosis of Elana's cancer and her prognosis was Steven Steinberg. Dr. Blinder is a psychiatrist, not a gynecologist. His statement about possible sexual transmission of cervical cancer is not correct. Public health clinicians agree that this kind of cancer can develop if a sexual partner has certain venereal diseases.

When the couple did have sex weekly, said the doctor, Elana didn't perform with enthusiasm. It was "perfunctory with no adequate words of affection." Since his wife's heart wasn't in it, testified Dr. Blinder, "Mr. Steinberg sought out professional contacts for sexual expression." This was an intriguing idea the jury was to hear no more of—the prosecutor's attempt to bring in evidence of Steinberg's sexual affairs was objected to by Bob Hirsh, and the objection was sustained by the judge. How did this man who worked twelve hours a day fit it in? Where did he get the money for those "professional contacts" when his wife supposedly took his entire paycheck? The whole idea just didn't fit with the image of the long-suffering good husband and father, but it was never to be explored further. Hotham lost the battle in the judge's chambers to introduce evidence of Steve's affairs in Phoenix. His investigator had found one young woman who saw Steinberg regularly, but the jury was not to hear from her.

"That's not proper and he knows it." Hirsh was furious. "Sex has nothing to do with it, and he's just trying to throw dirt on my client."

Generally a prosecutor in a criminal trial is not permitted to introduce any negative things about a defendant's past. Those things are called "prior bad acts," and the jury never hears about them except in very limited circumstances. Jurors are usually astounded after the verdict when they learn that a defendant had been in trouble with the law for years. The theory behind this is good—hearing about the defendant's past wrongdoing is too inflammatory. It doesn't mean that the defendant committed the crime that's before the court now, although the jury will tend to think so.

"He's bringing up what a great guy Steinberg is, Judge. I ought to be able to say what was really going on," the prosecutor sputtered. He lost this argument.

Hotham just wasn't a fighter in those arguments in chambers. "If he had yelled and screamed more, I thought he could have won most of them," Hylton told me afterward. "Jeff was too much of a gentleman and he was up against a street fighter. He didn't want to be like that; he had a certain disdain for defense tactics."

That wasn't the whole story, though. While Hotham did read all the insanity cases, what he wasn't aware of was that in an insanity defense the "prior bad acts" rule goes out the window. The state supreme court had said, in *State* v. *Skaggs,* that the jury was entitled to hear *all* the things in a defendant's past —how else could they judge if he was insane? "Since the defendant is permitted to disclose his personal history and is not restricted to any particular acts or conduct for the purpose of showing he was insane, the state may also explore the same area and present evidence not disclosed by the defendant to prove his sanity," wrote the court. In simpler terms, what is sauce for the goose is sauce for the gander. Knowing about *State* v. *Skaggs* would have solved a lot of problems for Hotham. It's one of those things that has to be anticipated well before trial—it would be best to have *Skaggs* photocopied and ready in your trial briefcase.

Back in the courtroom, Dr. Blinder was demolishing Elana Steinberg. He spoke in a free flow of words—Bob Hirsh scarcely interrupted. The jury was rapt. Some were taking notes on their pads; a few looked amazed as the story unfolded all during that long afternoon.

"During their fifteen years of marriage, Mrs. Steinberg became increasingly critical of her husband who could never do right. She viewed him as a source of income—he never seemed to make enough to please her. His opinions meant nothing. He would come home one day to find new furniture in the bedroom, a new rug. She never consulted him on domestic decisions," Blinder began.

Elana had a terrible character, the doctor said. All she cared about was "appearance, material wealth, status," while Steve's love and deep feelings were "not a part of her emotional vocabulary." All she cared about was her house, jewelry, Cadillacs. Their friends were chosen, by Elana, only for their wealth.

"The arrangement was a simple one," said Dr. Blinder. "He earned the money, she spent it. Each week he would turn over his paycheck to her and he received nothing back. The money that she 'squirreled away' in the bank she would never let him touch.

"He didn't have any credit cards. She had the credit cards," said Dr. Blinder. When Steve gambled he only did it to "get strokes from Elana." He borrowed money so that he could "give her smiles to get the strokes, and the smiles were in short supply."

Steve was the real businessman in the Steinberg/Singer family: "Steve felt he was the only reliable member of the family in business; Barney lost business. Mitch, for all of his five-and-a-half-million-dollar house, was all show. Steve was the guy who put in the work, who kept Mitch's business afloat as long as he could, and nobody gave him credit for it."

It went on this way for several hours. There was nothing good to be said for Elana—even the pride of her life, her love for her daughters, was destroyed. "Elana rode Traci and drove her nearly crazy and Steve was powerless to do anything about it." It was a long afternoon. Fortunately, or maybe unfortunately, Edith Singer was not there to hear it.

After Dr. Holmes's and Dr. Blinder's testimony back to back, the jury was reeling; there was nothing too awful for Steven Steinberg's late wife to have said or done. According to the psychiatrists, this man's life had been fifteen years of abject misery. He was married to a monster and her family, and they tortured him. Elana was a caricature of a spendthrift nagging wife; Edith Singer, the worst of mothers-in-law; Barney Singer, a ne'er-do-well who looted cash registers and forced Steven Steinberg to take up gambling against his will. There were no restraints in these stories told by the two doctors, nor was any of it questioned in any respect.

Case histories are stories, and Sigmund Freud told stories when he was writing about his patients, too. It was the heart of the psychoanalytic method, but the case histories of Freud's neurotic violet-scented ladies in Vienna do not contain venom directed at others as these psychiatric autopsies of Dr. Blinder and Dr. Holmes do. Should a medical report be able to double for a story in *Cosmopolitan*? Psychiatrists like Blinder or Holmes are really testifying as if they have firsthand knowledge of all of these offenses of the dead woman. The character assassination is being done by a doctor. Steven Steinberg should have been the one on the witness stand saying these terrible things about his dead wife and his in-laws, but he wouldn't have to do it now. When it was Steinberg's turn to testify, he could, and did, adopt a noble, high-minded approach, saying things like "I truly loved my wife, Mr. Hotham," while he cried.

Legally there is something suspect about this technique. When the psychiatrist who makes the statements about the victim's words and conduct is asked about the truth of them, he can only respond, "That's what the defendant told me, and I believe him." The prosecutor can rant and rave, and criticize the doctor for being naive, but the damage can't be totally eliminated. When a doctor repeats what the defendant has told him, he gives it believability and the aura of medicine. When Martin Blinder said, for example, that even though Steve was out of work "his wife was out test-driving a new Cadillac and looking for larger houses," it could never be refuted. Dr. Blinder had never met this woman, and she was dead and silent. Theoretically there is no limit to what a criminal defendant can say through this kind of psychiatrist, because these little "incidents" are part of the defendant's clinical history, as Dr. Blinder says in his textbook for lawyers.

But there is a problem, and the problem is the hearsay rule. I don't even like to say those words, since the rule has bad memories for me from law school. Law students take a course called Evidence, usually in the second year of school. Half that semester is taken up trying to get a grip on the hearsay rule. Just when you think you have it, it slips away in the forest of "exceptions" to the hearsay rule, and it is gone. There are some people who are born with a talent for the rule; others struggle on and never feel quite comfortable. The worst part is that a trial lawyer has to recognize hearsay instantaneously and be on his feet in trial. The need for such immediate reaction is probably one of the reasons trial lawyers burn out so quickly. They can never relax and sit quietly in a half-doze at the counsel table; every fiber of the body must be alert to jump up and object before the actual hearsay, or what you think is hearsay, gets out. There is no time for delay, because once the answer is out, the damage is done. The rule is simple: "Hearsay is not admissable." People think this is just one more of the technicalities in the law that make them cross; why can't jurors hear every single thing? They get the impression that the trial is skipping all around and under the evidence and there are big gaps in between. But there is a solid idea behind the hearsay rule. Evidence in a court of law is supposed to have a certain quality; it has to be considered trustworthy, to be related by someone who has firsthand knowledge of the events, someone whom we can look at and evaluate ourselves as he or she describes those events. Repeating what someone else supposedly said outside of the courtroom is just not good enough.

Let's take an example. When Dr. Blinder said, "I talked to Shawn and she told me, 'Mommy always needed money and Daddy couldn't get it,' " not only is that a very damaging statement, it is also hearsay. Hearsay is a statement made by someone else outside of the courtroom and offered to prove that something is true; hearsay is particularly offensive when the person who supposedly made that statement is "unavailable as a witness." This would cover both the dead Elana, who was certainly unavailable, and also six-year-old Shawn, whom the law considers not old enough to be a witness. The problem with hearsay is that there is no way to know whether this is a reliable statement, whether Shawn actually said that, what else Shawn may have said, or what Dr. Blinder's question was in the first place. The *quality* of this statement is not good enough to be a piece of evidence in a trial upon which important things rest.

Now, some people are very special when they are witnesses, and doctors are among them. First of all, doctors are "experts," and because they are experts, they are allowed to give an *opinion:*

"Do you have an opinion, Doctor, as to the defendant's state of mind at the time of the murder?"

"Yes, I do."

That is a question that cannot be asked of you or of me when we are witnesses in a trial. Only "experts" can give an opinion. The reason for that is that the law says they are qualified to enlighten the jury because they have had special experience and training. When they testify, experts can also refer to a variety of sources that would otherwise be hearsay—things like hospital charts with nurses' notes, a doctor's report from back in St. Louis, the content of a textbook on orthopedics. Those secondhand resources are allowed because this is the kind of material an expert usually relies on when he is shaping his opinion. That kind of material is reasonably trustworthy and not likely to be made up or distorted, and so it is an exception to the hearsay rule.

Something totally different happened at the Steinberg trial. Dr. Holmes and Dr. Blinder were not talking about blood-pressure readings and hospital charts from St. Louis. They were making very damaging statements about "incidents" in the life of Elana Steinberg that could never be verified. It takes an objection from the opposing lawyer to bring hearsay to the attention of the court. Jeff Hotham did not object. A judge does not step in spontaneously and reject hearsay, or remind the opposing attorney that he should be objecting to it. That's for attorneys to do. The judge is a judge, not a partisan. If one attorney misses a point and then it's too late, he has to live with it.

The content of these two reports was devastating to the prosecution, and to the reputation of Elana Steinberg and her family. I've tried to think what could have been done about it. Objecting to this kind of psychiatric report would have had to be done well before the trial even started by bringing a motion to keep it out before it happened, a motion *in limine*. The defense testimony might be restricted, but I doubt it. Judges always bend over backward in first degree murder to let almost every kind of evidence in for the defense, because the stakes are so high. It would depend on whether a judge was willing to stick his neck out a little bit on the evidence. It's easier for the judge not to do this, and to let everything go through for the defense. Then, if the defendant is convicted, the trial record is clean and it's not likely that the case will be reversed when it goes up on appeal. Trying to limit the testimony would be experimental. I assumed that's why Jeff Hotham didn't do any-thing about it here. He knew what was coming. He had the reports in his hand months before the trial, but he thought the attack on Elana was inevitable. "That's the way the game is played," he told me later.

The more traditional strategy is to be aggressive from the start. I don't understand why the prosecutor didn't do this. I don't believe he could comprehend that the jury would buy the idea that the killing was somehow understandable. A prosecutor could take the offense himself from the start—take it away from the defense at the very beginning, in the opening argu-ment. He could let the jury know what was going to happen, saying, "Now you're going to hear a lot of mud and trash thrown at this dead woman, just to get your mind off what this man did." He could play the tape of that police telephone call himself—not wait for Hirsh to do it. He could tell the jury, "You're going to listen to this guy, the defendant, perform on a tape—you're going to hear a real performance. It's show time, ladies and gentlemen."

This is most important. Before the trial a prosecutor should take the psychiatric report and tear it apart line by line, phrase by phrase, so that when the trial comes he can go over every line, saying, "Where's your source for this statement, and this statement?" He could have copies made for each juror and pass them out, so they could follow along as he goes. Jurors like that. It gives them something to handle, and they feel a part of things.

Steve was very selective about what he said to his psychiatrists. There were a lot of things left out that he didn't tell them. Right before the trial, a prosecutor could send the defense psychiatrists a whole list of things that were never mentioned in their reports, like all the missing money from the cash registers, and the other bushy-haired robbers in Des Plaines, and the rest. Hotham could have sent the doctors a letter listing these incidents, asking them to read it. Then at the trial he could have asked them about those events—"When you made your report, did he tell you about the bushy-haired men back in Chicago? Did you know about the Toronado in New Mexico?" If the defense was going to drive a hearsay truck in, so could the prosecutor. It cuts both ways.

Hotham relied on a serious approach when he cross-examined the defense psychiatrists. He tried to go into different diagnoses and theories, treating their work as a science that could only be rebutted with science. Trying to pin Dr. Blinder down was like trying to pin Jell-O on a wall. Sarcasm, in my opinion, would have been more effective with him than cool courtesy. Reading Martin Blinder's writings would have been very revealing. I would read passages to the jury, particularly the section that describes how to go about trying the victim, where he deals with the subject humorously. A list of every time Dr. Blinder came into the state to testify and what the diagnosis was in each one of those trials could have been compiled. He was very vague on previous testimony. "I don't recall what I said in that trial, or what the diagnosis was," he'd say, but if you had the cases all listed, you could see the pattern.

For example, the jury wasn't really aware that Dr. Blinder diagnosed this extremely rare dissociative reaction twice in two days—first in Phoenix, and then the next day in Safford, for William Gorzenski. A prosecutor really has to do his homework on an insanity defense, particularly when it is one like the Steinberg case.

Sometimes inflammatory psychiatric reports of a defendant's history give the sense that it is a story perfected long before, probably before the forensics ever came in. It's very much like a scene from *Anatomy of a Murder*. When the lawyer sees his client for the first time in the book, he is getting ready for an insanity defense, because there is nothing else. He says to the client, "Now you're going to tell me what happened that night, and if what you tell me is like this, I might have a chance to win this baby." You can imagine the story his client told him.

Neither Donald Holmes nor Martin Blinder would agree that their testimony in the Steinberg case was nonscientific. They remain convinced today as they were when Martin Blinder testified, "I think I have a pretty good sense of who Mr. Steinberg is, and he's not a killer. . . . I remain certain that Mr. Steinberg did not have his wits about him at the time of the homicide."

Next stop, Safford.

CHAPTER EIGHTEEN

"SHE WAS A VERY DEAR, CLOSE FRIEND OF MINE"

"She was a very dear, close friend of mine, one of my closest friends," one woman told the jury when Bob Hirsh asked her to describe her relationship with Elana Steinberg. A lot had happened to friendship since Elana had been killed on that rainy night nine months earlier. The witness's answer to the next question asked her by Steve Steinberg's attorney was more telling.

"And you've come down here without a subpoena, have you not?" said Hirsh.

"Yes, I have."

Now that may seem like an innocuous question, but to a trial attorney the meaning is clear. This woman, and probably all of the witnesses who were going to pass in review on February 10 and 11, had declared their allegiance—they were defense witnesses solid and true. These witnesses were not reluctant or shy or troubled about what they were going to do in this trial. If they had ever had any mixed feelings or ambivalence about testifying for Steve, those feelings had been resolved. The defense attorneys knew that a single phone call would bring them to the courtroom on the day they were needed. Without a subpoena, Hirsh had no power to compel the appearance of any of these witnesses. The tactic was a display of his utter confidence in their loyalty. The defense attorneys knew that these witnesses would not have cold feet about the trial, have a sudden attack of influenza, or have to go to an aunt's funeral in Chicago. They would be there because they *wanted* to be there. There were probably few jurors who comprehended the import of the question he had just asked, but Bob Hirsh wanted to let the jury know that these people were, in a sense, volunteers. They might deplore the murder of their friend, but they were willing to put that aside and testify for her husband when it counted.

Not all of the Steinberg friends were there, because Bob Hirsh had an unerring touch for choosing the witnesses. The reason he had been so discriminating after those defense meetings in Diane Lindstrom's living room now became clear. The friends who were going to testify in the trial had to be psychologically committed to the acquittal of Steven Steinberg. There was a price to be paid for this display of loyalty to Steve. It was not going to be enough for witnesses to say that Steve was a "wonderful guy, warm, caring, all of the children love him," even though just appearing at the trial to say those things was enormously helpful and showed that Steve was not a pariah to his contemporaries. Hirsh had to be sure that these people were not the type who would then go on to blurt out a statement like "but he shouldn't have killed my friend Elana," thereby destroying the effect.

For some of the more daring of the defense witnesses there was another price to be paid. Not only did they have to give Steve a good character, but they would also have to say certain derogatory things about their late friend Elana. Bit by bit and piece by piece the defense attorneys were going to paint a picture of the dead woman as a "Jewish American Princess," shopping, decorating to excess, nagging, shrill-voiced. She had to be so terrible that the jury would believe that Steve Steinberg had "snapped." Each little bit of testimony helped to contribute to the desired portrait.

There was no overkill in the anti-Elana testimony of the friends. It was delicately handled. Each witness was quizzed about one or two incidents of Elana's extravagance, mainly dealing with interior decoration, which seemed to be the underlying theme of the trial. Hirsh would ask, "How did the house look to you?"

"It would seem like every time we went there we found there was something new that we hadn't seen the time before," Steve's mother contributed. One response drew smiles from some of the jurors. It hit home with them when one of Steve's friends said, "The house was like it stepped out of *House and Garden.* It's the kind of home you are afraid to sit down in. You know what I mean—afraid you might break something."

Adverse vignettes were sandwiched in with saying good things about the Steinberg family life as a whole. The friends all testified that the Steinbergs never quarreled, that they were both wonderful parents, that they seemed to be very happy together. Still, the cumulative effect of the comments criticizing Elana was strong—trial observers noticed it. When I asked one reporter her impression, she told me that "all of Elana's friends slammed her." The friends who testified for the defense were probably unaware of the impact of what they were doing on these two days of the trial. The only part of the trial that each witness saw was his own brief period on the witness stand, since witnesses were excluded from the courtroom unless they were testifying. It is conceivable that they did not recognize the cumulative effect of the damage that was being done to the memory of their "very dear, close friend."

Steve's sister, Gloria, led off the stream of defense witnesses. Hirsh and Benchoff had an embarrassment of riches, since there were so many. Gloria said that Steve's family life growing up in Chicago was very close and everyone was always in harmony. Whenever Steve Steinberg's stepfather, David Goodman, was mentioned, Bob Hirsh portrayed him as a refugee from the persecution of Jews in Nazi Germany. It was a strange and bitter counterpoint in this trial in which, at the same time, the dead woman was being described as having the worst of "Jewish" traits.

> Q. Did your mother then marry a gentleman by the name of David Goodman?
> A. Right.
> Q. Is David Goodman, or was he, a citizen of Germany in the thirties?
> A. Yes, he came to America in 1938.
> Q. And was that in the thirties; do you know, during the Nazi—
> A. I don't remember the year, I'm sorry.
> Q. But it was in the thirties, wasn't it? During the Nazi—
> A. Yes, uh-huh.

The word "Nazi" is finally out.

Gloria testified that after she and Steve were both married and living in Chicago, the couples did not socialize very much because Gloria and her husband "didn't live that particular life-style. . . . We'd go to a movie or bowling or something, we didn't go out to expensive restaurants." Steve and Elana were happy in their marriage, said Gloria, but Elana was the dominant person.

> Q. Why is it that you say that?
> A. Well, after my father died, Steve and I took care of my father's grave—can I explain how a Jewish grave is taken care of?
>
> Jewish graves are raised above the ground about six or eight inches, and some people plant flowers on the top. And we try to keep them neat and elevated so that nobody will step on them. Steve and I used to go to the cemetery and take care of the grave, and when we both moved out West we could no longer do it.

And my father's sisters in Chicago wrote to me and said that the grave needed repair and could we do something about it. It would cost us forty dollars to repair it, and then there was a total of two hundred and fifty dollars to take care of it in perpetual care. I wrote Steve to ask if he could help with taking care of the grave, and Elana wrote back that they would share in the forty dollars but they wouldn't share in the perpetual care.

Steve called me from work one day and said that he really wanted to do this and he'd get the money to me somehow. And we left it at that even though Elana objected to it.

There was a dual impression left here: first that Elana was so mean that she wouldn't take care of a Jewish grave, and also that Elana controlled the purse strings so completely that Steve had no cash even for this religious obligation to his dead father. No one inquired if this was the same man who was spending thousands in betting on Monday-night football, the man who friends said "always carried a big wad of bills, always."

Gloria said that Steve had never talked to her about any problems at home, and he had never asked to borrow money, although she and her husband, Barry, would have been happy to lend him money. "I simply had no idea of any indebtedness," she said. She brought in the photographs of her son's bar mitzvah in May—the candle-lighting and the party in the backyard just ten days before Elana was killed. Everyone is smiling and happy.

Hotham did not cross-examine Steve's sister or any of the defense character witnesses with any depth or intensity. This is not unusual. Cross-examination of a character witness is usually a disappointing and unproductive exercise for a prosecutor in a murder trial. But this case was different. There were intriguing areas which could have been explored on cross-examination had the prosecutor chosen to do so. Did Steven Steinberg's sister really know nothing about her brother's gambling, which had begun years ago when he was in high school? If this was true, wouldn't it tend to show that he had deceived his mother and sister for years? Did Steve ever pay his share of the $250 for the father's grave? Since her brother was in such desperate financial straits when the family went to the bar mitzvah in California, why did he not feel free to discuss the true situation with his sister, to tell her that the roof was going to fall in when he returned to Arizona? What kind of "warm and close" relationship was that?

Steve's mother had a brief turn on the witness stand. Her son was nonviolent, she said; "Everybody always loved him." Had she known he needed money, she and David Goodman would have helped Steve out without question. Ironically, Steve's mother was the only one on that day to be complimentary to Elana. It slipped out when Bob Hirsh was asking the standard interior-decorating question.

"How did that home look to you?" the defense attorney asked.

"It was gorgeous, absolutely beautiful. Elana was a wonderful housekeeper. She was a good mother and I believe a good wife," her mother-in-law said. Bob Hirsh got more than he expected here.

After Gloria and Steve's mother came the Steinberg friends. Hirsch never asked this woman about her husband's function as the conduit for Steve's gambling. The word "gambling" was never mentioned with her. She saw Steve as "very attentive and very warm, even publicly"—the word "warm" reappeared constantly in the friends' descriptions of Steven Steinberg and was a favorite word in the trial; Steve and his relatives were "warm," the Singers were "cold." Steve was a worker, very dedicated—early in the morning and late at night —and according to this particular friend, Elana understood that. It was the nature of the family business.

Hirsh asked her, "In terms of the relationship between Steve and Elana, did you see a tendency for Elana to dominate Steve?"

"To a certain extent, yes," she answered. "She never was really abusive of him in public in any way, but there were subtle tones that we could tell that Elana usually got what she wanted, and he was very willing to give her what she wanted, and that kept both of them happy."

"Did you ever see her purchase exotic, unusual things for the house?" Hirsh was going back to the leitmotif of interior decorating.

Unlike some of the other defense witnesses, this friend described Elana's decorating as a matter of taste, good taste, rather than excess. "Elana had very good taste. She wanted nice things, and Steve was willing to provide . . . to keep Elana happy, yes, sir."

This woman and some of the other witnesses who were to follow on these two days, were the same people who had written bail letters to the judge nine months earlier. They had praised Elana then, and seen Steve as a "good provider," but by the time some of these witnesses got to the courtroom things had changed, and now there was a subtle difference in the approach. Elana was seen as materialistic and frivolous and her living standards outside the norm for the rest of the group, an interesting evolution. The defense must have gelled in the months before trial.

Why did that happen? My guess is that Elana had stepped over the line in some way with at least a few of the women, upsetting the very fine balance of what was acceptable for this circle. They were all consumers, obviously, but each group has its own limits. Elana was very much a free spirit, and she was breaking out from the mold. A closed-in group like hers can be very cold, very unrelenting, if you stray. She must have stepped on a lot of toes.

The next witness, the wife of a Phoenix stockbroker, was not hesitant when Hirsh asked if she had any impression of Elana's feeling about money and property. The elegant and well-dressed Judy Alpert answered with an anecdote:

"There was an incident, I was shopping at Bullock's looking for a comforter, and I ran into Elana and her little girl, Shawn. And I mentioned to her that I was looking for a comforter for our bedroom because we hadn't gotten a bedspread yet, but that I had more or less changed my mind because it would mean getting rid of our king-size sheets and pillows and buying new ones. And she said, 'That really should not make any difference. Since they have come in style, I've gotten rid of all of our bedspreads and sheets, and I just went out and bought all new ones.' And she said, 'That's all you have to do.'

"I thought that was extravagant to do. If they have holes in them I could understand it, but if they were good I simply couldn't fathom doing something like that."

Mrs. Alpert said that Elana was domineering, recalling an incident: "She mentioned to me that Steve had been asked by Mitchell to go to Albuquerque and have it be his baby. I asked her if they were going to be moving there, and she said, 'Absolutely not. I do not want any part of it. Steve will just have to go there and come back and forth. I absolutely refuse.' And I mentioned to her, 'Don't you even want to go to see what it's like?' And she said, 'Absolutely not—he will have to go by himself.' "

Hirsh pointed out for the jury that Judy Alpert was happy, even eager, to be a defense witness. "And you've been waiting around here for two days to testify?"

"All I can tell you is that Steve is just a very warm and gentle person and a loving father and a loving husband. And I wouldn't spend two days in this room if I didn't think a lot of Steve."

One woman gave the most extensive testimony about her view of Elana Steinberg. Her testimony stands out—she was the lead among the friends. She began in low key by saying that she thought the Steinbergs had a very good relationship; they never argued and they were good parents. But then the ax began to fall. Elana was an extravagant spender:

"She loved shopping," said her woman friend. "She would go out shopping I think almost on a daily basis. She used to kid around and say that the women in the department stores, the salespeople, all knew her name as well as the children, because she used to take Shawny with her shopping."

"Did she characterize herself as a professional shopper?" asked Hirsh.

"Yes. There was always something new. You know, over a

period of years something new would appear in the house . . . everything in that house was of concern to her."

This friend acted as a guide for a tour of her dead friend's house, presumably so the jurors could see the decor for themselves and marvel at it. The defense lawyers made a series of forty photographs, in color, of all of the rooms in the house on Via de Luz, and Babs Spero was the guide as Hirsh introduced the photos into evidence, one by one.

"This is the living room, this is the closet she turned into a bar, these are the chandeliers, they are all in the dining room . . . " It goes on and on.

The relevance of these photographs to the murder of Elana Steinberg on the night of May 27 is obscure. Were they intended to inflame the jury with envy or some other emotion? The prosecutor had no objection to her walk through the house on Via de Luz. It was probably much too late for him to make any meaningful opposition had he chosen to do so. The trial had now obviously been turned on its head and the person being tried was Elana, not Steve.

She was not through. She told the jury that she had one argument with Elana in the five years of their friendship. "You couldn't get a word in edgewise. When Elana wanted to make a point, it was a run-on sentence. You didn't stand a chance against her, and I never argued with her again because there was no point. She was going to win.

"She was a carbon copy of her mother, Edith. I mean, Elana was a product of her environment, just as much as anybody else is. It was black or white with Elana. It was, you know, either/or: she had certain things that she felt were important in life, and you had to measure up to those."

Hirsh said, somewhat amazed, "Despite all this you were still a friend of Elana's?"

"Well, you're bringing up the bad traits. As in anyone, Elana had good traits too."

The jury had to wait to hear about those good traits until the cross-examination, when Jeff Hotham asked about them. The witness did not volunteer anything good about Elana Steinberg.

"She loved her children. She obviously was a good house-keeper, and she was a lot of fun to be with."

Hotham was in over his head. By now he was beginning to perceive that shopping was going to be an issue in this murder trial. "When you talked about her being a professional shopper, did you mean that she was thrifty, shopping for a bargain?"

She quickly put an end to that. "No, I can't say that that is true."

Hotham asked her if she was aware of Steve's gambling.

"I am now. Was I then? I knew that he gambled, but everybody loves a winner, and when he won, I knew about it. Once he won an enormous amount of money in Vegas and he bought her a Cadillac. But I never heard them argue about gambling."

The husbands from the charmed social circle in Scottsdale were more sympathetic to the dead Elana than were their wives. Their testimony by and large was normal character evidence—Steve was nonviolent; they thought the Steinbergs were happy. Either the husbands were too circumspect to criticize Elana's character or the defense attorneys may have believed that it would have been overkill to have both spouses say the same thing. Only one man was overtly critical. Hal Brin said that he was a regional sales manager for a videocassette company and that he used to go to B. B. Singer's two and three times a day, because he liked Steve so much. He too praised the Steinberg charm.

"You just would meet him and you would like him. You couldn't help from liking him. . . . He could have borrowed money from me anytime, but he never asked me," said Brin.

"What was Elana like?" Bob Hirsh was sure of his witness here. A skilled trial attorney never asks a question like this unless he is confident of the answer.

"Well, Elana was, in my opinion, a very status-conscious, materialistic type of person that always seemed to be the center of attention no matter what was going on. . . . She would more or less call the shots, but I never found any problems with them

when they were together, if that's what you're trying to refer
to."

Like some of the other witnesses, Brin had a single anecdote to tell that reflected adversely on Elana.

"Once we were having a party at my home for a friend, an
entertainer who was appearing here in Phoenix. And I introduced this entertainer and I said, 'This would be a good man
for you to know, because maybe you could get a job at B. B.
Singer's. He runs B. B. Singer's." And then before anybody
could say anything, Elana spoke up and said, 'Well, he doesn't.
My brother runs B. B. Singer's.' I personally felt very embarrassed for Steve."

Only one of the defense witnesses seems to have been able
to cross both lines and be a character witness for his friend
Steve and yet display affection for Elana. He was the person
who had known the Steinbergs for the longest time. Paul Ackerman had been in Steve's platoon in the National Guard back
in Chicago, and the two families had socialized for fifteen years.
Ackerman's wife had been depressed after the murder and was
still not up to par. Hirsh had approached her to be a witness for
Steve, but she told him she couldn't testify. "I would just fall
apart," she said. She was still grieving for Elana and the little
girls. The Ackermans were the only social friends of the Steinbergs who were not Jewish. They are also the only couple who
have kept in touch with the little girls over the years since
Elana's death. Apparently there was something inhibiting about
the friendships of the rest of the Scottsdale circle that would
not permit them to make an unsolicited comment at the trial
like that of Paul Ackerman: "I liked Elana very much."

A few of the defense witnesses on these two days agreed to
talk to me about how they felt about the trial in retrospect. The
rest did not wish to discuss it. I can understand how they felt
—they had been caught in a difficult dilemma. None of them
knew just how to act when one of their friends killed his spouse.
Unfortunately, they were being forced to choose sides. One man
expressed his feelings about his motivation in helping Steve.

"Well, you have a friend and you just stay with him. You
don't abandon him. I really like him. He had this special quality

that made people like him. And you don't want your friend to go to the electric chair. It's natural to help. About Elana? She really wasn't bad. It just sounded that way because no one asked the right questions. I'm sorry now that it looks like I said bad things about her. I really didn't know her that well, and she was no different from anyone else. She was a typical Jewish American Princess—I'm Jewish, you know, and my wife is a princess, what's so terrible about that?"

"Did the group meetings make a difference to you—that there were other people doing the same thing?" I asked him.

"I went to two of the meetings beforehand. It was just like everybody was just zonked up with the spirit of it or something. We were all just exhilarated. There were so many lawyers there and all of their secretaries, and it was exciting. You're right about the group psychology. It was a group project."

He would do it again, he told me, but the next time he would have more insight into what was going on.

"Would I do it again all over? I would help a friend by being a character witness for him, of course. But I think I would be more sophisticated now about anything else I'd say. I would question, 'Hey, what's the big picture here?' But you never ever expect something like this to happen to you or one of your friends, and I don't ever expect to be in that position again. I don't really feel good about it."

The defense attorneys had arranged a masterful witness sequence. In between the Scottsdale friends, whose life-style seemed to baffle the jurors, Hirsh called three humbler witnesses. They were former employees of the Derby, which, like the other restaurants, had come to an abrupt end two months after Elana was killed. They all liked Steve. The bar manager said that Steve was a workaholic. The bookkeeper, somewhat given to exaggeration, said Steve worked "twenty-four hours a day." Mitchell Singer was a bear to work for, they said, and Steve had to jump and do what Mitch said. No one was critical of Elana, but Hirsh wanted the jurors to know that she called her husband at work a lot.

"How many times a day would she call him?" This was an important point with Bob Hirsh, and he asked it of everyone.

One answered, "Five times a day." The bookkeeper said it was twenty-five times.

The head chef said he loved Steve "like a brother." Afterward, this man told me that he thought a lot of Elana, too. "She was always interested in everybody's family, a really classy girl." He seemed surprised that no one had asked him about Elana at the trial. "I would have told them if anybody had asked me," he wanted me to know.

That day of the trial, February 10, 1982, was not a day when anyone wanted to hear anything good about Elana Steinberg. Nor was the next day.

CHAPTER NINETEEN

MURPHY'S LAW

M urphy's Law was in operation for the State of Arizona in this trial—if anything could go wrong, it did; if anything would be misunderstood or underinvestigated, it was. But of course in a trial there is another way to look at Murphy's Law. For Steven Steinberg, everything was going right.

The prosecution's next problem was that one of the state's psychiatrists, the heart of Jeff Hotham's rebuttal, had planned a ski trip to Vail. Hotham's original choice for a psychiatrist was seriously ill, and the prosecutor had substituted Howard Gray, an ambitious and businesslike doctor who was the medical director of a private psychiatric hospital in Phoenix. His background was not as public as that of Martin Blinder, but he had fifteen years of solid and prestigious private hospital practice. Gray had done forensic work for years, but he was tailing off now because his private practice was booming—*State v. Steinberg* was to be one of Gray's last court cases. The ski trip was set to begin before Gray would have testified in his normal spot, and the psychiatrist had no intention of missing Vail. Dr. Gray would simply have to be accommodated earlier or Hotham would have to go without his services. Normally, having to call a witness "out of order" is not a terrible blow for a lawyer in a trial. It often happens, particularly with expert witnesses from out of town and with doctors. It is always better if this can be avoided. The flow is disturbed. In some instances it can be a disaster. The timing that was finally worked out for Dr. Gray was particularly bad because he had to be squeezed into Bob Hirsh's series of witnesses on one of those days when Elana Steinberg was taking a battering from her dear, close friends in the courtroom. Gray's appearance on this devastating day made it seem to some of the jurors as if he were actually a witness for Robert Hirsh. Some of the jurors thought he had crossed over. Of course, Judge Riddel announced that Gray was actually a witness for the prosecution, but that didn't solve the problem. By the time the dust had settled, no one on the jury was exactly positive who the doctor worked for. It was bad luck, or good luck depending which perspective you were taking.

The state had two psychiatrists, Gray and Michael Cleary. They were both a disappointment to the prosecutor. He was particularly chagrined at the performance of Gray. The doctor droned and lacked enthusiasm; he obviously wanted to leave as quickly as was decent. Neither of Hotham's psychiatrists had any verve or enthusiasm in their testimony. They were a poor match for the showmanship of the psychiatrist from San Francisco as he told his stories of frustrated sex and the meddling mother-in-law, the valve on the pressure cooker and the beef brisket. The state's psychiatrists didn't tell any little stories; they were restrained and, frankly, dull.

The key to neutralizing Dr. Gray and Jeff Hotham's second expert, Michael Cleary, was that they were both immobilized by their belief in the diagnostic labels of their profession. To doubt any printed diagnosis was almost like doubting psychiatry itself. They had to acknowledge that there was such a thing as "dissociative reaction," even though neither man had ever seen a case in actual practice. The diagnosis was listed in the psychiatrists' bible, that list of every diagnosis numbered and put in neat categories, called the *Diagnostic and Statistical Manual of Mental Disorders,* or *DSM* for short. When something was listed there, it became an element of their faith. Gray said he had never seen a dissociative reaction in all of his years of practice and he was suspicious of it because of the possibility of malingering, or faking. Not only that, he had little or no evidence upon which he could tell what happened on that night nine months earlier.

"I can't form an opinion about his state of mind because there is no objective evidence for any condition—the interview was the sole technique that was available and I did not think I could look back in the past," he said. "If he is telling the truth, then it is possible he was experiencing a dissociative disorder, but I have no way of determining whether he is telling the truth or not."

Hirsh put "truthfulness" back in the case after he had taken it out earlier in the state's case—now, truthfulness was the key ingredient to his defense. "And it's a fact, sir, that you simply had no evidence that caused you to believe that Steve Steinberg was not telling the truth? That's a fact, isn't it?" The defense attorney raised his voice, advancing on Gray in the witness box.

"Yes."

It was disappointing, weak. Hotham was disturbed, because he had expected more from Gray. It seemed almost as if he were not interested. Worst of all, the jury was confused— why was Gray's testimony, which should have been so important, sandwiched in between Bob Hirsh's witnesses against Elana?

The gods were smiling on Steven Steinberg throughout this trial, and luck rolled again when Michael Benchoff received a telephone call one evening in the middle of the case. The caller was Jean Marie Tims, the wife of an Arizona corporation commissioner, who had lived next door to the Steinbergs three years before the murder. She offered herself as a volunteer. Mrs. Tims told Benchoff that she wanted to be a witness and made an appointment to see him the next morning to discuss it.

There were technical problems with inserting her in the

trial. Mrs. Tims's name had not appeared on the witness lists that had been exchanged by the prosecutor and the defense attorneys before the trial, and the state had never heard of her.

In Arizona the rules of criminal procedure call for a wide range of what is known as "discovery," unusual in criminal law. There is supposed to be a mutual exchange of witnesses and exhibits and an opportunity for interviews before the trial; no one is to be caught by surprise. It was perfectly possible that the judge would decide to preclude Mrs. Tims from testifying if Hotham raised an objection to it; at the very least the prosecutor could demand sufficient time to have a meaningful interview with the belated witness, perhaps even a postponement for a day. No objection appears on the trial record. The prosecutor agreed to let Mrs. Tims testify. Unfortunately, Hotham never talked to Mrs. Tims before she stepped on the witness stand and he had no idea what she was to say.

The houses on the cul-de-sac where the Steinbergs lived had little privacy. The cul-de-sac was a small tight circle with pie-shaped lots; the fronts of the houses were virtually on the sidewalk. The neighbors were very, very close. As far as Jean Marie Tims was concerned, she was entirely too close to Elana Steinberg. Mrs. Tims said that she "liked them both" but then pulled out all the stops. According to this neighbor, Elana was "not very nice to Steve." She described Elana Steinberg as very domineering. While Steve was affectionate and loving, the affection was never returned. Most of the problems between Mrs. Tims and Elana involved the Timses' maids, said Mrs. Tims. "From time to time Elana would hire them to baby-sit so that she could go to the restaurant and go out and do things. And she had a tone of voice with them that definitely let them know what their place was."

According to Mrs. Tims, Elana's voice was particularly irritating. She had a high-pitched and shrill voice and was a compulsive talker, said Mrs. Tims. She would yell, "Steven, answer the door," "Get me something to drink," or "Do this" or "Do that." When Steve would come over to talk to the Timses when they were playing Ping-Pong in the garage, Elana would scream, "Steven, have you brought the bread home?"

"If he was cleaning out the pool, he wasn't doing it right. If he was carrying out the garbage, he made a mess. I didn't hear him raise his voice to her. The most he would say was 'I can hear you' when she was yelling and he was just a couple feet away in the backyard.

"I said to my husband, 'I really don't know how Steve manages to work in the store all day and then go home to what he goes home to at night.' "

The vehemence and the tone of voice that Jean Tims used in her testimony was damning. She played the parts, first mimicking Elana's voice and then Steve's. Some trial observers saw her as overacting—some as a "nosy neighbor." But the jurors bought it totally. Of all the defense witnesses Jean Tims was probably the most emphatic about what was what at the Steinbergs' house. There was no cross-examination, but that was probably for the best. Mrs. Tims was obviously dug-in and excited, and further questions would only intensify her angry description of Elana Steinberg.

Her testimony has a harsh and bitter note, even on the pages of the trial transcript. When I talked to Mrs. Tims about it four years later, her feelings hadn't changed much. She believes that she had enormous impact in the trial, and she is proud of it. "Why did I do it? The papers were so vicious to Steve the first day. I read it and I said, 'I've got to do something to help him.' I didn't want to hurt my husband politically, but he said I could do it if I was strong enough."

I was mystified by her reference to the news stories about the trial. The reporting was low-key and factual, but perhaps Mrs. Tims read something in there that I couldn't see. She told me she had a hard time finding Steinberg's lawyers, but she located Benchoff and saw him the next morning. He must have thought he had a real bonanza.

She was amazed that she was able to talk so freely, without interruption, she said. "I never talked to the prosecutor, and I just thought, and Mike said, 'Now he'll object to this,' or 'We won't get this in.' But he never did, he just let me ramble on, and I never expected that to happen. But it was all true. You know, I thought that Steve would get the death penalty, I really didn't think that he would just walk away. I don't know exactly what I thought would happen, but not that, either."

There was something significant that Hotham could have done. Jean Tims by no means exemplified the feelings of the rest of the neighbors on Via de Luz. It would not have been hard for the prosecutor to find a witness to testify on rebuttal who didn't share her feelings about Elana Steinberg. I talked to one of them who cried when she remembered Elana.

Three years before the murder, the Timses had sold their house on Via de Luz to a young couple from India. They, not the Timses, had been living there during the critical time period. I drove up to the house one sizzling summer day in August. I didn't know what kind of reception I would receive. For all I knew of the neighbors on Via de Luz, Jean Tims was the rule, not the exception. That was not what I found, and particularly not from Pawan Nandam. She told me she missed Elana, even now.

"I miss Elana. I think about her all the time," she told me. "She and I would talk every day, take turns picking up the children. She was very nice to me and to them, and that is comforting when you are in a strange country. Elana said to me, 'I'm so glad you came to live here. You're so much nicer than the other people who lived here used to be. He always looked at us as though we were way beneath him.' "

I told her generally how harsh everyone had been to Elana at the trial—how she was portrayed as a materialistic and nagging woman. Pawan saw her differently.

"Well, let's put it this way. In every marriage, and this is true in India just as it is here, there is one person who is the boss, the more aggressive person. And that's the way Elana was. And you know when the more aggressive person is the wife, people here as well as people in India say she is bossy. If it were the man, no one would think anything about it. Elana had the habit of just speaking out; she always said exactly what she thought, although sometimes it might not have been the right time for that. You know, some people just can't cope with that kind of outspokenness.

"A Jewish couple moved in down the street, and I told her, 'Elana, don't worry about me. I would think that you would want to go and be friends with her,' because they really were the only Jewish couple on the street then. And Elana hugged me and said, 'No, I like you the best.' "

Everyone talked about the house, and Pawan told me about it right away. "You would come home from there and think, 'I've got to clean up or something,' because your own house would look so bad in contrast."

The worst of all was what happened to the little girls, she told me. "I sometimes see them at the school, those dear little things. Elana was very, very nice to my children, and would take them places with her and pick them up at the school—a good neighbor."

It would have been interesting to see the effect of Pawan as a rebuttal witness as she talked about her neighbor with misting eyes, a total departure from the strong-voiced, angry Jean Marie Tims. But the jurors were not to see that, nor did they ever learn that there was any other point of view about Elana Steinberg in the neighborhood.

Another surprise witness appeared after the trial had started—June Belva Donavan, who owned a furniture store in Phoenix. Mrs. Donavan actually didn't know Steven Steinberg, but she said that she had seen him once in 1975, six years before the murder, and she had observed Elana "shouting at him with a very shrill voice." Apparently she was not a character witness for Steve, because she didn't know him—she was a witness *against* Elana, the victim, a category for which the law makes no provision in a murder trial. The tonal quality of Elana's voice was very disturbing to Mrs. Donavan, and Bob Hirsh wanted the jury to know about Elana's voice—that was important to the defense strategy for some reason. "How did Elana talk to you?" Hirsh asked.

"When she called me she was never satisfied with what she got, and she would call me and start to scream on the phone. And I use the expression 'scream' because her voice was a high pitch, and she always came across like she was angry with you. I tried to explain to her that if there was anything wrong we would take care of it, but she would not listen, and she would just scream on the phone and go on and on."

"Did you ever argue with her?" Hirsh asked.

"I would take the phone and just hold it out and let her go on. And I could hear the voice coming out of the phone, and every once in a while I would say, 'Yes, Elana,' and then I'd just hold it back."

"Did you think she was being unjust about your furniture?"

"There was nothing really wrong with it. She just got my nerves on absolute edge. I could not deal with her."

Why did she come in? The record is silent on that. It is surprising that the prosecutor did not object to the late appearance of Mrs. Donavan or object to the relevance or timeliness of the testimony. A tradesperson who did not like a customer who was later murdered would seem totally out of line—should the prosecutor go out and find tradespeople who had liked the dead woman? By now the trial had turned itself inside out—it was as if the caption on the indictment should have been changed to *State of Arizona* v. *Elana Steinberg, et al.,* with the *et al.* being Elana's parents.

These two painful days of *State* v. *Elana Steinberg* finally wound to an end with another character witness, a priest named Anthony Beauchamp, who was the former pastor of the Greek Orthodox church in Phoenix. Beauchamp told the jury that he had met Steven Steinberg when he ate at B. B. Singer's with a parishioner. He had responded immediately to Steve's personality when he came to the table.

"As a priest, when I'm served in restaurants I appreciate the personal touch in one who works with people. And that's how the relationship developed between Steve and I, and that is why I visited the restaurant often. He called me 'Rabbi Anthony.' And the ladies knew who I was when I called and said, 'Reserve a table for three o'clock for Rabbi Anthony.'"

The priest testified that he came frequently after that to eat at B. B. Singer's, all the way from Scottsdale to Central Avenue, and all because of Steve's charisma.

"And Steve would say, 'Gee, rabbi, I'd love to sit with you but I'm busy, I hope you understand.' And then he would still come back to see if everything was okay. He was starting to make his own bread, and he brought it to me to taste before he gave it to the customers. 'We're trying something new, father. Give me your opinion.'

Father Beauchamp said that he had been a volunteer working with jail inmates in a work furlough program, and that he could always call on Steve to get jobs for the probationers at B. B. Singer's. "Steve would provide employment for anybody I recommended to him." The day that Steinberg was arrested he called Father Beauchamp, and the priest went to the jail to see him.

"There was a glass separator—I was on one side and he was on the other. And he was crying constantly. He said, 'Father, I don't believe what happened to Elana. I didn't do it. I don't know what happened.' And he was reaching with his hands out on the windowpane, and grief-stricken. A tragedy had beset him."

Father Beauchamp talks in poetical form. "Finally he put his arms down and was just sobbing and sobbing and saying, 'Father, father, help me.'

"It is not a Steve Steinberg act. It is not the Steve I know or I wouldn't be here today and I wouldn't still love him and respect him."

Tom Fitzpatrick, the columnist for the *Arizona Republic*, wrote, "When Father Beauchamp walked past the defendant on his way out of the courtroom he reached his hands out to him and embraced him. These things are not lost on juries."

When I began to look for Father Beauchamp, I had a shock. His church had disappeared, replaced by a supermarket —the congregation had moved far to the north. Eventually, I found him. He was living in an Eastern city and working in a sectarian job now. It was easy to see why Anthony Beauchamp made such a forceful witness—he was articulate and personable, with a deep, rich baritone. He wanted me to know that he hadn't been prepped by the defense attorneys for the trial.

"The papers wrote it up afterward as though I was trying to wear my clerical clothes to give bigger emphasis to the fact that I was a priest, but that is not so. I always wore them, and that is the way I would always talk. I met with the defense attorneys when I got off the plane, but they didn't work with me at all, they just said, 'Just answer and be yourself.' Steve was a great guy—warm, friendly, full of energy. Like most Mediterranean and Jewish types, he was what I would call a 'toucher,' you know, they tend to touch each other, talk a lot, and are very demonstrative, and he was like that. I would have liked to have been a friend of his, but it was really more of a business acquaintance. I really didn't know much about his personal life, and I never heard him talk about his wife. I just said what I knew and experienced, and I don't know whether he was guilty or innocent, or whether she was guilty or innocent."

I asked him what he meant by that intriguing comment, "whether she was guilty." He was mysterious.

"There is an old Arabic proverb—I am Lebanese, you know—and that is, 'We planted the ifs, but they didn't grow.' " I don't know what he meant by that.

A priest in clerical garb is something to be cherished. He is impervious to cross-examination: it would make the opposing attorney look foolish to ask any searching questions. Father Beauchamp's testimony was interesting because it shows how much Steven Steinberg must have enjoyed his role, center stage, as the host, the owner, the baker of bread, the provider of jobs, the greeter at the restaurant that Mitchell Singer said had never had a month in the black since it opened.

The defense was almost completed; there was only one witness left, and that was Steven Steinberg himself, scheduled for the next day. Two friends of Steve's in Chicago were standing by to come to Phoenix, but they were called by the defense and told confidently, "You don't have to come. Everything's going so well we won't need you." Judge Riddel told the jury at the close of the day that they had not many days longer to serve: "We hope to have this to you by next Wednesday," said the judge. The trial was moving at a swift pace.

Steve's defense witnesses could go home now: Jean Marie Tims and the furniture store owner, the three Singer's restaurant employees, and, of course, those very dear, close friends of Elana Steinberg's who had needed no subpoenas.

CHAPTER TWENTY

NOW, WE'RE NOT GOING TO CRY, ARE WE?

Steven Steinberg is a big man, and that was a surprise. When Dr. Blinder and Dr. Holmes told the story of Steve Steinberg's life they left the image of a man who was short and slight, the kind of person who would be henpecked and underpaid at work, easy to push around—in short, a wimp. But Steven Steinberg is six feet tall and well-built. There must have been a lot of power behind those stabs, and Elana didn't have much of a chance to fight him off. Jail had had one beneficial effect. Steve was puffy and out of shape before all this happened, but he had lost weight and looked fit in his new clothes.

Another surprise was how much this man cried. At various times during the trial he wept uncontrollably, putting his head down on the counsel table, his shoulders shaking. There were always tears in his eyes; the *Republic* columnist said that he had "a hangdog look." Bob Hirsh had organized the witness list masterfully, almost as if it were a symphony or a tone poem. If Steven Steinberg were an instrument in this musical work it would be a violin or perhaps a harp with a glissando passage fading off sweetly across the room in inexpressible sadness. Some of the jurors wept with Steve, mingling their tears with his. His lawyer took him through the direct examination quietly, carefully, as one would an invalid.

Q. And when did you and Elana get married?
A. We got married May 29, 1966.
Q. All right, and you had a big wedding, didn't you?
A. Yes.
Q. With Barney and Edith and your mother and Dave Goodman?
A. Yes.
Q. And they all helped throw the wedding, did they not?
A. Yes—my parents helped pay for it.
Q. And we're not going to cry. We're going to get through this, all right?

Hirsh's client was crying. There was something about paying for that wedding that was sensitive still.

All of the awful things that could have been said about Elana Steinberg and her family had already been said. They had been said by Martin Blinder and Donald Holmes in the language of the doctors. If the man on trial had ever had to say these things about his wife and her family in the face of the jury, would his image have been tarnished just a bit? It is impossible to know. Steve Steinberg had only to take the high road. At the soft urging of his lawyer, he talked about his life with Elana.

"As far as I knew it was a good marriage. It was based on love, I thought, but I guess when I look at it now it was based on money a lot. As long as I could provide a lot of money we were happy. I was happy. We had nice things. I always wore nice clothes. We drove nice cars and I was happy and I believe Elana was happy. . . .

"I don't want to keep saying things or putting Elana down,

because we had a lot of fun. I mean, she was a good mother. She kept a beautiful home. When we would go out we always had fun. We never argued once we left our home. I didn't know I was unhappy or that there was anything wrong."

"You didn't know?" Bob Hirsh is incredulous that anyone could be happy living with Elana. "No, I didn't. I guess I just didn't want to admit anything wrong. We never discussed anything. Elana and I did not talk to each other, we talked at each other. There was never a discussion. We didn't know how, I guess." Steve would handle things differently now that his eyes were open, he said. "If Elana was here today, maybe we could talk."

Steven Steinberg had said a lot of things about the Singers to his psychiatrists and they had dutifully repeated them all, but when the defendant himself was testifying it was a love feast. Steve was always happy when he was with his father-in-law, Barney; he felt "sorry" for Mitchell. He didn't even have a bad word to say for his mother-in-law despite what he'd said to his doctors about Edith. A little petulance crept into his testimony only once, when he talked about Mitchell making money and not sharing it with him. "He couldn't give me a twenty-five-dollar raise when he was buying his Mercedes," he said bitterly. Otherwise it was hard to believe that this was the same man who had filled the psychiatrists' ears with horror stories about his marriage.

Direct examination was short, but Bob Hirsh wanted Steve's gambling out in the open; he wanted him to make a public confession. "I am a gambler, I admit it." Hirsh's client told of betting sums that he couldn't even estimate, maybe "a hundred thousand dollars" or maybe "ten million dollars, I couldn't dispute it, I have no idea." Steve bet two thousand dollars on single football games; he lost ten thousand dollars on the Super Bowl in 1980. The bets escalated from hundreds to thousands, he told the jury. At the end the man who had had so much cash was reduced to pitiful handouts. On the day of Elana's murder, he was scrounging spot cash from his wife. He explained his financial situation on the day of Elana's death to the jury.

"I borrowed five dollars from Elana for gas but I only put three dollars in the car so that I could have telephone change because I had to call some banks in the hopes that I could get a loan and have the money on the 28th and be able to pay some of the interest on the loans that were out or coming due within the next week. . . . I'd been scared before, so it wasn't anything new. But as the night progressed I'm sure I was nervous because I knew that I had to meet with George Morrison at the Continental Bank the next day and see if I could get another ten-thousand-dollar loan."

Steinberg, now weeping copiously, told the jury that he couldn't tell his Elana or any of his family at the bar mitzvah about his problems because "they would think I was a failure." He might be baring all about his gambling in Phoenix, but he was notably reticent about his gambling in Chicago.

"Well, in Chicago I would just go to a racetrack sometimes for dinner in a social situation with my wife, or play poker every once in a while, or sometimes I would play parlay cards, a two-dollar card—nothing extensive."

The *Arizona Republic* columnist in a dramatic column described Steinberg testifying about his wife's death. "His face was ashen and he seemed only inches away from total collapse" —there was the "terrible pain in his eyes." At that moment, wrote Tom Fitzpatrick, several jurors and half of the courtroom were in tears as well; for some reason hearing about the bushy-haired strangers always made them weep.

The prosecutor's strategy for Steinberg's cross-examination was hard to figure. Asking about the killing itself was blocked by the brick wall of Steinberg's purported amnesia and the hallucination. He didn't remember hiding the knife, opening the dresser drawer, or throwing the underwear on the floor; all he remembered was the men with the plastic gloves.

"Every time I close my eyes in my cell at night I see those bushy-haired men, I'm telling you, I saw them," Steinberg said with tears in his eyes. At least two jurors began to cry again. Frustrated, the prosecutor's next plan was to try to show that Steinberg's financial bind was not as bad as he thought and that he could have gotten money from his family or Elana's family if he had just looked around. The reason for this is obscure; Hotham told me afterward that he didn't want to dwell on the gambling debts too much for fear that the jury would sympathize with the defendant—"the poor guy, he had all these gambling debts and naturally he snapped, anybody would snap."

No one said anything about the fact that with Elana dead, Steve's finances would momentarily brighten: he would have the CDs that Elana had so carefully protected, and have the house, the jewelry, and some small insurance policies on Elana's life. It was a strange performance. The most critical omission was that the prosecutor never mentioned the earlier bushy-haired pair back in Des Plaines, the six burglaries at B. B. Singer's, the man with the gun on the chopper, the jewelry that was taken on the vacation trip with the Goldfarbs from the MGM Grand in Reno, the missing diamond watch, and all the other strange burglaries and robberies. Steve had received a free pass—it was a miracle.

"Edith, what's going on in there is bad. You've got to do something. They keep talking about how terrible Elana was and how much she spent on her credit cards," wailed a family friend on the telephone.

It was February 12, 1982, and this morning Tom Fitzpatrick's column in the *Republic* was headlined "Witnesses for Steinberg Paint Portrait of Wife as Free-Spending Shrew." Edith Singer was still not functioning well at the time of the trial and she hadn't been briefed on the defense strategy, but she was becoming aware of what was happening to her daughter's memory in Judge Riddel's courtroom. Edith thought she should do something, but she didn't know what to do. It was the day that she and Barney were scheduled to testify. When she got to court, Edith cornered Frank Hylton. "Frank, what's this about Elana's credit cards in the paper? What does it mean? What's wrong with them? When I get in there, what should I say?"

Hylton tried to calm her. "There's nothing out of the ordinary. They're just normal credit cards, Edith. They're just like my own wife's, don't worry."

Edith cried and hung on Hotham's arm before they went into the courtroom. "What will I say?" The prosecutor decided to meet the issue that was worrying Elana's mother head-on, at the beginning of her testimony.

Edith was still upset, but it was time for her to walk into the courtroom. The Scottsdale detective's reassurance wasn't what he really thought—Hylton could tell that things were going wrong in this trial. No one was talking about it, and Frank believed that it was out of his hands. It was obvious that there had been an enormous shift at trial. Everything was one-sided now. Bob Hirsh seemed to roam the courtroom at will, striding, talking, bursting in with speaking objections, and above all masterfully drawing out his own witnesses so that they made no false steps. The prosecutor's cross-examination of all the defense witnesses had seemed weak, almost ineffectual. He had scored no points that Hylton could see. Now, in his direct examination of Elana's mother, the prosecutor was trying to mend the damage done by the tales of Elana's shopping, rather than concentrating on Edith's grief.

"Edith, your daughter has been portrayed as a professional shopper. Do you think that term applies to her?" Hotham asked.

"Well, I'll be honest with you—I don't even know what a professional shopper is. Sometimes she'd meet me for coffee and we would go into Bullock's or Goldwater's and look around and we would be gone for a few hours and then she would go her way and I went my way. Sometimes we would buy something and sometimes we'd just look."

Hotham kept at it. "Was Elana a thrifty shopper?" The prosecutor had apparently abandoned his own case and given in to the dynamics of Hirsh's try-the-victim defense. He was trying to justify Elana's purported shopping as "looking for a bargain"—and this strategy was not exactly endearing Edith Singer to the stern-faced jurors. They had wept over and over again with Steven Steinberg when he told about the bushy-haired men and the plastic gloves, but they had turned to stone for the dead woman's mother. Edith Singer didn't know that what she was saying was putting icing on the cake. She perceived that there was a problem, but she didn't know what it was or how to handle it.

"Oh definitely, she'd look for bargains. If Traci needed a dress, she'd go from Goldwater's to Diamond's, you know, to see if she could get a better buy here or there. I do the same. That's how we are. . . . "

"Did Elana spend extravagantly when Steve was out of work?" asked Hotham. "We've had people say that here—was it true?"

"No way. She never spent with extravagance, even before. If her charge was overrun, she wouldn't buy anything. She just wouldn't," Edith said eagerly.

This was a chance to spike the credit-card story, which she still didn't understand.

Her daughter was a good wife, Edith said, as the jury looked on coldly. "She built him up, Steve, when he was out of work she would say to friends, 'He's going to sell commercial property or maybe go back to the pool and patio business again. I have confidence in him.' Elana would never, never put him down. She loved him. Only one time I heard her criticize him and that was when he came back from Vegas and she said 'Ma, he lost everything.' "

Bob Hirsh came in soft as a kitten. The slashing angry ridicule that he reserved for some of the state's witnesses was muted. He handled the bereaved mother with great solicitude. There weren't any points to be made by trashing Edith Singer to her face. That had already been done by the psychiatrists in their part of the defense. Hirsh wanted the jury to see that he had sensitivities, too—that he wasn't trampling on the victim's mother.

"We've met before and I've called you Edie, right?" Edith nods.

"And you've called me Bob?"

"Right."

"Can I call you Edie today like I have in the past?" Ever polite and smiling, Edith said, "Of course."

"Edie, remember once when we talked you gave me a characterization of her, remember how you described Elana? I think it was a JAP—your characterization. You said she was a Jewish American Princess?"

"If that's what you think."

"No, ma'am. You remember you told me when I asked you what Elana was like?"

"She was my princess, she was my doll. She was my beauty. She was my whole life."

Bob Hirsh was not satisfied. He really *wanted* this phrase.

"And you saw her that way, the Jewish American Princess?"

"No. I saw her as the most beautiful daughter in the whole world."

Edith was sobbing, and Bob Hirsh wanted it ended right then, because Edith Singer's tears, once begun, might never end. "Thank you very much, ma'am."

After the Steinberg trial, Bob Hirsh told me that when he heard Edith Singer on the witness stand he knew the trial was over. "She was one of those witnesses that has to volunteer, it's hard to control them. She wanted to talk about the credit cards and all, and that just made it worse." He believed that it was a terrible mistake to call Edith and Barney on rebuttal, rather than in the prosecutor's case in chief.

The Singers should have been strong witnesses, because their grief was so overwhelming. Edith never really recovered; it was as if she were killed that night too. Elana's mother seemed silly and frivolous when she talked about the shopping; the jury couldn't understand why she was doing it. It wasn't a good idea for her to touch on this subject, but she had read the newspapers and she had heard the warnings from her friends. Edith was trying to take things in hand herself, and she didn't have the skills to do it. It would have helped if Barney and Edith could have testified about their son-in-law by proxy, just as he did about them. Elana's parents could have used someone like Martin Blinder to put their thoughts into polished words, or someone to write a medical report that told a different story. But it was too late for that; the damage had been done already and it couldn't be repaired.

After she was finished, Edith asked humbly if she could

stay in the courtroom for Barney's testimony. There was no objection. The prosecutor had made some peculiar choices for Barney's testimony. He tried to say once, without much success, that he had seen Steve lose his temper. He would jump on a salesman if he didn't like what he said, Barney said, and the salesman would get scared and run out of the restaurant. Barney wasn't very convincing. On cross-examination, he was destroyed.

"When I interviewed you, sir, and asked you to tell me about those times Steve was violent, you told me the only time you knew about was at the restaurant when some cowboy insulted a little girl, isn't that right, sir?"

"Yeah, that's right."

"And you said it was justified, that you might have done the same thing yourself, right?"

"It's possible," Barney admitted. "But I told you he does get violent once in a while, he does."

At this point one of the jurors turned to another and smiled, Frank Hylton told me, and wrote something on his pad. Hylton didn't think it was a good omen.

All of the burglaries and robberies that had occurred were left untouched by the prosecutor, although the Singers had described them all to Jeff Hotham—the money missing from the cash registers, the holdup in the pool store, the stolen jewelry, and all of the strange tales of assaults that had followed Steve. Hotham was using none of this. He told Barney and Edith that he "couldn't get it in." They wondered, but they were quiet.

Edith Singer had had an artificial heart valve replacement two years before the murder, and she is frail and tires easily. When they got home from court, Barney called their doctor. He put Edith in Scottsdale Hospital for a few days, because the strain was getting intense. Barney brooded at home in silence. He had recognized the hostility in the courtroom for what it was. The Singers were alone.

A reporter for one of the local papers told me that it was pretty sad to see the Singers at the trial. He came away, he said, with the impression that they simply were not shaken too much, that they could forgive and forget the son-in-law who "treated Edie like a queen," as Hirsh had said. After the trial was over, when controversy was swirling in Scottsdale, the reporter went out to the Singer house for a follow-up story. "It was gut-wrenching," he told me. "That raw grief didn't come out, not at all, in court."

Edith Singer told me that there was one thing she really regrets about her testimony that day. It was when the defense attorney asked if he could call her "Edie" and she had agreed.

"I wasn't thinking 'all right,' " she told me. "I wanted to scream, 'Not while you are sitting next to that murderer who killed my darling.' I wish I had done that. I wanted to."

In retrospect, the Singers could have used a lawyer. There are some states, one or two, that permit the victim, or the victim's family, to hire an attorney to sit in and assist the prosecution. It would have the potential for more confusion, but there are occasions when the victim's interests are not being adequately represented in a criminal trial.

A friend in court would have helped Barney and Edith Singer, because they were not up to coping with everything that was said about them and their daughter, and the prosecutor was not responding adequately to defuse it. With all the hurt that this savaging in the courtroom brought upon his family, Elana's parents and her two little girls, it would have been understandable for them to have some kind of legal representation, but that's not the way the system works in Arizona.

The use of the Jewish American Princess phrase in the trial was meant to be inflammatory. In essence, Bob Hirsh's defense said, "See what she is like, that's what Jewish women are like, that's what Jewish men have to put up with, no wonder the guy went bananas."

Ironically, as I found out later, this jury did not have a clue as to what the words were supposed to mean. Unless you grew up in Cleveland or New York or somewhere else "back East," you would never hear the phrase in Arizona. There has never been a large Jewish population living there, because the state was not an area of first settlement for immigrants from Europe. The folklore and the Yiddish phrases that are part of

the Jewish big-city culture are just not widely known in Phoenix. This is cowboy country, Bible belt, senior citizens. If you
said the words *Marjorie Morningstar* or *Goodbye, Columbus,*
you would draw a blank every time. Arizonans would catch the
word "Jewish" but not much else. If the phrase was meant to
be a gently humorous comment, as Jewish humor generally is,
it misfired in this trial—the jury didn't see it that way.

CHAPTER TWENTY-ONE

CALL IN THE STARGAZERS

I'm not sure who else you can call—psychiatrists are the experts of the time. Back 2000 years ago they could call in the stargazers.

—SCOTTSDALE DAILY PROGRESS, *April 7, 1982*

It was ending. The big punch for the state at the finish was intended to be Hotham's two psychiatrists, back to back for maximum effect, just as Bob Hirsh had done with Holmes and Blinder. The traditional "battle of the experts" is one of the least attractive aspects of the insanity defense, an embarrassment to some psychiatrists. There are usually equal numbers of forensics on each side—numbers are supposed to be important. So when Dr. Gray went skiing and testified on that black day for Jeff Hotham, instead of at the end of the trial, it hurt. It made it seem as if the state couldn't find as many doctors for the battle as the defense could.

This was expensive time. The lengthy interview before trial, the trip to Phoenix for the trial, all the preparation—the whole process can add up to thousands of dollars. Despite the implication that the state was the only party to have "paid guys," the Steinberg insanity defense effort was costly indeed.

Michael Cleary, Jeff Hotham's chief forensic psychiatrist, was an old hand at the battle of the experts. Dr. Cleary is a tall handsome Irishman with a thick brogue, educated in Dublin.

He had the deepest forensic background of all of the doctors. Menninger-trained, Dr. Cleary had spent years as the director of the maximum security facility at the Arizona State Hospital. He has worked with prisoners for years in a forensic setting. He hadn't backed down when he was interviewed before the trial by Hirsh and Benchoff, but he has a quick temper, and it shows.

Like Howard Gray, Cleary was caught by the necessity to accept that something called "dissociative reaction" exists, despite its skimpy treatment in *DSM* and the lack of objective techniques for its diagnosis. Obviously, he regards dissociative reaction with skepticism. Cleary said that in his years as director of Arizona's state mental hospital and in twenty years of practice, he had never personally seen a patient with that diagnosis. He had reviewed the records of the short-term-care center, the county hospital, and found only three diagnosed cases of dissociation in 2,600 admissions—a one-in-nine-hundred ratio.

"When I see that diagnosis advanced in homicide cases, which is usually where you see it, I look very carefully to see if the individual had any past episodes that would give it credence, and I've never found any," the doctor said in his rich Irish voice.

He found no support for such a rare diagnosis in Steve Steinberg, Cleary told the jury. "His amnesia pattern was wrong, because he said he remembered some things, and not others. His past history was negative; he did some reality-oriented things that night that contradicted an altered state of consciousness. I found him to have no psychiatric illness." Hotham's direct examination was strong, well organized. He felt good about it.

Cross-examination of Dr. Gray was really just the dress rehearsal for Bob Hirsh's furious attack now on Michael Cleary. Hirsh's insults were contagious, and they rubbed off on some of the jurors. The most damage was done when Hirsh said that Cleary took, and did not pass, the boards in forensic psychiatry. He had fun with this.

"And despite the fact that you have chosen forensic psychiatry as your subspecialty and you put your name on your office door like that, you nonetheless flunked the boards in forensic psychiatry in Toronto in 1978, isn't that a fact, sir?"

Dr. Cleary was board-certified in general psychiatry, which Hirsh's Dr. Blinder was not, but when Jeff Hotham had tried to do the same thing with Dr. Blinder, the defense psychiatrist was better equipped to handle the question. "I feel I *am* certified," Blinder said confidently. "I have been honored by my colleagues with fellowships and being chosen for positions of responsibility." The jurors told me afterward that only Cleary had failed an examination, he had "flunked," while everyone else had passed. Not only that, Cleary was "paid."

Bob Hirsh devoted a good deal of energy to discrediting Michael Cleary, but it was not really needed. The Irish psychiatrist did no major damage to Steinberg's position. Although he, like Dr. Gray, had never seen a dissociative reaction, Cleary had to acknowledge that it existed, that there was such a thing. If Steinberg was telling the truth, said Dr. Cleary, the diagnosis would be "a good bet"; if Steinberg was lying, it was not. And, pressed Hirsh, did Dr. Cleary have any reason to believe that Steinberg was lying? After all, didn't Bingham, that experienced police officer from Scottsdale, say that he believed that Steve was telling the truth? "I have no way of telling whether an individual is actually telling the truth or lying," said Cleary in a weary voice. The effect was flat, spiritless.

Hylton said later that the state's doctors could just not compare to the other two. "First of all, Blinder just looked so professional, an expensive suit, and just a manner—ours looked like country. Cleary had on short sleeves and a bolo tie —that was a mistake, I thought. They didn't enjoy testifying like the other two did, obviously, they didn't sparkle or talk a lot—they really didn't have anything to say."

Dissociative reaction caught everyone by surprise in the Steinberg trial. It was so amorphous. It couldn't be tested, traced in history, or anticipated. Apparently it was seldom, if ever, seen in a private setting—only in a murder trial. In this trial both sets of actors played by the same rules and accepted the medical existence of a trancelike state without question.

Today it would be different, because the rebels have appeared, those psychiatrists who are really debunkers. If one of them was called by the prosecutor in a trial like this, he would take a completely different tack. Someone like Lee Coleman, a leading debunker on the West Coast, would tell the jury that psychiatrists just don't have the ability or the tools to see what was in someone's mind on May 27, 1981. If anyone were to say that he could do that, says Dr. Coleman, the jury should just disregard it.

A debunking forensic would say, "Let's look at the method. How did he arrive at this conclusion? By *conversation,* that's what it was, and nothing else. He talked to the man in the jail and he wrote it all down and he accepts everything he heard as true." Dr. Blinder and Dr. Holmes both said the same thing—that they had been psychiatrists for twenty years, and had talked to hundreds of people, and knew when someone was telling the truth. To a debunker, that's no different from calling someone as an expert witness who reads tea leaves: they could make the same claim based on their years of reading the leaves. The debunkers don't believe that this method is scientific. Some critics have said that psychiatrists are not particularly good at evaluating truth, that, in fact, they're very poor at it. They see lying as just a facet of their patient's illness. They call lying denial or malingering and consider it an interesting symptom. Psychiatrists are not trained to be judgmental about their patients.

These rebels are pariahs, for the most part, in their profession, because there isn't much room for criticism from the inside in forensic psychiatry. They're concerned that if there is a tiny crack in any diagnosis the whole structure might disappear, like the emperor's new clothes. After *Steinberg,* though, the debunkers were in Arizona to stay. The battle of the experts has enlisted new personnel since the *Steinberg* insanity defense, and it will no doubt change again. Everything comes full circle.

The evidence had ended on an anticlimactic note, with Bob Hirsh almost having the last word. In the rebuttal there were no witnesses called by the prosecutor to speak kindly of Elana Steinberg, no neighbor such as Pawan or any of the employees at B. B. Singer's who had liked Elana. In fact, the state didn't really know that such people existed, because the power of the defense was such that the prosecution had almost accepted the premise themselves. No one gave a thought to the possibility that there could be others who had a different viewpoint.

On February 17 the lawyers settled the jury instructions. Hotham had been pushing for first degree murder throughout the trial, but now he wanted an instruction for second degree murder—an intentional killing without premeditation. In the law of first degree murder, the word "premeditation" means time enough to deliberate calmly. It isn't necessary to think about something for three days to constitute premeditation—sometimes even getting the murder weapon is sufficient. Judge Riddel thought about this overnight and returned the next morning to reject the prosecutor's request for second degree murder instructions. Hirsh was silent. The judge's basis for her decision was the length of the walk that Steinberg had to make from Elana's bedroom to the kitchen and back again—sixty-six feet each way, a grisly journey which took considerable time. To Judge Riddel there was no other way to look at that journey than time to "premeditate" within the scope of the law. Hotham was worried that the jurors wouldn't understand. "It would be possible for the jury to say, well, no, premeditation means to me that he planned this thing for a couple of weeks or something like that," he argued.

"We've got certain facts that are undisputed," said the judge. "She was killed in the bedroom with this knife in bed. And maybe I have overlooked something and I sure don't want to. But the knife somehow got to the bedroom. It wasn't there before, and, other than speculation, what have I missed that can show an intentional killing without premeditation?"

" . . . Well, Judge, our understanding of premeditation is not what the jury's understanding of premeditation is. And it may choose to disregard it and if they choose to say I don't understand premeditation but he did intend to kill her, then an instruction on murder second degree is appropriate and I respectfully request it."

"I will not give it because I think everything that you say goes to show that in this case it was premeditated or nothing at all."

Jeff Hotham was correct. The jurors, or so some of them said afterward, had a totally different understanding of the word "premeditation." To them it meant "plan," and that walk of sixty-six feet to get the knife simply did not fit their definition of a plan. It was a strange irony that the judge thought the walk to the kitchen and back could only be interpreted as premeditation while the jurors thought that the walk was not sufficient. It was miscommunication on a grand scale.

In the end the judge gave the jury three choices—not guilty, not guilty by reason of insanity, or first degree murder. It was all or nothing. The jury was going to have to find that Steinberg had time to deliberate, or he was going to go free.

Hirsh's closing argument to the jury does not read that well on paper and is one of the weaker points of his otherwise brilliant performance. Though the argument rambles, the jury was already totally in Hirsh's control. They obviously loved his flamboyance, and almost everything he said in the closing argument was ultimately adopted by the jury. There was a certain amount of simplistic emotional appeal in the argument—it wasn't exactly intellectual. It appealed more to the gut feelings of the jury and particularly to their attitudes about money. The major theme, if there was one, could be that "money does not buy happiness," and the jurors could be glad that they didn't have any. Hirsh used phrases like "All Elana wanted was money, money, money." In Hirsh's closing, Steve's gambling was not a desperate passion that was consuming his life and his family, but the equivalent of a day of work at the office. He was trying to earn money for his family with those frantic bets, Hirsh said, and "to get smiles from Elana."

"These are the dynamics, Mommy always needed money and Daddy couldn't give her any. He couldn't. How does he try to make money? He gambles. He is a good gambler. Don't you think they stroked him? They stroked him plenty when he won because that is how he got loved. That is how he was one of them."

Hirsh hits a solid point—he goes through the list of those witnesses who testified on those two black days for Elana Steinberg. "The women who were Elana's friends, they knew that he killed Elana, they told you the same thing. He is a good person, a family man, loves his children. Do you think they were lying? Were they cross-examined by Jeff? Did he dispute any of it with one piece of evidence? . . . Did he tell you any dynamics, the whys, the hows? He had months on this case; he knew what the defense was. And what are we left with? Cleary, saying yes, it could have been. And Gray said, yeah, there was not one thing to indicate Steinberg wasn't telling the truth. They support us. Ask Jeff to explain that," Hirsh said sarcastically, turning to Jeff Hotham, who was sitting at the counsel table writing furiously.

Mitchell Singer, who by this time was bankrupt, would be surprised to learn that Hirsh in his closing argument had given Mitch a "five-and-a-half-million-dollar home" and not one, but two Mercedeses. Hirsh did not forget any shred of evidence that could have a favorable import. Chris Bingham, the Scottsdale detective, was referred to over and over again: "Bingham thought Steve was telling the truth, and that's what he does for a living." Hirsh said that the knife was held by the blade—'See that print? It didn't slip.' The stab wounds were aimless, perfunctory, nothing serious. Steven Steinberg lived a life of "thirty-seven years of virtue," he was scared, alone, weak. Elana Steinberg and her family were terrible, said Bob Hirsh, "and did the prosecutor ever tell you anything else?" The two state psychiatrists are "paid, their boys are paid eighty dollars or a hundred dollars an hour—that's a good bill for you," he tells the jury in irony.

But despite all the terrible things that everyone did to Steve Steinberg, he still wasn't mad, Hirsh said.

"He wasn't mad at Elana that night. He says he loved her, and how did he love her? She was a bitch. Well, I'll tell you. He loved her because of the love he had for her was just like the love he has for the children."

Now it was time for the prosecutor's final portion of the closing argument. In a way, it was his best performance. His language was eloquent and the argument well organized, but it was too late to mend the damage of what had gone before. Belatedly the prosecution seemed to realize that the previous Thursday had been "smear the victim day," as Hotham put it.

"The defense attorney implies that the victim is responsible for her own death and a perfect example of that is Mr. Hirsh telling you that she was a bitch. And last Thursday, smear the victim day, they brought out a lady who had a grudge against Elana Steinberg for five years and a nosy neighbor who wanted some free campaign publicity."

Hotham's attack on the defense psychiatrists was strong. "Can you really believe that it is possible for someone to talk to an individual, three months, six months, ten years after a crime, and be able to tell what his state of mind is? That's ridiculous. Do you believe that someone could be perfectly normal for thirty-seven years and then dissociate for five minutes and then be perfectly normal and sane ever since? That's ridiculous. Let's move away from this fantasy world of mumbo-jumbo phrases like psychogenic fugue, ego dystonic, and somnambulism and move on to the real world where words have real meanings. Let's talk about anger and hatred. Let's add a knife and twenty-six stab wounds and you have death.

"The simple fact that Steven Steinberg killed his wife does not mean that he is insane. There is something wrong with all murderers but that doesn't mean that they are all insane. The defendant decided that it was time for Elana Steinberg to die. And who turned this loving mother with two children into this bloody body? Steven Steinberg. This was not sleepwalking. This is first degree murder. The state has proven the defendant guilty beyond a reasonable doubt and it is your duty to find him guilty."

It was late in the afternoon of February 17, 1982. Steven Steinberg's fate was now with these twelve people. Hirsh felt confident; he could sense that acquittal was in the air. The room was filled with attorneys, who had come to watch Bob Hirsh, and reporters, who know a good show when they see one. It was going to be a long night for everyone.

CHAPTER TWENTY-TWO

A WALK TO FREEDOM

It's a serious moment when the jury files out of the box, crosses over in front of the court, and disappears into a door that leads to the unknown. A murder trial is stylized drama, and there are certain times to do things; certain words are said over and over again like a litany. There are only a few moments of high drama in which the jurors are the actors, but these few moments are dramatic and significant. Jurors seem to know by instinct how they should act, and they invariably rise to the occasion; no one smiles inappropriately. They look neither right nor left, and shoulders are back.

For the last two weeks the jurors had been getting acquainted. Since they were not able to talk about what was going on in the trial they had been thrown back on their children, their cars, or, for the three military men, old war stories. No one on this jury was remotely like the witnesses that had been onstage in *State* v. *Steinberg*. They had never been in the pit at Caesars Palace or gone to Lake Tahoe; they were not likely to have been customers at B. B. Singer's or bought bed comforters at Bullock's Scottsdale. None had gone to a bar mitzvah and they weren't exactly sure what one was. No one had ever heard the words "Jewish American Princess" before, nor any jokes about JAPs—they wouldn't have known where to laugh. There was a charismatic religious flavor in a portion of this panel, and everyone was aware of it. There was a little group that spoke together about being "a good Christian." These jurors recognized each other immediately through some unknown chemistry, and there was a certain distancing between them and the rest of the panel. Prayers had already been voiced in the jury room, and no one objected, although some of the jurors felt slightly awkward around spontaneous prayer—they were not accustomed to it and it embarrassed them.

The room where the jurors deliberated was monstrously uncomfortable, small and cramped and furnished with county metal chairs and a table. The overhead lighting was cold and unflattering, and there were no windows. One member of the jury asked for a prayer before deliberation began. She talked so familiarly and eagerly to the Deity in her prayer that it was obvious that she did this often. It was about three o'clock in the afternoon.

At four, the jurors sent out a question through the bailiff, and the two attorneys were called into the now empty courtroom. The jury asked for a tape recorder. Hotham knew that this was not a good sign. The jury was going to play the recording of the call made to the police that night, with Steinberg's hysterical voice at the outset: "Hurry up! Hurry up! I was robbed and my wife is dead. . . . Oh God, help me please!" Hotham and Frank Hylton thought that Steinberg's emotion on the tape sounded phony and contrived, but the jury could well think differently. Bob Hirsh and Benchoff were rejoicing quietly. The jurors' interest in playing the tape was a good sign as far as they were concerned—it meant that they were thinking on the right track. Hadn't Blinder and Holmes said that the tape was legitimate and not faked? There was not much time left on this day after the jurors got their recorder, and everyone went home at five-thirty to a restless sleep.

By ten the next morning, the jury indicated that they had a verdict. They had deliberated barely three hours. This is not a record for speedy deliberation in a murder trial, but it is extremely brief. According to courthouse lore, a short deliberation time usually means a guilty verdict. Edith Singer was not in the courtroom on this day—she was still in a Scottsdale hospital for observation, and Barney was with her. Only Mitchell was holding the fort for the Singer family. Hotham had told Frank Hylton he didn't have to come back the next day. His gesture was symbolic of the lack of teamwork between the two. Hylton felt dismissed and isolated by the prosecutor.

The court was packed with defense attorneys who had come to watch the legendary Bob Hirsh, and with that strange breed of people who watch murder trials as a hobby. An elderly couple from Michigan who had been there throughout were talking to Pat Sabo, the reporter for the afternoon paper. All three of them agreed that Steinberg would be convicted. "I thought Jeff's closing argument was very strong," Sabo told them, and the Michigan couple agreed.

Steven Steinberg was brought over from the jail by his friend the deputy. He was paler than usual and shaking. He could barely walk. The attorneys were cold and clammy in the air conditioning, although they had done this many times. It is hard to imagine the tension of such a moment for those who have a stake in it. There is an emotional surge; the stomach drops and the heart beats in panic—if blood-pressure cuffs were put on attorneys in the courtroom waiting for a verdict, they would indicate a hypertensive crisis. A big trial, and this was a big trial, is what makes trial lawyers drink, lose their wives, burn out, and have coronaries at forty-seven on the jogging track at the YMCA. Prosecutors have an easier time of it. Jeff Hotham had been in murder trials many times before, and he had always won. The strain sat more lightly on his shoulders.

When I talked to the prosecutor about that moment years after the trial, he told me that he knew immediately that he had lost.

"I watched them walk back in and I kept my eye on one of them that I thought was with me all the way. He was a retired military guy. During the trial he had body language that I thought meant that he was listening really intently, and he would nod at the right times, you know what I mean. When they walked back in the room that man turned his head away and he wouldn't look at me straight in the face as if he were saying, 'I'm sorry about this.' I knew what the verdict was then."

The foreman the jurors had chosen was a thin serious man in his forties with a short haircut, a white short-sleeved shirt, and a pocketful of pens, a quality-control man from one of the Phoenix utility plants. To a hushed courtroom, the bailiff read the verdict; "We, the jury, find the defendant not guilty by reason of insanity."

Steve Steinberg's head went down on the table. Everyone was embracing him and crying. Father Anthony had said that Steve was a "toucher," and this was an occasion for touching. Everyone wept—his mother, Diane Lindstrom, some of the jurors. To the astonishment of the reporters, two of the jurors walked up and embraced Steinberg. "God bless you, Steve," they said as they mingled their tears with those of the handsome defendant. Some jurors slipped out through the side door and did not join in the happy chaos in the courtroom. The prosecutor left the room immediately and talked to no one.

There was more to come. Arizona law requires that when a person has been found not guilty by reason of insanity the prosecutor should be ordered to begin civil commitment procedures—to file a petition asking for a mental health examination. If Steinberg was examined for commitment to the state hospital, the examination would have to determine that he was a "danger to himself or to others" before he could be sent to the state hospital—commitment is not automatic in Arizona under these circumstances.

Everyone was looking for Jeff Hotham so that the commitment process could begin, but the prosecutor had disappeared without a trace. The bailiff put in calls to the major felony bureau without success. No one could find him. While the court was waiting for a trial supervisor to appear in Hotham's place, the jurors had assembled for their final meeting in the jury room, exchanging addresses and picking up their belongings. When a smiling Steven Steinberg walked by in the corridor, one of the women called out as she saw him pass, "We all love you, Steve . . . God loves the sinner." He waved to them. Finally Marc Budoff appeared for the state in the empty courtroom.

"Your honor, Rule 25 says that this court shall order the prosecutor to commence civil commitment proceedings. I believe the court is at the posture now where it must order that," Budoff said.

Hirsh was ready—he said that Rule 25 permitted the judge to consider the trial testimony to determine whether any further examination was needed under the commitment statute. Hirsh argued that there had been four psychiatrists in the trial and each one of them had said there was not a thing wrong with Steven Steinberg—there could be no basis to order commitment. Mike Benchoff broke in to recall a comment Hotham had made in chambers when they had been discussing jury instructions. Apparently Hotham had argued that there was nothing wrong with the defendant and had conceded in advance that there would never be any commitment for the man—"He said so himself," Benchoff argued, and the judge agreed.

"There is no factual evidence and no expert opinion that at this moment the defendant has any mental disorder, illness, or disease. There is nothing to indicate that he is presently a danger to himself or a danger to others; ordering the county attorney to file a Rule 25 petition would be a useless and futile act."

Then came the words that Steven Steinberg was waiting to hear.

"There will be an order at this time releasing the defendant from custody."

Judge Riddel asked Steinberg if he would like to make phone calls in her office, "Make any calls you want, Mr. Steinberg. I know you want to talk to your grandmother back in Chicago," she said graciously. Steinberg wept; he called his relatives while sitting in the judge's chambers. A photographer took his picture as he left the courtroom to be picked up by one of those loyal friends. Steve wore one of the suits from Sears that Diane Lindstrom had bought, but the collar on his shirt was loosened; his persona was already beginning to change. He had his comb in his hand and his clothes in his nylon suit bag. The expression on Steve's face struck just the right note. It was pleasant, but not gleeful. "Escort to Freedom," read the caption on the photograph when it was printed the next day in the *Arizona Republic.* It was over.

CHAPTER TWENTY-THREE

JESUS MEANT FOR ME TO BE ON THIS JURY

It took me almost two years to find the jurors. In the end I couldn't locate them all. Some had moved, one juror had died, and a few had just disappeared. That's not unusual in Phoenix. Most people don't have roots there, and five years is a long time. The jurors that I did find were interested in what I was doing, and they all agreed to talk to me. The trial was as fresh in their minds as it had been in 1982.

Jurors don't always reveal what they really thought when they were deliberating, and I can understand that. Their thoughts are their own business, and they're rooted deep in each juror's subconscious and are perhaps inexpressible. I believe the people I talked to were telling it like it was. I'll let them speak for themselves.

The first juror I talked to, a man, caught me totally by surprise. When I called him to make an appointment, he had a precondition: "Before I talk to you, lady, I want to ask you one question—are you Jewish?" I told him I was not, but I wondered. The next day when we met, I asked him why he had asked that.

"I said that because I was afraid if you were a Jew, you would tend to favor the Singers and not Steve Steinberg. You would be on their side. He lost everything, the poor guy, he lost his children, and I'm afraid that anything you would write would be in favor of Elana and the Singers. You know that family was not fair to Steve after the murder—they had the children. But I want you to know that my decision when I was on that jury didn't have anything to do with religion."

It was such a strange thing to say. I told him I was writing a book because it was the general perception in Arizona that this verdict was unusual. He didn't agree. Steve Steinberg's justification for killing his wife was clear to him. He spoke with a certain anger, all directed at Elana.

"I don't know why anybody would think it was a strange verdict. It was just so clear. The guy shouldn't have been on trial. He should have had a medal. He just put up with so much. She nagged him and nagged him and he just snapped. Why, the last thing she said to him was to bring the Cadillac home early so she could use it."

He said, "You have to consider the facts that led up to the event, Steve went out to her car to put in a TV set and she bugged him for the umpteenth time. That man went through so much for fifteen years. Everybody said it. The consensus was that she was an overbearing, nagging broad."

I think he may have wanted me to know that he wasn't a misogynist, because in the next breath he went on to praise the judge. The judge was wonderful, he said; Marilyn Riddel was really a gracious, wonderful woman. "Every morning when we came there, there would be a plate of cookies that she had made that night for us—she baked them herself. And she would always say every morning, 'How are you? So nice to see you.' A lovely lady."

The points that Bob Hirsh had made with the medical examiner about the knife had really scored with this juror. I think this testimony impressed him as scientific, and obviously the jury had talked about it.

"About the knife, that's one of the things I really paid attention to. It was clear that he held it by the blade, the expert said that. He was in such a trance that he just didn't feel the pain."

"But even if he didn't feel pain, wouldn't the cuts have been there?" I asked.

"He was in such a trance that he didn't get cuts either, it wouldn't cut his hand. Once he grabbed the knife, his grip never moved. That showed he was insane. I don't know who said that, it might have been Bob Hirsh, somebody said it."

Not everyone had agreed, he told me—there was one dissenter, and a fascinating experiment. "There was one guy who wouldn't go along. He bought a lot of hamburger on the way home one night and tried to stab it. He said, 'I've skinned a lot of deer and elk and that never happened to me with a knife.' But I said to him, 'Did you hold that knife perfectly still?' Case closed. He didn't have anything more to say about it after that." The juror smiled at the memory of this.

I asked him if the jury had resolved the evidence of the faked burglary—the open drawer and the underwear thrown on the floor. Did this seem like an attempted cover-up to them? His theory on this went back to Elana and was inconsistent with the testimony about the dead woman's habits. It had been agreed that neatness was one of Elana Steinberg's bad points. He told me, "Well, maybe Elana did this when she was talking on the phone to her mother, just opened the drawer, threw those things out, and left them there. She talked to her mother all the time."

He believed in "that dissociative state," he told me—Steve hadn't known what he was doing when he walked out to the kitchen, and all the psychiatrists had said so. The whole experience of being a juror was a thrill for him, and he would do it again. Unlike some of the other jurors, he wasn't criticized after the verdict—people he knew agreed with him, he told me.

"I loved being on that jury. That and breaking the sound barrier were the two greatest experiences of my life. I hope you are going to be impartial, and I gather from you that you're in favor of Elana and you won't be. The fault is with the legislature."

The next juror was more introspective. To her, the verdict was more a failure of proof on the part of the prosecution. And just as Jeff Hotham had feared, she had a concept of "premeditation" totally different from the judge's.

"I wasn't happy about it. I didn't think he should have gotten off without anything, but we didn't have any choice. We never thought he was insane, never. I know that that was the verdict, but we couldn't say just 'not guilty'—we all knew he was guilty. The main thing for me was that we couldn't find premeditation. It had to be premeditated, and he didn't *plan* it. 'Plan' means to plan it out in advance. Doesn't it mean that in the law?" I explained the judge's reasoning about the time it took to make that walk to get the knife.

"I wondered why some of the jurors talked about how far it was to the kitchen and that kind of thing. That's new to me. I'd have to think about that."

I asked her if she shared one juror's belief that Steve Steinberg should have been praised, rather than tried for murder. Her answer was revealing—she didn't approve, even though she accepted completely the devastating picture of Elana the psychiatrists had drawn.

"Did I think he should have had a medal? No, I'm shocked that anyone would say that. I couldn't agree with anybody who said that his wife deserved it. No one deserved to die, not even her. Some things you have said to me might have changed my mind, like if I had known that he had said 'Shut your fucking door' to the little girl, it really would have changed my mind. Sleepwalking and talk like that? No way."

It was as if the prosecutor had been licked from the start, beaten, she said. Bob Hirsh would just go after him and he would do nothing. "Was he experienced at all? We talked about it in the jury room—'Why doesn't he do something?' Hirsh is a very good attorney."

She told me that she was much more knowledgeable now

and if she did it again she would talk more in the jury room and look into things more. "I'm kind of quiet and I don't speak up. I was surprised that nobody asked me any questions when they were picking the jurors. They really didn't know a thing about me. I would have a hard time convicting anybody—I would think they want to know that." This woman was perceptive enough to see the limitations of the voir dire.

She would be a juror again, she told me. The experience hadn't soured her, but she would be more questioning now. "Why didn't we know some of these things you're telling me, like about his background and all, and the jewelry? I think you should know everything."

Serving on the jury wasn't a bright spot for one juror. She told me, bitterly, that she was very much criticized at work and that she would never do it again. I asked her all the same questions I had asked the other jurors, but the responses were a little different. She was impressed by the psychiatrists, especially Martin Blinder.

"We all listened to the doctor from San Francisco—after all, he is a doctor and he must know what he's talking about. We don't know anything. I respect the fact that he is a doctor."

I was amazed at the depth of antagonism that some of the women jurors had for Elana and for the Singers, presumably because Barney and Edith had raised Elana and that made them guilty too. Elana was looked upon as a bad mother, a cruel characterization that even those dear, close friends would have protested, had they known. Traci and Shawn would have found this judgment heartrending; mothering was Elana's strongest point.

"He was so good, and she was so bad. Everybody said that. Even her friends said they didn't know why he put up with it. I don't remember exactly who said that. She drove him to it by wanting things. Steve killed her because he loved her. He only gambled a little bit, he had a little gambling problem. Nobody said one good word about Elana. I am shocked that the children are with her family. I thought the little girls would go with their father or the father's family after the trial, because they shouldn't go with her family."

As for the trial and jury instructions, she commented, "There was a definite difference between the prosecutor and the defense attorney, and we all noticed it. It was the system that beat us. We didn't have any choice, but we all thought he was guilty. Would we have come in with a verdict of manslaughter? I don't know, maybe. I don't want to talk about it anymore, I'd like to forget it." She was obviously uncomfortable, and I left.

Next I met the man who was apparently the sole dissenter. The rest of the jurors were united from the start, or they had quickly forged a consensus. He told me that he thought Steinberg was guilty and that he felt terrible afterward. If he had to do it again, he said, he would not have gone along with the rest. The man told me that he didn't know he could hang the jury. "I thought I had to convince the other eleven to change their minds, and I knew I couldn't do that." He said that he had become resigned and given in at the end because he had spent a lifetime taking orders.

"In the military you just don't go off on your own from the rest, and that's what I did, I went along with everybody else. Every time I said something the rest of them would say, 'That wasn't in evidence so we can't consider it.' I wanted to look at the pictures and pass them around and have people look at things in the pictures, but the foreman said no."

His being chosen in the voir dire surprised this juror. He had thought he wouldn't be chosen, he told me, because he had a "hillbilly accent," and came over like a weak sister, a typical government employee.

"I never thought that he was crazy. And certainly I never thought he held the knife by the blade—how dumb. He held it right on the handle. I thought he was guilty and felt terrible afterward. He was walking around and it was a terrible sight to see how vicious it was. She did look terrible after the testimony —if he took the garbage out she criticized him. But why didn't he get a divorce? I had an unhappy marriage, there were times when I was plenty mad, but you get a divorce. I regret that I was not stronger in this trial."

The next juror was anxious to tell me that the trial was, for her, a religious experience, as was everything in her life. She had a beatific expression on her face when she told me her convictions about Jews, and justice.

"I am a Jesus freak—I was born again and I praise His name forever. There were a lot of devout Christians on that jury, and they had peace written all over their faces. There were prayers, sure, but they were very short, sort of 'Help us to communicate here,' nothing that would bother anybody."

She told me that the minute she walked into the courtroom she knew God wanted her to sit on that jury. "Was justice done? God is my judge, and He's fair. The Jews are special folks. God said that they are special people, He said that we were commanded to pray for the Israelites. I love them; it was because the Jews didn't believe in God's sovereign plan that made it possible for me to be a Christian. If you are not serving God, He doesn't have much to say about your life. If you're not serving Him, you're serving the devil. There would be no purpose for God to jump in there, in the trial."

I had to break in. "But aren't you expecting too much from these people? They are Jewish, and they're not likely to convert to Christianity and take Jesus into their lives, as you're expecting them to do," I protested.

She was enthusiastic. "That's not true. It *is* possible to be a born-again Jew, it happens all the time. There are many closet Christians. God will deal with the Jewish people differently than other people, and that will be interesting. God is still on the throne but Satan is still the prince of the powers of the air. Killings are the work of Satan, Satan has access to the throne room twenty-four hours a day, but Jesus intercedes and you are forgiven. It's not right but it's just what we have to deal with until the Lord returns. I'm not ashamed of the Lord. Sometimes people avoid me at work."

After this, we talked specifics. She shared the feeling about Elana and the Singers. The "psychiatric autopsy" had been devastating. There was no sympathy for Edith Singer—"She just lost a shopping companion, that's all." She told me that she was impressed that no one, especially her friends, had anything good to say about Elana. She was also impressed by Jean Tims, in part because she thought, inexplicably, that Mrs. Tims was the governor's wife.

Steve Steinberg was seen as an innocent victim, and she could understand why he hadn't gotten a divorce. It was because he loved his children so much, she said. "He was content to let her go on her own way with credit-card buying and her blown-up perceptions of money. They went to stores, fancy stores, I would never be able to go in them. And their houses were so fancy."

Bob Hirsh's tour of the house with Babs Spero had been effective psychology. The bit with Chris Bingham had paid off, too. She told me it was important when that policeman from Scottsdale "who was supposed to be good at what he did" said that Steve was believable. "Bob Hirsh did a real good job with that," she told me. She seemed to have an appreciation of his skills, even while realizing that things were not what they seemed.

Finally, there was the element that lawyers can never anticipate in a jury, when a juror sees things that no one could possibly anticipate. "I felt there must have been some involvement with the Mafia. I thought it was possible that maybe there were two bushy-haired strangers after all, I'm still not sure," she said seriously. "And then I knew he was insane because he didn't pick a good knife—I looked at one of the photographs of the kitchen drawer. I could see that there was a better knife in that drawer that he could have used."

That was a bonus Bob Hirsh could not have anticipated. I was stunned after this interview. Later I went back again, a year later, to talk to this woman and see if her analysis had changed. She told me that I had misinterpreted her comments about there being no justice for Elana because she had not accepted Jesus. That wasn't what she meant, she told me. She had a calmer air than when we had first met.

"If I said there wasn't any justice for Jews, I didn't really mean that, you know, the way it sounds. New Christians are very enthusiastic and want to tell everybody about it, and I got sort of carried away. Being on that trial jury really changed my life."

Another juror was more predictable. He was serious, reflective, and one of the very few who thought that having other jury instructions would have made a difference. The other jurors, I thought, would not have convicted Steven Steinberg of anything. They were thoroughly convinced that he was the victim, not Elana.

"What was important to me? Well, when people said that it wasn't like Steve's personality to do something violent, even Elana's own brother and father said that. And also the prints on the blade on the knife and there was no sliding down the hilt to the blade, I don't know who said this, but somebody did. And also it was very important to me that there was no attempt to cover it up."

I told him about some of the religious commentary I had been hearing. Did he think that was important? "A lot of the jurors were Christian—you know how they come in and start talking about how they are Christians. I kept waiting to hear what they had to say because I thought their viewpoint would be interesting, but really they didn't add anything. They didn't say anything bad about Jews, and, of course, I don't feel that way.

"I do think it probably would have been different if we had instructions for second degree murder or manslaughter. We just didn't think that it was premeditated. We couldn't say just 'not guilty.' He did it, that was clear from the start. So we had to say the other."

Martin Blinder got raves from another juror. Bob Hirsh's strategies had, one by one, struck home. Cleary was seen as "working for money." The tape recording of the police call, because it was so dramatic, meant a lot. I guessed that it was this juror's idea to play it back in the jury room. "The psychiatrist from San Francisco was very impressive. And the state's doctor, that Dr. Cleary, he looked bad because it was shown that he only works for money and for the state. And I was also very impressed by the tape recording of the police call. It was so emotional that he must have been crazy, he was screaming, everybody was screaming."

This juror was impressed by Dr. Jarvis's testimony that the wounds were superficial. He said it was as if Steve didn't mean to do it. "I was impressed by the way Steinberg held the knife halfway down by the blade. He didn't have his wits about him to hold the knife that way. And then the state just didn't show me that Steinberg didn't 'like' Elana, so why would he kill her?" he asked me. He wanted a motive, and he thought the state hadn't brought it home.

It interested me to compare the reasoning of one juror against another. I asked him if they had talked about the burglary setup in the bedroom. "Did the jury decide that Elana had thrown the underclothes around? That didn't sound like her," I told him.

"No, I thought throwing the underpants around was just like this—you come to your senses and you say, 'Here I am holding a knife, what have I done? I'll try to fix it up to look like a burglary.' That doesn't conflict with him being insane. It's just like a normal thing to do."

This man was serious and sober. He wasn't about to castigate Elana Steinberg, and unlike some of the other jurors, he never criticized her. When I asked him if the jury thought that somehow the killing was a form of justifiable homicide, he demurred. "I didn't notice that she was portrayed as a bad woman," he told me, "but some of the women talked about it. They talked about that Mrs. Tims and they were critical of Elana. That wasn't me," he wanted me to know.

"Bob Hirsh did a very good job. I don't think I'd tend to go to the prosecutor if I ever wanted a lawyer. I was impressed by the way the woman lawyer—what was her name, Diane?— she watched the jury all the time for their reactions. I'm impressed they all went to so much trouble."

I told him about the bushy-haired men that Steve had chased back in Des Plaines. "If the jurors had known about that, that he'd used the same story before, would it have made any difference?" Probably not, he said, which surprised me, but was probably a correct appraisal of the sentiment of this jury. Nothing could have changed their minds, I think, after those two terrible portraits of Elana Steinberg by Holmes and Blinder.

"Some people wouldn't talk to me afterward. I still think we did the right thing. I am a Christian and I took a Christian oath and I did what I had to do."

The next juror whom I located was a pleasant middle-aged woman in the suburbs. Perhaps because we were somewhat alike, I seemed to understand her more easily than the other jurors. The "sane, beyond a reasonable doubt" standard made a difference to her.

"Well, it has been a long time. I didn't really feel good about it afterward," she told me. "I don't think that he should have just gotten away without anything. But when you have that many psychiatrists that say, 'Well, there is this thing called dissociative or whatever it was, and we don't really know whether he was in it or not,' what can we say? But getting off scot-free bothered me. He should have been treated or something. We didn't think it was premeditated, either. That means thinking about it, at least a little bit. It is possible that the jury would have gone for manslaughter, but I can't be sure."

Every little thing that happened at this trial had an impact, everything. It bothered this juror that Steinberg's mother and his family were "hovering around in the halls" and passing the jury room. She said it made the jurors feel awkward when they would run into them all the time in those close quarters. Judge Riddel's sharing of the back offices with the defense had its own effect. Like everyone else, this juror thought that the prosecutor had been outclassed, and it bothered her.

"I thought there was too much emphasis on how bad she was, and it bothered me. I remember I kept thinking, why doesn't somebody come up with something? Why don't they do a better job? There must have been some way to not make so much about how terrible she was and how good he was. I realize that the prosecutors don't have as much time as a regular lawyer does—they have a lot of cases, maybe that's why."

She continued, "I got the feeling no one was prepared. I'll give you an example. They didn't even have a floor plan of the house, drawn to scale or anything. They would just get someone up there and say, 'Draw me a picture of the house as you remember it,' and it wasn't the right size. I thought, why aren't you ready so you could see where he went and how far he went?"

This juror was the only one who worried about what might happen in the future. "No one was happy, not really. He looked so nice and he cried at all the appropriate times, but you still worried. I hope I don't have to pick up a paper someday and wonder whether this man has killed someone else."

We talked about the change in the insanity law, that instead of the prosecutor's having to prove the defendant was sane, now the burden was on the defendant to prove he was insane, a subtle but very important change. She told me that it was important to her because it was the only redeeming aspect for her—"Really, I was embarrassed to even be associated with the trial, but the change in the law is one good thing."

The last juror I found was a trim, pretty woman with a lot of energy. Of all the charismatics on the jury, she was the most expressive. Her words just flowed, particularly when she talked about her religious convictions. From the first, she told me, God had meant for her to be on the Steinberg jury—she had known it when she walked in the courtroom.

"I was praying to be on it, it was meant to be. If I hadn't had Jesus I don't know how I would have survived the things that have happened to me in my life. There were some good Christians on that jury."

She explained, "Steve just had so much and he snapped, she tortured him and he didn't have any way of getting it out. There was so much evil. She hadn't been raised with the right values."

"Do you think there can be enforcement of the law for

someone who isn't a Christian?" I asked her. "One of the other jurors said that, at least I think that's what she said, and I found it a little disturbing, because I'm a lawyer. I didn't think religion had anything to do with it."

She told me she didn't agree with the other juror—even if you didn't accept Jesus, there was justice. Nonetheless, it was clear that she regarded Steve Steinberg as a potential convert to Christianity.

"I forgive other people. But you know that people have choices. I don't hate Jews, Jews are God's chosen people; Jesus was a Jew, but they rejected him. They rejected Jesus because He was humble and they are looking for something flashy, like a king. We make these choices to reject Jesus. I told Steve afterward, "The Lord hates the sins but loves the sinner. You have to bring Jesus into your life."

"The paper said that some of the jurors embraced Steinberg after it was over. Do you know why they did that?"

That was Satan, she told me, who wrote that story in the *Republic*. That was really Satan, that's how Satan worked, writing things up and distorting them. "What I was really saying was that Jesus is compassionate and he will forgive you. I didn't want Steve to grieve and blame himself, but I thought he had to change his life and take Jesus in. I would have been happy to talk to Elana's family too," she told me, "but they left. I feel compassionate to them just as much."

Satan figured again in the trial, she told me. He was the bushy-haired strangers that Steve saw. Satan was very real to this juror, a palpable presence that explained a lot of things. When she talked of more earthly things, her sentiments were the same as those of some of the other jurors. Steve was not responsible for his frailties, she told me. If he gambled, it was only to buy Elana things she wanted. She had read about the insurance fraud with the jewelry that the police were investigating after the trial. "If he did that, report all those things stolen when they weren't, like they said in the paper—it was only because of Elana," she said.

"The mother was flippant; she called Elana her little princess. What does she mean, calling her a princess? We all talked about that, that was terrible. No, I never heard the word JAP, I wouldn't know what that means. We didn't think that her mother should take the children because she wouldn't bring them up right and they shouldn't be with her or the grandfather, we all talked about that. Did we think that Steve should have them? Well, I don't know, I suppose so."

She told me one of the jurors was a troublemaker, "but we straightened him out. There is always a troublemaker."

We talked about the idea that all murderers could be said to "snap." Would that make them all temporarily insane? This one was different, she told me, but she didn't know why, unless it was because he had stabbed her so many times—that meant he was crazy. "Would he do it again, if the circumstances were right?" I asked.

"We all thought he would get some counseling; he needs some help. There were some questions I would have liked to have asked him, like 'What was in your mind that night?' We'll never know. Would I reach the same verdict again? Oh yes, but I don't think it will ever happen again. People have to take Jesus into their lives. I hope Steve is not grieving too much."

CHAPTER TWENTY-FOUR

BIRKAT HAGOMEL

"I'm taking my son home with me tonight," Steven Steinberg's mother said as she waited with friends in the courtroom after the verdict. Reporters were pushing in, scrabbling for comments from anyone they could find, and the jurors were not very cooperative; few wanted to talk. After a verdict the winning attorney usually is exuberant, mingling with the players, laughing and talking, but Bob Hirsh was serious when he talked in public with his client. "You owe something," he said sternly to Steinberg. "It's time you learned how to help people now." Hirsh's comments for public consumption were made as the successful pair sat in the judge's office waiting to make phone calls, flanked by reporters amazed at the verdict.

If Steve Steinberg's mother hoped that he would stay at home that night and if Bob Hirsh expected his client to begin a life of self-sacrifice, they were both going to have to wait for a while. That night was one for celebration. Steven Steinberg made the rounds of Scottsdale night spots—the ones where former employees of B. B. Singer's were working after Mitchell Singer's restaurants expired in the summer. Steinberg's journey on this evening did not go unnoticed, and it has since become a piece of Scottsdale history. The memory of the trial does not die in this city. Years later, people like to say that they had a part of it. Either they knew Mitch or Edith and Barney Singer, or they ate at the restaurants, or, the favorite story, they were there, actually there, on the night that Steven Steinberg came into the Jockey Club or Under Three or Pops right after he got out of jail. It wasn't exactly a triumphal progress. One man remembers an unfriendly atmosphere. "Everything just got still—they had recognized him or they heard him say who he was. There was a real cold feeling in the room." At one of the restaurants, a former Singer employee working the bar told me about that night.

"There were a couple of us working there that night, and we all knew him from Singer's. He came in about nine o'clock and he had a friend with him; I got the impression that the man was watching over him or something. I always liked Steve until that night. But that night I saw something different, and I didn't like what I saw. Everyone that was there felt the same way. We just didn't know what to say to him."

He continued, "I didn't think that he showed any remorse, none at all. He said that the only thing that he regretted was that he had to stay in jail for nine months. I remember this— he went up to some woman who was sitting at the bar and he put his hands on her breasts and laughed and said something about being in jail for so long. I don't know whether he knew her or not. We were all disgusted. Whatever sympathy everybody had for him evaporated."

For Mitch Singer, the whole night was an insult. "He was out celebrating, look at me, I got off—what kind of a person would do that?" Mitch said. Steve called Edith Singer, and in the course of the conversation with Elana's mother, he marveled at the odds he had beaten with the verdict. "Do you know how many times that could happen?" Edith's son-in-law asked her happily. Edith was amazed. "It was like I would think it was a good thing, he didn't seeme to realize how I felt, he just wanted to say how lucky he was."

Back in the courtroom, everyone had left and the paper was being swept up. The clerk had gathered up the exhibits. The judge had thanked the jurors with her usual graceful speech and returned to her office in Division Five. It is difficult to have business as usual on the rest of the day after a murder verdict like this comes in, but the atmosphere was generally calm in the judge's office. It was deceptive, though, for a storm was about to break around Marilyn Riddel that would last for months.

The controversy began immediately, when reporters interviewed Larry Turoff, the head of the major felony bureau and Jeff Hotham's supervisor. Turoff admitted that the County Attorney's Office had been beaten and congratulated the defense attorneys, but he had something important to say as well: the jury should have been given an instruction on second degree murder. "Being the prosecution," said Turoff, "we can't appeal." There is no second chance for anything that goes wrong for the prosecutor in a criminal trial. After an acquittal, the case is at an end, no matter what error may have occurred to hurt the state's case. While Turoff could complain, that was all he could do. Only the defendant can appeal in a criminal case, never the state.

Now the reporters had something to hang their hats on, and the idea was a solution to the otherwise inexplicable acquittal. During the weekend, the notion took hold. Tom Fitzpatrick wrote about it in the morning paper in a double-size column headlined "Steinberg Might Be in Prison If Judge Had Not Restricted Jury." Editorials began to appear with headlines like "Killer Goes Free." In all of it, the blame was placed on the judge's refusal to give the jury any alternative to not guilty other than first degree murder. It was a simplistic answer to a verdict that expressed complex emotions.

The letters and telephone calls that Judge Riddel received after the Steinberg verdict were a new experience for her. She filed the letters in the court file and took all the phone calls, even though some people just breathed on the phone. It is possible that the adverse publicity in the conservative Phoenix papers was the most distressing to judge; she was a conservative Republican who was used to nothing but approval from the press.

What happened next was extraordinary. The pressure was so great that Judge Riddel began to give interviews to discuss her jury instructions. "I was absolutely right," she justified herself in one interview. "If the evidence shows only one thing, and that is premeditated murder, and the defendant pleads insanity, you just do not give instructions for lesser offenses."

Legislators in the Arizona senate and house called for an investigation. "This is a travesty of justice," said the chairman of the house judiciary committee. The months passed, but the controversy did not die. Judge Riddel continued to explain her jury instructions in *Steinberg* at meetings and on the luncheon circuit. In front of one group, she said that the furor over the insanity defense the trial had caused was exaggerated. "It must have been a dull week for news and there was nothing else for the media to write about. When *Steinberg* came along, they all decided that insanity was some new invention of Procter and Gamble." Judge Riddel had some powerful defenders. Prominent members of the state and county bar rose to the judge's defense: she had done the right thing, they said, and judges must be free to exercise discretion without having to justify their decisions later. If there was fault, it lay with the insanity defense itself. The judge's husband, also a lawyer, wrote a response to an editorial in a Scottsdale paper: "Marilyn Riddel is no friend of the criminal. After all there was a jury in this case —she is being maligned."

Some of the callers and the people who wrote letters vowed to defeat Judge Riddel in the next election, but that has never come to pass. She has never had a problem being reelected.

The public criticism of Judge Riddel was partly the result of superficial news coverage. The press had missed the real issues of the trial. The phrase "Jewish American Princess" never appeared in print. No one discovered that Martin Blinder was the "Twinkie" psychiatrist. There were no articles about sleep-walking or the dissociative reaction. And no reporter ever bothered to find out anything about Elana Steinberg. It was shallow reporting, typical of most trial coverage. Trials are dull most of the time, and reporters wander in and out—a long-range view of what is taking place is usually lacking. It was easy and provocative to lay the blame for what happened on the jury's instructions. The controversy left a scar on Judge Riddel, but she stood her ground. Lawyers backed her in a solid front, and that almost never happens. All in all, it was a strange and never-to-be repeated occurrence in Maricopa County. No judge has explained jury instructions since the Steinberg verdict.

And Robert Hirsh? Three days after the triumphant conclusion of the Steinberg trial, Hirsh moved his trial headquarters to Safford. Less than three weeks later, the Gorzenski verdict was in. The jurors had stayed out only long enough to eat their dinner before they found the hard-drinking Gorzenski not guilty by reason of insanity. Hirsh's trial technique was again to try the victim, as he had so successfully tried Elana Steinberg. The dead Sandra Gorzenski caused her husband to snap, said Dr. Donald Holmes, by her "flagrant act of infidelity" in going out with another man before her divorce was final. It was another incredible triumph for the dazzling Robert Hirsh and the two psychiatrists, and, of course, for the dissociative reaction. Unlike Marilyn Riddel, the judge in the Gorzenski trial had given every jury instruction for homicide that was known. The result had been the same. It took some of the sting out of the criticism of Marilyn Riddel. Jury instructions were apparently not the sole cause of the *Steinberg* problem.

After the Gorzenski triumph and Hirsh's appearance on *60 Minutes,* it seemed as if there could be no end to Hirsh's success. Certainly a good deal of business came his way.

Hirsh still treats each trial with his full concentration, and the stress is beginning to tell. Things don't come quite so easily anymore; temporary insanity acquittals are hard to come by since the *Steinberg* verdict and since the legislature passed a new insanity defense law making it more difficult for defendants. A new breed of psychiatrists is springing up—the debunkers. Prosecutors are becoming more savvy and not as easily intimidated.

Hirsh continues to receive the ultimate accolade for a criminal defense attorney: whenever a policeman is in trouble Hirsh is the first attorney sought. He has lost some big trials. The "sanctuary" trial of church leaders in Tucson received national attention. Bob Hirsh's defendant was a Presbyterian minister, of impeccable character, who took a moral stand on providing sanctuary for refugees from Central America—everyone thought there would be an acquittal, because the defendants and their moral position had so much appeal. The government agent had infiltrated the church's prayer groups wired for sound, and many people found that offensive. The unthinkable happened. Hirsh's client and some of the other religious figures were convicted of smuggling aliens, a conviction which is now on appeal. Like everything in life, defense techniques have to readjust and reform. Nothing stays static in the law, and Hirsh's own success is making it difficult for him now—but his difficulties won't last forever. Robert Hirsh is too inventive and too motivated to slip into the background.

And what happened to the handsome young prosecutor? Jeff Hotham was crushed on the day he disappeared from the courtroom. Hotham didn't know how it had happened, but he cherished the thought that the jury instructions had sunk the case, and that if the judge had given the option of second degree murder the jury would have convicted Steven Steinberg. The damage done to the victim's reputation didn't really sink in until years later for Hotham. He was distressed by Howard Gray's testimony and felt that the psychiatrist had not given his full attention when it was needed.

Fortunately, there was work still to be done, and that was the best medicine for Hotham. He plunged into his next case, the ugly rape and murder of an eight-year-old girl who had been kidnapped and left in the desert to die. Police had used a tracking dog brought in from California to identify the defendant's scent on the victim's bike and underwear as part of the evidence. It was difficult evidence to present, and Hotham did it brilliantly. In this trial, the jury did not cry with the defendant, but stared at him coldly. Of course, no one suggested that the eight-year-old had caused her own death. It was another death-penalty sentence for Jeffrey Hotham, his sixth.

Still, he was never the same again after the Steinberg trial. Losses like that leave a lasting mark on an attorney's confidence. A year later he asked for a transfer to the civil side of the County Attorney's Office, retiring voluntarily from the combat of the criminal courtroom.

When I interviewed him four years later, he was still there, in a small office away from the excitement of the major felony bureau. There was a certain air of melancholy about him. We had lunch together, and he told me that it was the first time he had been able to talk freely about the Steinberg trial with anyone except his wife. It was too painful, he said. "That trial was the worst miscarriage of justice I have ever known," the prosecutor says now. "The system failed Elana Steinberg. I always wondered what I could have done better, but when you're on the receiving end of something like that you are not the most objective observer."

I asked him what he thought went wrong, from his standpoint. I told him some of the things I had learned, and he seemed genuinely surprised at the reasoning of the jurors. "I think the voir dire was a problem. It was not extended enough for the kind of trial it was, and it would have helped to have known more about these jurors. But I certainly didn't get any negative feedback from them while the trial was going on. I thought they were with me. I'm still amazed—how could the jury look at those photographs and say that the stab wounds were superficial? These are terrible wounds. I can't understand that kind of thinking," he said, shaking his head in amazement.

There were dozens of questions I wanted to ask him, but I found it impossible to do it. They were the "Why didn't you do this" questions that were so obvious to me now in the full glory of my legal hindsight. Why didn't you bring in Elana's friends, friends like B.J. in Chicago? Why didn't you ask him about the bushy-haired men in Des Plaines, or about forging Elana's sig-

nature on the loans? Why didn't you bring in another pathologist? I couldn't say those things—they were his to say to
himself now. If Jeff Hotham had any second thoughts about his
strategy or preparation, he did not share them with me.

"I knew that they were doing a hatchet job on Elana, but
that comes with the insanity defense; it's part of the program,"
he told me. "I don't believe that there is any way that I could
have stopped it. Of course, I did hear the words 'Jewish' and
'JAP' being said, but they really didn't signify anything to me at
the time," he said.

"You know, I'm just a simple middle-class guy from Illinois, and it never entered my mind that anything like that
would influence a trial. In retrospect, it might have been a good
idea to have a Jewish prosecutor from our office try the case—
he would be able to pick up on the nuances and turn things
around."

When the legislature changed the insanity law, it was a
direct result of the *Steinberg* verdict. "It's the one good thing
that came out of it," Hotham said. "It wasn't a total waste." He
was skeptical of the forensic psychiatrist's ability to testify about
what was in the defendant's mind in the past. "Jurors put too
much weight on what the psychiatrists say; they're not capable
of being critical and analyzing this testimony. The average juror
is in awe of the doctors."

Finally, Hotham asked me about Elana's family. He
thought they blamed him, and it made him unhappy. "I feel
bad about the Singers," he told me. "I know how they have
suffered."

Jeff Hotham's long period of self-imposed exile came to an
end in 1987 when he was selected by the governor from a list
of five candidates to be a new Maricopa County superior court
judge. He now will be giving jury instructions himself. He sent
me an invitation to his swearing-in ceremony. The courtroom
was packed with Hotham's friends. Everyone was delighted. In
his remarks at the ceremony, Judge Hotham remembered his
five years in the major felony bureau as the best in his career.
For the first time since the Steinberg verdict had come in on

that February day in 1982, he seemed truly happy. If there were failings in his prosecution of Steven Steinberg, he had served a long penance.

If anyone learned anything as a result of the verdict, it was probably the Scottsdale police. Frank Hylton says that even though he knew things weren't going well in the trial, he never doubted that there would be a conviction. "It shows how naive I was. I wouldn't think that now." Hylton says there are a lot of things he would do differently.

"I would not let myself be backed off the case as I was in this one. I now recognize that when you have an insanity defense, it's a totally different ball game. Scottsdale police don't have much trial experience; we seldom go to trial and we don't to this day. When we do have a murder trial, it's kind of a first for everyone, but after *Steinberg* we are aware of the worst that can happen and we don't take anything for granted."

Cecil Kirk had been astounded, but he had another experience two years later that helped him understand the power of the try-the-victim defense, particularly when the victim is a woman. Kirk testified in another trial; the defendant had shot his ex-wife and her boyfriend in bed. The jury brought in a guilty verdict for the male victim's murder, but not for the attempted murder of the ex-wife. As a verdict, it didn't make sense—the act and the motive were the same for both victims.

"Afterward I was in Goldwater's one day buying something and I used my police ID card for identification," Kirk told me. "A woman came up and told me that she was on that jury. I asked her how they ever arrived at that verdict of not guilty on the woman who was shot and she said, 'We all just thought that the bitch deserved it.' I guess that says something for juries, but you know cops always get down when they lose." Kirk was fatalistic.

Traci and Shawn are fine, amazingly. In a triumph of will and courage, they have both done well. Elana's spunk lives on in her daughters. Traci has always been a leader in school. She says she wants to be a lawyer, and she is almost ready for college. Shawn is the image of her mother; people are amazed when they see how much she is like Elana. She adores Barney

Singer and doesn't want to let her grandfather out of her sight. She also does well in school. Shawn is a diver and a budding actress. These girls are not shrinking violets. They have not seen their father since their mother was killed, except for Traci's tearful meeting with him in the courtroom the first day of the trial. The girls want it that way. The break is complete.

There was no custody battle after all. Steven Steinberg signed an agreement permitting Barney and Edith to be the girls' guardians, and the Singers did not contest Steve's acquisition of Elana's estate. It seemed that no one had the spirit or the money for a prolonged battle after the murder trial. When Steve, Bob Hirsh, and the foreman of the jury appeared on the television program *60 Minutes* in a segment about the insanity defense, Steve was unidentified and photographed in shadow, but everyone in Phoenix knew who it was. The program was not a celebration of the insanity defense, but it upset Traci. Afterward she wrote a letter to the program's producer: "Why don't you tell people how we feel about it?" There was no answer; Traci Steinberg's letter didn't make the program's mail call the next week.

For the Singers, Steve's acquittal made everything worse, although neither Edith nor Barney comprehended what had happened to their daughter and themselves in the courtroom. They had only a more primitive thought in mind, and that was retribution. Steinberg's freedom was a perpetual affront. Edith's grief was never resolved, and five years after Elana died, that grief was as fresh as it had been when she was sitting *shiva*.

Mitchell Singer's business had been on the ropes before Elana was killed and it never recovered. Mitchell never really went back to work after that—he abdicated control of the restaurants to his new partners from New York. In three short months, all of the restaurants were gone and Mitchell had filed for bankruptcy. At the end of that summer, Barney begged his son, "Give me something to do—I can't stand just sitting around the house." The Platts let Barney work at one of the Central Avenue restaurants. One day late in August, Barney arrived in the morning and found that there were no eggs for breakfast—that was the end of B. B. Singer's.

The Platts, of the big cigars, went back to New York with all their personnel. In the bankruptcy hearings that followed, Bill Platt testified that he and his father had lost all their investment, a huge sum, in the three months that they had been associated with the restaurants. No one could tell exactly what had happened, because there was a fire one night in the Brass Derby office on the second floor, the same office where Bill Adamowitz had found the empty safe on that rainy May night. Most of the financial records were destroyed. There were some angry rumblings from the creditors in Mitch's bankruptcy, and the last of the employees were never paid. The suppliers, by and large, took a bath, and Mitchell and Bonnie lost everything themselves. The Brass Derby, where Steve Steinberg once held forth as manager, greeting Father Anthony and all of his friends, is now a Chinese restaurant. B. B. Singer's in Scottsdale has been through a whole range of names and cuisines since the murder trial. The restaurant business in Phoenix is a cruel one and there have been many casualties—Mitchell Singer is not unique.

The Scottsdale friends from the happy barbecue days have changed too. There have been some shifts in friendships, a few divorces, and a general "drawing in" among the friends who were once so close. Some of them have run into the Singers in restaurants. Scottsdale is still a small town, and it's hard to avoid seeing people on a Saturday night. These meetings tend to be embarrassing for everyone concerned. It's hard for Steve's friends to look at Edith and Barney after what happened. At last report, no one had ever paid Ira the $6,200 from the get-out bet, but he is still hopeful.

None of the friends in Arizona seemed to want to talk about Elana to me. The very mention of her name caused carved Spanish doors all over north Scottsdale to close and close firmly. Young matrons in tennis socks found a hundred reasons to be somewhere else rather than to remember Elana Steinberg. Of the circle of friends that had once been so close and intimate in Arizona, only one couple had even kept in touch with Elana's little girls over the years since their mother had been killed. Only the Ackermans remembered the girls' birthdays and called Barney and Edith Singer periodically, to the Singers' great pleasure. For the rest of the group it was as if Elana Steinberg had never existed, as if the entire family they said they knew so well from pool parties, gourmet dinners, and bar mitzvahs had suddenly disappeared from the face of the earth. The trial and the defense of Steven Steinberg had seemingly sapped all of their energy for friendship. It was a mystery I was never able to understand.

The day after the verdict, Steve Steinberg went to the Scottsdale police property room to pick up the evidence, which was basically Elana's jewelry. The rest of the evidence had little value, and no one claimed it. It was just bloody sheets and a carving knife with a bent tip, and those are the kind of things that stay in police evidence lockers forever. When Steve and his mother emerged, a bank of newspaper photographers waited outside. They were there because by now something new had surfaced—the gold-and-diamond earrings found among the jewelry in the bedroom that night matched the description of earrings that Steinberg had reported stolen in the MGM Grand burglary in Reno. There was a possibility of insurance fraud, Hotham told newspaper reporters, and the Scottsdale police were investigating.

The county attorney, Tom Collins, called off the investigation in an exercise of prosecutorial restraint, much to the dismay of Frank Hylton and the police. Collins's decision was probably wise. It smacked too much of being a vendetta—"We lost the trial, so now we will try something else."

Mike Benchoff told the reporters that Steinberg was not profiting from Elana's death; "Half of all the assets would be placed in trust for the little girls," Benchoff said. After the cost of the Steinberg defense and the paying off of all those bank loans, it was unrealistic to expect that there would be anything left. Steve never funded any trust for the girls, and the Singers never expected it. It took almost two years to find a buyer for the house on Via de Luz. Ethical real estate practice required an agent to disclose the tragedy to any potential buyer. It was a real detriment. Finally, there is a family there again, and the neighbors are delighted. The ones who remember Elana and the girls are generally critical of the verdict. There is a sadness when they speak of Elana and a sense of embarrassment about the trial.

Just as had happened in California after the Dan White verdict, the state responded to the Steinberg trial with an attempt to change the law. Everybody in the legislature was crying for insanity defense reform after *Steinberg* and *Gorzenski,* and those names were waved like battle flags. The legislators tried to be calm and actually waited until the next legislative session so that there could be hearings. No one seemed to be able to put a handle on what was wrong. The legislature in Arizona is not given to thoughtful analysis, but its members knew they didn't want a repeat of *Steinberg.* In the new statute the burden of proof was changed, and that seems to have made a difference. Now a defendant has to prove that he is insane by something called "clear and convincing evidence." In Steve Steinberg's trial the state had to prove "beyond a reasonable doubt" that the defendant was sane—and as soon as psychiatrists arrived on the scene that was almost impossible. The second part of the new law had to be abandoned. It called for 180 days of commitment to a mental health hospital after someone was acquitted, but this was struck down by the Arizona supreme court almost immediately. An acquitted defendant has to be treated like everyone else, said the court, and it must be determined that he is "dangerous" or, like Steven Steinberg and William Gorzenski, the acquitted defendant will walk out of the courtroom. Daniel M'Naghten would have been amazed, but then he never heard of such a thing as temporary insanity.

Steven Steinberg did not stay long in the community which had been so understanding of his frailties. It seemed best to get a new start in life. He left Phoenix almost as soon as the trial ended. Some people say that Steve went to Israel, but that doesn't really seem likely, because he comes back to Paradise Valley on certain occasions. People have seen him in Scottsdale restaurants, they say, but that could just be part of the Steinberg legend. Most of the friends who testified for him so enthusiastically are now cool and distant. It is curious, but it is as if they had set a force in motion that was more than they expected. Steve's friends from elementary school in Chicago have been the most loyal, but then they didn't have the experience of the trial—it was the trial that made everyone pensive and quiet afterward.

And then, too, there was the thanksgiving blessing—Birkat haGomel—that caused shock waves all over north Scottsdale; its echoes even rumbled as far as Chicago. It was a large miscalculation of public opinion for Steve to come back for the blessing. The Jewish community in Phoenix was outraged; members called each other, called their rabbis, and buzzed with irritation. It was the end of any public approval of Steve Steinberg in Scottsdale, and even the defense witnesses were a little shaken.

It is customary in most religions for there to be a special prayer of thanksgiving for someone to say after being delivered safe from danger. The Jewish blessing of thanksgiving is known as Birkat haGomel, and like most parts of Jewish ritual, its roots are ancient indeed, carrying one back to biblical times to find the dangers for which the blessing was appropriate. There were four kinds of people who were obliged to say the Gomel: one who safely completed a voyage on the ocean; one who had passed through the wilderness and survived; one who had been dangerously ill and recovered; and one who had been imprisoned and then set free. Later commentaries on the blessing expand to include a whole new range of Old Testament disasters —the Gomel could be said if a person was gored by an ox or escaped from a preying lion, or was attacked by "night bandits" and was saved. There is no commentary about the type of imprisonment that would be right for reciting the blessing, but there is a flavor of the dungeons and chains of the Pharaoh, of Jews who were prisoners because of their faith. Somehow the Gomel does not seem to encompass anyone who was accused of killing his wife in Scottsdale and was acquitted because he was walking in his sleep. But times have changed since preying lions were a hazard to be contemplated, and a modern interpretation of the Gomel says that the blessing is for anyone "who has passed through a harrowing experience that has endangered his life."

To Steven Steinberg, spending nine months in the Maricopa County jail was certainly a harrowing experience, even if it didn't exactly endanger his life. When he asked to be allowed to recite Birkat haGomel it must have posed a philosophical problem for the rabbi at the Scottsdale temple. Elana's murder was an embarrassment for the Jewish community, but nonetheless a jury had found this man to be without fault. The secular law had apparently spoken, and it was hard to fly in the face of that. So it was arranged; Steve would be called to the Torah for an *aliyah* and he would recite Birkat haGomel.

It is a distinct honor to be called up for an *aliyah,* a "going up," just as it is an honor to be called to participate in any part of synagogue ritual. It means that the person called to the Torah is someone who deserves recognition, who deserves the chance for spiritual merit in the eyes of the congregation. Birkat haGomel is supposed to be a public, not a private, prayer, and the person who is requesting it says the blessing out loud after the second blessing over the Torah. All eyes must have been on Steven Steinberg on that Sabbath morning as he recited the ancient Hebrew thanksgiving for his own personal deliverance from danger; there must have been tears in his eyes, because this was a man who wept easily. It was a dramatic moment in the temple as Steven Steinberg said:

"Blessed are thou, Lord our God, King of the Universe, who bestows favors on the undeserving, for having shown me every goodness."

Now the congregation must respond, and they do:

"May He who bestowed every goodness upon you continue to favor you with all that is good . . . forever."

EPILOGUE

I first began to study the Steinberg trial because I wanted to look inside it, and I have tried to do just that. In a way I regret my actions, because what I found there was disturbing. This verdict was different, and everyone in Phoenix knew instinctively that it was different. It had pressed the judicial system as far as it would go. I didn't think there was anything very momentous in this trial in a legal sense. There were very few objections to evidence to break the flow of the trial, and there were no dramatic breakthroughs in the law. The trial just sped along without a hitch. It was a test of lawyering, though, and above all it was a test of trial preparation. The things that needed to be done in this trial, for the most part, should have been done before those jurors ever walked into the courtroom on February 2.

The preparation of the defense attorneys was a masterpiece. They didn't miss a thing, they talked to everyone, they found the best witnesses, and then they handled the witnesses they chose with a beautiful delicate touch. When I interviewed the judge who presided over the Gorzenski trial in Safford, he made an interesting comment that I think holds just as true for the Steinberg trial. The judge said that the jury had been presented with an "information overload," and it all originated from one side. "They were just overwhelmed," he told me. The information overload that the jury was fed on Elana Steinberg was almost too much to absorb. Some of the jurors told me that they were perplexed that they weren't getting more from the prosecutor; they knew that the balance was askew, and it was making them uncomfortable. In my opinion, it was close. If there had been a little more about the badness of the dead woman, perhaps what Martin Blinder calls the "equities" of the trial would have tipped over and reversed themselves—you can go too far sometimes, and Americans like to root for an underdog. In this trial, the underdog was certainly Elana Steinberg. There was just so much put on the jurors' plate, and it was all put there by Bob Hirsh. After that, I suppose that the verdict was inevitable; a jury has to work with what it has.

I like to think that every trial has a theme that guides the strategy of one side or the other. I have a feeling that this trial did. When Bob Hirsh and Mike Benchoff first talked to their client in the jail, a reporter noted the two men smiled at each other and wrote something on a yellow legal pad. I think that what they wrote on that pad was the theme. Elana Steinberg was going to be the real villain of the piece—she was going to be the stereotype known disparagingly as the Jewish American Princess. Certainly the structure of the defense would bear that out, the constant talk about decorating, the emphasis on shopping, the criticism of the dead woman's voice—all of it was building a picture that meant something to these men and that they hoped would mean something to a jury.

Assuming that you recognized the theme—and I don't believe Jeff Hotham ever did—it could have been turned inside out. A prosecutor could have made it his own. The minute that you read the phrase "Jewish American Princess" in all of the psychiatrists' reports—and Steve Steinberg was the one who put it there—you could have made your own plans. Instead of being all injured feelings and outrage at the not-so-subtle religious slant, you could run with it. A different prosecutor—and I agree with Jeff Hotham that it would have been preferable for him to be Jewish—could have taken it away and made it his own theme. He would never have stopped; he would never have let those words rest. He would have jumped on Dr. Blinder and Steven Steinberg and made them repeat those words over and over again; he would have made them talk about them until they were blue in the face.

After he was through with that, he could talk about Auschwitz and the gas ovens and the Nazis, and by the time he was through, the defense witnesses would have been sorry they had ever heard of a Jewish American Princess. That's called turning the defense strategy inside out. I think it could have been devastating. At least no one would ever call the victim a "bitch" in closing argument as the defense attorney did in this trial.

The curious thing is that while the concept meant everything to the defense, the jury didn't have a clue. The jurors had never heard the words before; to these people, Jewish women and Jewish men were interchangeable. They didn't know that there was this feeling, this bitter joke, about American Jewish women that had grown and flourished in the mouths of Jewish writers for the last two decades. The objects of the joke are the daughters and granddaughters of the women you see in those poignant faded photographs of immigrants taken on shipboard in New York Harbor with the Statue of Liberty in the background. The objects of the joke are the daughters and granddaughters of the women with grave expressions who hold bundles of household goods and babies in yards of dresses, the women who were to be so vibrant and alive on the streets in the cities of America, the women who worked and peddled and scraped to keep everyone alive on the Lower East Side in New York and on Maxwell Street in Chicago. The same energy and survival qualities that these first-generation Jewish women had have somehow become an embarrassment and a figure of fun to their offspring, and that embarrassment takes a peculiar form.

Stereotypes about Jewish women in America are immensely complicated. The sociologists are just beginning to write about this, but so far they consider it a combination of misogyny and Jewish self-hatred, a form of inward anti-Semitism practiced by some Jewish men against Jewish women. The stereotypes and jokes seem to be saying, "See, this is what Jews are like, these are the real Jewish things, those loud shrill voices, those women always buying things and wearing jewelry and being greedy. But that's not me, I'm not like that, see, I can even make jokes about it." The Jewish mother and princess are two stereotypes that are distinctly American, and it is sobering that for the first time the stereotypes became lethal.

The Steinberg jury was never on the same plane as the lawyers when it came to this. They didn't know the jokes, they had never heard the phrases before, they knew "Jewish" but not "Princess"—there was a cultural gulf there. And after all, wasn't Steve Steinberg Jewish himself? Didn't this take some of the sting out of his portrayal of his wife? It was my impression that the tactic was to portray Elana as a combination of all things that bigots considered specifically Jewish, while picturing Steve as a Jew trying to break away from all this. It was Elana who wanted "money, money, money," not Steve, they said. According to Steve and his doctors, even little Traci was not immune—he called her a "Princess in Training." In the end the whole shorthand concept of what was a princess was lost, because the jury, and most of the courtroom spectators, may have had the sense that these unattractive qualities given to Elana Steinberg were also qualities supposed to be typically Jewish—they may have understood that—but didn't really understand what the lawyers were talking about. In New York City, Cleveland, or Philadelphia, people would have been able to relate to the stereotype immediately, but not in Arizona; they didn't find it humorous or "cute" to be a princess.

It was a strange defense, and very close to the line of permissibility. When I asked my Jewish lawyer friends how they felt about it, they all said they didn't blame the defense for thinking of it. Winning is the main thing, my friends told me, and you do what you have to do to accomplish the desired result. It just meant they were good lawyers. The defense left a strange and uncomfortable flavor behind, and people generally are aware of it even though the newspaper stories never mentioned it—it spread by word of mouth. To me it helps explain the drawing in of the Paradise Valley friends after this trial, their almost absolute refusal to think about Elana anymore. What was said about her was too close to the bone.

There was information overload about the bad qualities of Elana Steinberg and her family, but there was one bit of information that was untouched—the pathological gambler. The trial was an unforgettable picture of the disintegration of this kind of gambler. Steven Steinberg is an absolute fit for the profile. Steve had had the adolescent death experience that Dr. Custer describes; the web of bank loans, the sweating scene in the pit at Caesars Palace, the "get-out" bets he made on the sports spectaculars like Super Sunday—these are classic episodes. Elana Steinberg was a little different, though, because the wife of a compulsive gambler tends to be passive and almost helpless. The gambler generally has the upper hand, but that wasn't the case in the Steinberg marriage. Elana was outspoken and bossy, but she too must have been very unhappy as the spiral of the gambler played out. The decision to leave him was just as difficult for her as it was for other gamblers' wives, and she waited too long.

It is possible that Elana Steinberg didn't heed the warning signs, but she must have seen them in that last scene at Lake Tahoe, on the way to that bar mitzvah. Unfortunately, the jury had zero information about the compulsive gambler, and in the end Elana was blamed for her husband's gambling as well as for everything else.

At the very end, when almost all the writing was finished, I was able to meet Steve Steinberg in an airport coffee shop far from Phoenix. We sat there eating eggs and bagels from those molded airport trays and talked awkwardly. I would never have recognized him; he had changed so much from the old news photos at the trial and the wedding pictures at the Blackstone.

Almost everyone had told me about Steinberg's charm— the almost hypnotic way he had of making instant friends. Men had told me, "There was this thing about Steve. You just met him once and you loved him." Father Anthony had testified that he was struck with him immediately when Steve came to his table at the Brass Derby. I was prepared for that, but the charm was gone, or it eluded me. If I had to describe him I would use the word "blurred." He was tentative, very ordinary, and somewhat sad. The glamour days were obviously gone, and it was difficult to imagine that they had ever existed.

He cried often while we were sitting there—usually when he talked about his family and how good they had been to him. I think he misses Phoenix, but is astute enough to know that it is gone forever for him. We didn't mention gambling.

Steinberg said that he knew that the jury instructions had caused a firestorm. "It's not the judge's fault," he told me. "She went one hundred percent with the letter of the law. The prosecutor is the one. He kept insisting, over and over, that it was first degree, premeditated—that's why I never got out on bail. The judge had no choice. I'm just grateful that the system worked."

I told him that the things that had been done to Elana in the trial disturbed me, as well as the general strategy of the defense. He understood that, he told me. "I don't think that the victim should be the one on trial. Unfortunately, that's the way it works. When someone is drowning, and I was, you snatch at anything. Anyone would. It was a matter of circumstances, and the system dictates how you act or react. I'm not proud it happened."

We shook hands, and we both left and didn't look back. I felt deflated, in a way. It wasn't quite what I had expected—he seemed so harmless, so average, to have been the center of all that had happened.

Finally, looking back at the verdict, I concluded that it took luck. Everything had to be right, or everything had to be wrong, depending on your perspective, for this verdict to happen. The jury had to be just the right combination of twelve men and women. One person could have changed the outcome. I believe that a strong juror could even have turned the verdict around completely and brought in a conviction. And this verdict took a combination of other things—a psychiatrist who wanted to go skiing, friends who didn't know quite what to do, a Scottsdale police disaster months earlier, doctors who believed in Twinkie poisoning and sleepwalking, jurors who believed in Satan and a knife that could be held by the blade, and a judge and jury with totally different understandings of what it meant to "premeditate" a murder. Will it ever happen again? I don't think so—this was a once-in-a-lifetime verdict.

ABOUT THE AUTHOR

SHIRLEY FRONDORF worked as a psychiatric social worker before becoming an attorney. She was a member of the *Law Review* at Arizona State University and has written and lectured on criminal and civil legal issues. She has practiced law in Phoenix, Arizona, for thirteen years as both a prosecutor in the Arizona Attorney General's Office and in private practice, where she specialized in constitutional issues. She is married to a Phoenix businessman and has three grown children.